1986

# The Compleat Chauvinist

# THE COMPLEAT CHAUVINIST

## A Survival Guide for the Bedeviled Male

# EDGAR BERMAN, M.D.

MACMILLAN PUBLISHING CO., INC.

NEW YORK

Macmillan Publishing Co., Inc.
866 Third Avenue, New York, N.Y. 10022
Collier Macmillan Canada, Inc.

Library of Congress Cataloging in Publication Data

Berman, Edgar.
    The compleat chauvinist.

    1. Women—Anecdotes, facetiae, satire, etc.
2. Sex—Anecdotes, facetiae, satire, etc.
I. Title.
HQ1233.B47      305.3      81–20892
ISBN 0–02–510120–X      AACR2

10    9    8    7    6    5    4    3    2    1

Printed in the United States of America

# Contents

# A Chauvinist's Paean
# to the Feminine Female

To that marvel of womanhood who is satisfied in reaching her potential as a female but is envious of no other males or females in the way they reach theirs. She is neither Steinemesque nor a Totaled Woman. She is as fulfilled being the mistress of the home, civilizer of the male animal, and the principal creator and molder of the next generation as she might be running a drill press five days a week, buying and selling commodities on the futures market, or playing viola in the Philharmonic just because she wants to.

Not only is she happy to be a woman, but her consciousness as to a woman's worth is already high without the benefit of rap sessions or placard waving. And though she is for women's rights and equal salaries, she doesn't mind washing her husband's golf socks without pay.

She may have no inclination to compete for competition's sake with men in a coal mine, a boardroom, or a foxhole; picket an all-male Little League game; or even feel the need to call a manhole cover a *person*hole cover. It is no symbol of enslavement to wipe a kid's nose, and she knows that her toddler's gender role will be no different giving the little girl a ray gun and the boy a Barbie doll for Christmas. She is convinced that being with them before the age of six and counseling them at puberty is as important as writing an ad for a deodorant. She shows no signs of penis envy, is looking for no Mr. (or Ms.) Goodbar, and despite the fad, considers a vibrator something to mix paint with.

She may enjoy clothes, her all-female bridge club, and Saturday night out with her husband. And if she would rather spend her spare hours volunteering in a nursing home than in a gym practicing to lift three hundred pounds in the next Olympics, it doesn't make her a traitoress to the cause of liberation.

She may be just as talented and happy as those women "out of the house," yet complain less, in her role of creating the warmth and magic of a home, than that female account executive who lives it up with the martinied lunches or the city council*person* who drinks beer with the boys in the back room.

Despite her lack of time in manning the ramparts for abortion on demand, her lack of interest for or against lesbian liberation, and her confusion over ERA, she's not at odds with those that do.

Also, a proud admission of male chauvinism should in no way be construed as my personal pique against the archfeminists. In fact, I hope the exposure of both the fact and fancy of the species Persona Rabida Feminist shows not a shred of vindictiveness just because of those accusations of sexism that have been made against my person. Some of the more shrill Steingreers will naturally bring up my international chauvinist ranking (hot on the heels of Pope Paul VI, number one, and Teddy Kennedy, number two) and indict this book as a subtle ploy to bolster it. Nothing could be further from the truth. My respect and admiration is unbounded for that marvel of reasonable and skeptical womanhood who neither needs nor heeds the hot and heavy urgings of either the Abzugians to the left of her or the Schlaflyites to the right of her. This book is only a defense manual against the ravings and ravages of that more androgynous species—the militant feminist.

# The
# Compleat
# Chauvinist

## CHAPTER I

# Chauvinists of the World, Unite— You Have Nothing to Lose But Your B----

The female chauvinist pig is all bristle and pigskin outside and mostly hogwash within. Four years from now I hope she is happily extinct.

*Shana Alexander, female leader and commentator, in 1972*

She isn't—yet, ten years later.
*E.B.*

IF WE CHAUVINISTS (and let's face it, gentlemen: few of us aren't) had not gone to utter flab since World War II, the feminist movement would never have gotten to first base—much less to the Little League. We who inherited the earth let the meek take it over. We went soft, cowed by the most outrageous publicity onslaught since Barnum. That's all over now. Our gorge is up; our testosterone is boiling. We have had it with chair*persons* and midship*persons,* and if another bimbo throws up sexism, affirmative action, and consciousness raising once more, we'll boycott the singles bars.

## If You've Seen One Jock, You've Seen Us All

We're coming out of the closet and don't mind admitting that if you've seen one jock you've seen us all. When it comes to ogling Dallas Cowgirls or topless Go-Gos, there's not a dime's worth of difference between Burt Reynolds and Albert Einstein. Male chauvinism is the natural state of man—all men—from the five-year-old playing doctor (she's the patient) to the sixty-fiver sneakily riffling *Hustler* magazine at the corner drugstore. Show me a male with a micro-ounce of that golden male hormone circulating in his raunchy veins, and I'll show you a roving-eyed charmer and

[ 1 ]

a "male animal" of the "who's been shaving their legs with my razor" variety. And even according to the latest ABC polls, all of us (men and women) want our sons to live in, out, or all over the place with every female they can seduce, but our daughters better be in by 12:00 P.M. as chaste as a Vestal Virgin.

Though most of us have been overwhelmed in the past ten years by the raucous hassling of this ERA of sisterhood, it's now back to sanity and the Bohemian club or those others—"women admitted at side entrance on alternate Tuesdays and Thursdays."

## The Feminist Mystaque

What would our Neanderthal forefathers have thought of our succumbing to the outrageous myth of sexual equality? As Marvin Harris, professor of anthropology at Columbia University, has said: "Feminists are wailing in the wind if they think they're going to abolish sexism simply by raising consciousness. There is not a shred of evidence—historical or contemporary—to support existence of a single society in which women controlled the political and economic lives of men." Yet we whose chauvinism is rooted in the proud ancestry of the pawing bull and the wild-eyed stud fell for the feminist *mystaque.*

But no longer. Chauvinists of the world, unite. We are now out of the closet and on the move.

Don't get us wrong. Not a man-jock among us is against equal opportunity or equal pay for equal work. We know in our bones that, beginning at scratch, without affirmative action or a similar Rosie Ruiz, Boston Marathon-style head start, they'll never catch up. It's been shown that a good female can never beat a good male as a chef, a symphony conductor, or a tight end. Not that a few can't make it in certain select fields, but there is nothing more unnatural than a female at the head of a wolf pack, or a conglomerate corporation. And notwithstanding that one demeaning decade of the 70s, not a thousand ERAs or ten thousand NOWs can reverse Professor Harris's statement.

## *Designer Genes—Y Over X*

To be sure, a Genuine Risk filly comes along every sixty-five years and wins the Kentucky Derby; so also do a Golda Meir and a Margaret Thatcher pop up; but what happens in between? As Darwin demonstrated in his *Origin of Species*, we males have been born the fittest for three billion years. From that constantly on-the-make little treemouse (the lemur, father of all us mammals) to Mailer the magnificent, the DNA of the male Y chromosome has programmed us to lead our sisters—and we have done so like gentlemen. Since we are the dominoes, so our live-ins, mates, and secretaries born under the sign of the genteel female X chromosome are the dominees. No matter the rare Marie Curies or Brönte sisters; all of the affirmative action in the world won't produce more than a handful of them. Brothers! The gene-deep fact of male dominance is here to stay, come hell or high dudgeon.

In spite of this, we have no one to blame for our present *female troubles* but ourselves. In the past ten years our chivalry overcame our good sense and, with our usual gentlemanly noblesse oblige, we allowed them their fling. To keep peace in the family, we threw them a bone. But what did they do? In typical Abzugian fashion they turned and jammed that very bone down our throats.

Equality? Who said there's anything wrong with equality? But only in the mythology of the Amazons has the human male ever been ruled by the female. The bitter sting of it all is that we who—in our time, in our generation—gave the ladies the vote and allowed them a few other social and political amenities must now swallow a terrible lump each time we have to run out for our own sandwiches or take care of a hyperactive kid on a Saturday morning.

## *Double (Standard)—or Nothing*

As we sat idly by, we had to bear the final insult—the invasion of our ultimate sanctum sanctora. Would that giant of a jock, Leif Ericson, have allowed a floozie reporter within sniffing distance of the sweat-bedewed and liniment-fragranced locker room of his muscled oarsmen? Would John the Druid have given even his most-favored camp follower the privilege of drinking his sublethal mead elbow-to-elbow in a Stonehenge pub?

Not since we dragged those Neanderthal nifties from cave to cave to relieve our most prurient urges have the keepers of our hearths, our sex objects, and the sometime mothers of our sons so risked our ire. Never since the torch of domination was first passed to us from our tree-swinging ancestors has our way of life and our pursuit of the double standard been so threatened.

## A Message They Couldn't Confuse

Mea culpa; let us all say two thousand Hail Marys and slide down lava-hot Mount St. Helens on our blistered buttocks. For, coincidental with the fiftieth anniversary of women's suffrage, we sent them a message they couldn't confuse. Sodden with sentimentality and a surfeit of democracy, most of us sold ourselves down the river promising them a share of our pie—as undeserving as they are.

Marc Feigen, a typical Harvard bleeding heart, really fell for all the female sexist hype. This one went completely bonkers, taking his wife in as a law partner, absorbing her last name, Fasteau, and writing a rabid antichauvinist book, *The Male Machine*, which even belittles the violence of professional football. Well, we know which Fasteau wears the pants in that family. Some women, as the saying goes in the locker room, have the testicular fortitude of a tomcat.

It's not unlike the reversal that came about in the philosophy of that feminist hero John Stuart Mill after he married Harriet Taylor. As described by Gertrude Himmelfarb in her book on Mill, Taylor was a "humorless firebrand widow." In urging an Irish rebellion she said, "The Irish would, I should hope, not be frightened but urged on by some loss of life." Well, who wouldn't succumb to the charms of this docile lady? In his "On Liberty," Mill—obviously looking over his shoulder—not only reversed his decisions on approval of capital punishment and a harsh penal code and other conservative measures, but characterized his lady as "not only part author but inspirer of all that is best in my writings." What else could he do?

But we must be patient with those others like Ashley Montague who've fallen for other understandable reasons, namely celebrity status and money.

All of this was an invitation to a mugging, and the feminists went to work like a South Bronx teenager. Then to make sure we really got it in the neck, our peace-at-any-price politicians traded away our birthright for a mess of ballots—opening the Pandora's box of affirmative action.

## The Pope and Us

Now, believe it or not, our only champions in these still darkened days of the feminist ascent come from the most improbable source—our Italian and Polish popes. Not for one second has their sense of macho been in question. No female priests, no raging hormones in the confession booth—not even an altar girl (pill or pill-less) to serve the wafers. And who backs them up to the very heavens? None other than their brother under the cassock, the Archbishop of Canterbury.

Doubtless, most of our other brethren who went-along-to-get-along in the early 70s have since rued their decision. They did not understand how tough it made things for the rest of us. When a few of us objected, we were branded sexist (which we are), fascist, even at times, Republican. It was difficult to murmur dissent except, of course, in the freedom of the locker room.

Though all of us were still the same chauvinists under the skin, we hunkered down like a bunch of conventioneers caught in a massage parlor. And to make matters worse, there was Joe Namath, our lord of the jocks, on nightly TV, wearing his pantyhose, blowing his coif dry, Brut-ing his armpits, and flaunting a bejeweled necklace deep in the hair of his thorax.

## The Fifty-Year Itch

For the Steinzugs, this masculine cave-in was all too good to be true. They never expected such a male fold-up . . . what we got should not have happened to Samson. Those militant Delilahs unsheathed their shears and clipped us right down to the quick. The first rebellion against our male hegemony in fifty years was on its way. And what a shorning we took.

But deep in our chauvinist marrow we knew this too would pass. For in our collective memory—going back to the gospel—we knew that the sorry state of the 70s could not endure. So why bother? We knew those militant "muthas" of us all would rue the day they breached the portal of McSorley's saloon. For just as the rowdy kiddies of the 60s went back to home economics and dental school at the birth of the 70s, so shall this feminist uprising recede into history in the 80s.

Looking back, we have grown to expect feminist chafing at the bit at regular intervals—in fact, about every half-century. As any gynecologist will tell you, the female hormones are the culprits. Just as they bedevil woman with every wax and wane of the moon, so they have had a historic cumulative effect. They build up over the years until they reach right down into the medulla oblongata where, at the proper boiling point, they explode in hot flashes of a yearning for equality. The rhythm of these rebellions is not only predictable but well documented.

## *The Hot Stove League—from Neanderthal to NOW*

No male worth his salt should ever forget the conversion of Mr. Lot's wife when she looked back—defying that great Chauvinist in the sky. And her female followers quaked, seeing that a female's *lot* could be a very salty one.

From then on, little exercises in futility followed at regular intervals as surely as the rise and fall of the hemline. And after Ms. Lot was Mortonized there came Lysistrata. That Greek lady got her sisters to stretch *Never on Sunday* to a week-in, week-out affair. Imagine their wishful intuition, ever considering that withholding connubial rights could get their warrior spouses to cease and desist from their most favored sport. Though no chauvinist alive could but admit that the sweet smell of sex permeates every synapse of our male cerebrum and there is "nothing like a dame" —there's also nothing like a war. Didn't that Grecian lady realize that from the time Genghis Khan mushed ahead on the frozen steppes of Mongolia, to MacArthur's wading ashore in the South Pacific, the male has forfeited months, yea! years of sex for his more gory pleasures? It would be as unlikely as our beer-drinking, taverned brotherhood trading off a run-of-the-mill roll in the hay for a Super Bowl Sunday or Game of the Week Monday. No question, sex has the same high voltage as war, but it just does not have the staying power.

## When the Heat Is on the Hormone

Not to belabor this historic rhythm, but do you still think the present semicentennial vibration on the female Richter scale is just of recent vintage? What would you say if the absurd statements "marriage is a state of war" and "*Kinder* and *Kuchen* should be shared by husband and wife" were not original in Kate Millet's *Sexual Politics?* Those very words were taken from the French liberationists in 1650—and who knows, those ladies may have plagiarized those buzz phrases from the Dead Sea Scrolls.

Nevertheless, too many of us have sympathized with their cyclic upheaval. So what if some of our charming chattel have temporarily slipped the leg irons, abdicated the scullery, and rushed headlong from the eminent domain of maledom? We've been through it before—they'll come crawling back when the heat is on the hormone—and when the core cools, they will jell back to sanity.

## Gentlemen Jocks—the Time is NOW

But, gentlemen jocks, the time is now—hopefully for all time. This last episode has been pretty prickly—and it's gone on much too long. We must cut it short and bring our ladies back where they belong—*under us*. Though we took our lumps like men, and we have our scars to prove it, that day is done.

Even you of faint heart who went along in the 70s, make peace with your conscience and be cleansed of your guilt! But those of us who fought it through should take little credit. For though that selfsame rampaging female horde is now marching to a more muffled beat, we had little to do with their change in tempo. We may have dragged our feet on ERA and encouraged the Dallas Cowgirls with their T and A routine; and of course Ronnie Reagan's ascendancy hasn't hurt. But if the feminist movement is flopping as badly as we think it is, it's due to natural causes: they just can't shake their female ancestry and instincts. Their gentle genes which give them their rightful place in the male world are the real sexual harassers—not us.

Let us not prolong this. Once and for all we must put an unnatural cause to rest and save our yet unborn chauvinist brothers the slings and arrows we have suffered. Never again shall a few brawnies lead their shrewish legions to nibble away at our god-given rights. Never again shall our leers, our loins, and our sacred locker room lexicon bow to that on-again, off-again myth of the liberation of our women. Gentlemen chauvinists, we have just begun to fight.

## CHAPTER II

# Great Expectations:
# Up from the Washboard
# Paradise Lost: Back to Needlepoint

There has never been a matriarchal society. There never has been a
society where women were the dominant sex, and there's no reason
to believe there ever will be.

> Dr. Judith Bardwick, Professor of Psychology,
> Associate Dean, University of Michigan

Women should accept their place at home leaving responsible pur-
suits to men.

> Dr. Harold Vath, Senior
> Psychiatrist, the Menninger
> Foundation

As WE HAVE INSISTED all along, you can't send a girl out to do a
man's job. In the past ten years the fems have promised their
oppressed sisters everything—everything but the paradise they
lost in their quest for those impossible great expectations.

So now comes the moment of truth. Is little sister better off in
1980 than she was in 1920 B.L. (before liberation)? And after all
those bone-wearying marches and decibel-shattering conventions
has she lived up to the potential claimed for her? All right, even
*we* might not expect a Picasso, a J.P. Morgan, or an equal share of
Bonnies (without Clydes) in just ten or fifteen years—but in that
time shouldn't Little Bo Peep have graduated from merely minding her sheep? Shouldn't the movement at least have brought its
tiniest shepherdess to fulfillment in the marketplace?

Deborah Warner, a curator at the Smithsonian Museum of
American History, on her exhibition entitled "Perfect in Her Place"
said, "I want people to realize the extent to which women have
always worked—especially in low status, dead-ends jobs." Then

she repeats over and over again, "Women are still in these jobs [of yesteryear], and the attitudes [I assume male] articulated then are still very much with us."

## A Libber in the Woodpile

For the woman who has to work, it is not being the next Eve Curie that counts, but just earning a few more bucks and maybe eking out a little *spousehold* help with the homemaking drudgery. When the chips are down it's not how well the Libbnicks have done for the few at the top but how much for the many little ones at the bottom. They have their little sisters plunged in guilt if they are not among those few achieving females down on Wall Street buying and selling hog belly futures; or among those brawny-bodied ones out at Shea Stadium practicing their offside punts rather than dragging little Emily to have her braces adjusted. Well, we've seen and heard the fems brag of those few at the top a hundred times on the Donahue show, but we have not seen any real in-the-bank results for the bulk of those long-suffering little sisters. As Anne Tolstoi Foster, a high advertising executive, suggested, all they had [those with great expectations] were great excuses: "Women have such excuses for inaction. Work? We were having babies. (See Jean Kerr.) We were moving around. (See Coretta King.) We were sick. (See Elizabeth Browning.) We were young. (See Radcliffe's president, Matina Horner.) We were old. (See again Mrs. Meir.)" If they had been seminaring, cocktailing, and demonstrating less and working more, they wouldn't have time to complain about it.

Well, no matter the results after they nailed us chauvinists to the affirmative action cross. It had better add up. Though under duress we have sacrificed for that feminist shot heard round the world (as it's turned out, a blank if there ever was one), we want to know what they have done for the little ladies—lately. For in the process we ourselves have not been left unmauled. Still hanging in there with our stigmata oozing, we wonder whether our ignominious martyrdom to that shaky cause has not been in vain. This is what we found.

## The Hot Stove League

For all of the claims and hoopla, the run-of-the-mill female is still no less shackled to her typewriter and hot stove than were her oppressed ancestors of fifty or fifty thousand years ago. Her Neanderthal ancestors also had to sharpen the spears and poison the arrows by day, then stand over a blazing spit waiting for the lord and master to stagger through the cave door loaded to the gills on two-hundred-proof Moonshine Mead. What's more, are those who were lured out into the male world any freer, happier, or more equal just because they sweat it out making "Mother Miller's pies" at minimum wage under a foreman's eagle eye, rather than making husband's bed in an air-conditioned home between coffee breaks with The Morning show? As Margaret Mead, that curmudgeonly grande dame of feminists, warned, "Most of what is called equality is the right to go to the office everyday or work in the factory. Compared with looking after the children, what most men do most of their lives is dull, dull, dull."

Columnist George Will shouts to old Marge, "Amen." Most women are longing to "get out of the house and into jobs that are boring men to distraction. Women today are especially apt to live in perpetual anticipation and thus in unfulfillment."

## Out of the House—and into the Soup

The Department of Commerce statistics spell out this point in chapter and verse. They estimate that women make up two-thirds of the world's labor force, put in two-thirds of the work hours, but get only a tenth of the world's income. As the figures indicate, if she is now "out of the house" (somehow one of the great goals of feminism), she is in the frying pan behind the counter in the school cafeteria, in front of a big green filing case putting *F* after *E* and *L* before *M*, or in a white coat in a laboratory stuffing medicine bottles. The lowest wage-scale jobs which the black and Hispanic males won't touch are still reserved for those ladies who have "gotten out."

Not only that, but here we are with feminism past its peak and the wage gap between the female worker and her male counter-part still deeper than Sophia Loren's cleavage. In the past twenty-five years the gap has deepened further, and with each recession it grows more so. As usual the female hired is still the first fired. Today, according to *Fortune*, females still have a stranglehold only on menial office and clerical jobs. What's more, it has been found that sixty-five percent of those who have "gotten out" have done it out of necessity—to make ends meet—and now wish they were "back in." So what have the fems done for their hard-working sisters? They've gotten them out of the house and into the soup. Women now are making up seventy-five percent of the poor in the U.S. And as equality breeds more divorce it'll get worse, not better. Charlotte Stewart of the Women's Center in Dallas says, "Divorced women all end up in the same place. Down."

## A View from the Bottom

And then there's the very top, where the privileged female works more for fun than profit. But how many are at the top? Katherine Graham, publisher of the *Washington Post*, is the only female at the head of a Fortune 500 corporation (since her natu-rally overachieving husband died at such a tender age after tak-ing over her family's paper).

In another arena of traditional male supremacy, we patriotic chauvs allowed the number of women applying to medical school to increase four hundred percent at a time when this country was begging for more doctors. Similarly, females now comprise twenty percent of law school enrollment. But then, after squeez-ing hundreds of worthwhile male students out of those scarce spots, they give in to their compulsive homing instincts, and only ten percent ever practice law or medicine.

Even in high politics, as we shall see, it is not much different. Although between 1970 and 1978 the number of women in the lower echelons of state legislatures jumped, the number of women in Congress fell from eighteen to sixteen. In 1981, female members numbered eighteen, the same as in 1960, with two sen-ators, both hot antifeminists. In practically all parliaments, world-wide, and especially in those egalitarian Politburos from the

Soviets to the Bulgarians, the Steinzugs are no more powerful than before the Revolution. Also, now instead of four there are only two female chiefs of state in major nations; the one in England is about as popular as an epidemic of nasal catarrh; and the other's polls in India are running neck and neck with the Untouchables. Even the new Solidarity-minded democratic Polish parliament has only the usual token solitary female.

And last, but hardly least—to get away from politics and labor statistics—one of the most highly touted promises of the libber campaign, the clitoral orgasm, has been one of the greatest disappointments of all. This feminist innovation (once known as masturbation), which the ads in *Ms.* magazine have so lustily described to old maids, elderly divorcées, and the not-too-attractives, just never measured up to its billings.

So here we are with court decisions making it illegal for the male world to keep females from crawling on their bellies two miles below the earth's surface mining coal. Then there are those old HEW guidelines for hiring and firing. Also those affirmative action statutes assuring that there shall be a quota of women in the corporate hierarchy—even when most women are done in at home by that one great decision: when to toilet train their children. Yet with all the laws, guidelines, and that overkill of publicity, we can see the plunge back to sanity accelerating like a sky dive. Actually, some of the strongest opponents of feminism are the grassroots women. In a published poll, seventy-one percent of women still felt that wife and mother was the best job, and fifty-one percent of working professional women wanted back in the house. (Having dinner with a high-powered New York female publicity vice-president and a founder of NOW, the only sigh of contentment I heard came when she was talking of retiring (at forty-nine) and getting back into the house.)

## Making Less and Working More

As we look back now, those grassroot "in-home" females were smarter than their "out of the house" sisters. For not only is the working woman making less under the banner of feminist equality—but she actually is working more. And to compound the inequality, her extra home work is done gratis, free, "on the house." The newly liberated woman may be fulfilling herself on a power line at 102 degrees in the shade, but before she puts on her spikes in the morning she still has to get the kids off to school. And a female cop, whether walking her beat as a rape decoy or clubbing a drug pusher into submission, must hurriedly stash her gun, holster, and cuffs and beat it home to put the family dinner on the table. Whoever the feminist was who got the idea that the man of the house would share her drudgery must have had her hormones twanging like an electric zither. Right now, working wives are slaving away seventy to seventy-five hours a week as their working husbands put in their forty. As Ms. Newland of the Worldwatch Institute put it, "Husbands still do little to relieve working wives of domestic duties" whether in New York, U.S.A., or Magnitogorsk, U.S.S.R. As we chauvs have always known, nothing less than major gene splicing will even budge the male animal in the direction of the washing machine.

So far it looks as if our heroines are doing more in two jobs (one for less and one for no pay) without hubby's helping hand. But don't think these Superwomen (as the movement calls them) are not appreciated by all of us, especially on Father's Day, as we cheer them on from the hammock.

## Equality—a Way of Death

But that's not the half of it. Not only does she work her typing and diapering fingers to the bone, but from all the statistics it appears she is competing neck and neck with her husband for that first leap into the loony bin, and if this doesn't work, into the family plot. The National Institute of Occupational Health states that nursing, waitressing, and secretarial jobs claim the highest incidence of mental illness. Not only that, but as she works harder and under the sharp eyes of her male boss, she gets more nervous, thus smokes more cigarettes, and voilá, in the year of our Lord, 1982, for the first time women will place first in the All American Lung Cancer Sweepstakes. So now more than one Health and Human Services pamphlet warns, "Signs of a woman's social emancipation are now not only a major threat to her personal health but even to her ability to bear children." But that's not the worst of it; she's not only puffing but drinking away. The *British Medical Journal* reports that, among women, drinkers have twice as much cirrhosis as men on half the alcohol; convictions for drunkenness rose 64 percent in ten years; hospital admissions due to alcohol rose 137 percent; and deaths from alcoholism rose 130 percent.

Most of this, of course, is due to more occupational stress plus her unique physiology—then the add-on, her family responsibilities. This goes way beyond that which puts the average male into his early grave. Another study in Framingham, Massachusetts, published in the *American Journal of Public Health*, showed that married women, in combining work with their demanding family lives, precipitate disease of the coronary arteries, which of course leads to the kind of liberation not even a feminist needs.

## A Plop Heard Round the World

So far we have been dealing with female problems here in the U.S. But, in keeping with its usual superlatives, the movement is also boasting of easing women's plights from Tanganyika to Timbuktu. On the basis of what we know *has not* happened here in America, our already deepened skepticism prompted a little worldwide research. It was hard for us to imagine a peasant woman with nine kids, knee-deep in a Malaysian rice paddy, having to be sexually awakened by a vibrator. So it was not surprising for our far-flung correspondents to have searched in vain for progress. Even Friedan's *Feminine Mystique* didn't seem to have much effect on a Berber woman carrying no fewer faggots of wood on her back than those on her husband's donkey.

## Sick Gloria in Transit

The news, however, isn't all bad. After Gloria Steinem's visit to Asia and Latin America, there was a move to prevent the women of the house from pulling more than a one-ton cart on Sundays and holidays. In Africa, thanks also partly to the Pope's visitation, there was a gambit to break the back of polygamy, limiting the number of wives to three—except for high government officials.

The political progress in advanced nations does show a trend, but one which might only be effective in the next millennium. For instance, in that great nation of *liberté, égalité,* and *fraternité,* there are 0.7 percent of women in the National Assembly (in 1970 there was only half that). And in this Grande Patria of pâtés and patisseries there are twice as many female chefs in three-star restaurants (in 1967 there was only one; now there are two). On the other hand, in England there has been a bit of backlash: Since Germaine Greer's last visit, the national sport of wife beating has almost doubled. Then according to Tracers Inc., ten years ago there were three hundred runaway husbands to one runaway wife! Since liberation women have caught up; but the wives come back—the husbands rarely.

Most eloquently, the Soviet women have compared their freedom to rivet and weld steel girders sixty stories up to the sad plight of the capitalist nonworking females—at home, enslaved by their dishwashers, washing machines, and TV dinners.

## Equality: A Criminal Opportunity Employer

On balance, if women all over the world want to follow the feminist Pied Pipers and give up the good long life for an equal but shorter one, why should we chauvs worry? But, digging a little deeper, it seems even we innocent males may suffer from the side effects of equality. As Ellen Goodman puts it, "equality is a criminal opportunity employer." Well, as we always knew, women in crime were sort of a necessary evil. They ran the gamut of gun molls, bag women, and young Bennington radicals (who would gladly risk making the explosives for their Weathermen boyfriends and not infrequently went up in smoke for the cause).

We thought it was just an isolated incident when libber tennis player Rosie Casals battered an innocent male on the streets of San Francisco. But from the treatise "Crime in Society," the authors, Savitz and Johnson, state that American women are engaging in more acts of violence today than at any time in the past. In the last few years, for the first time, four women made the FBI list of the ten most-wanted criminals.

Not only that, but for heaven's sake, stay out of their way at "that" time of the month. An investigation into women's prisons revealed that over half the inmates committed their crimes at the time of their lunar symptoms. As they put it, "the hormonal changes" of menstruation make individuals less amenable to discipline and cause them to rob banks, mug senior citizens, or gun down cops.

This is serious, and if there is anything to the "rhythm theory" whatsoever, it is only right and proper that a woman should wear some kind of identification during that time or at least commit herself for a few days and save the rest of us a lot of trouble.

## *When in Trouble—Dial M-A-N*

But here is the rub. It was always within the realm of possibility for the feminists to have gone further and shown more progress for their constituents. As we said at the beginning, you don't send a girl out to do a man's job. We're now being very, very serious. It was actually possible at the very beginning (before they tried to put us down so miserably) for them to have called on us chauvinists for help. After all, who but the male had the wealth of expertise and know-how which for centuries has successfully bribed nations and exploited continents? By comparison, what experience did the female have? When a woman needs a plumber, a TV repair*person*, or a plastic surgeon, since when does she call another woman? Even Bella Abzug had a male campaign manager, and both Indira and Golda would settle for nothing less than an all-male cabinet.

It is understandable, their being a bit squeamish in asking for help at the start, especially as nasty as they were. But on the other hand, who knows better than some of their more feminine acolytes how convincing a bit of the cross-legged, slit-skirt maneuver can be. Can they so easily forget what conquests their heroines Eve, Mata Hari, and Elizabeth Ray made by the simple skin game? Our modern Sir Walter Raleighs might have happily laid not only their coats but their whole suntanned bodies across the equal-rights puddle. Could anyone doubt that, with the slightest wink of a mascara-ed eye, the management genius at Volkswagen or the marketing mogul at Gimbels would not have jumped into bed—with the fems? If those mavens could gussy up the sickest corporations and bring them back alive, why not the movement? Would those gents have done less in the name of equality than in the cause of IT&T or Lockheed?

## Home, Home at the Range

It's too late now. Though the libs may have shown that "Hell hath no fury," they didn't know about a chauvinist scorned. We have forgotten not one spit in our collective eye. And to try selling us on their good faith and humility now would be like convincing Masters and Johnson of the Virgin Birth. As one macho mogul put it, "Pull their gonads out of the oven after they've baked, parboiled, and scorched mine to a cinder? I may be a whoremonger, a warmonger, and a sexist pig—and all of those other favorite feminist endearments—but be nice to them? Let 'em eat cake." If Nixon had an enemy list a mile long, the beer-swilling, broad-chasing jock now has one from sea to shining sea. Each and every male who might possibly have come around is as gun-shy as a four-time loser invited over for Sunday dinner by Zsa Zsa Gabor's mother. So who among men can blame these average, even if mildly pockish, vice-presidents of personnel or shop stewards for casting a jaundiced eye on those female job seekers now. Knowing our male as we do, if he can help it—and he can—the female worker will have bumpy sledding getting ahead—up and over our corporate body. And if the Steinzugs think they still can bring up the now tattered affirmative action scare, they had better take a course in "Male Studies and the Loophole Makers." So at the first sign of a slowdown, recession, or pregnancy, most of those already in will find themselves home, home at the range. Once there were great expectations; now it's Paradise Lost.

## CHAPTER III

# The Fury Godmothers—
# Delusions of Glandeur

Betty Friedan is a hopeless bourgeois.

*Susan Brownmiller, author of* Against Our Will

Some feminists are female chauvinist boors.

*Betty Friedan*

Phyllis Schlafly and Bella Abzug deserve each other.

*Author Midge Dicter*

And here are the feminist leaders
In the Era of equals and peers,
The Millets won't speak to the Steinems
And the Friedans won't march with the Greers.

*E.B.*

IT HAS SURPRISED some of our egalitarian pundits that, in the greatest democracy on earth, the greatest scam on earth (the liberation movement) has not reached its goals when every other sting from tea-leaf reading to Geritol has made it big. To us chauvs it's simple: There is a basic defect in the feminist (not feminine) character. But before going into that, we must first separate the feminists from the feminine—the raging Brunhildas from Lancelot's Guineveres. But they aren't always that easy to recognize—they are a breed apart. As our plain-spoken Katie Hepburn told Barbara Walters in a TV interview, "We women are very confused sexually. Look at the birds and beasts and the male and female, and there are definite types. We're getting sexually confused."

So until we can pinpoint all of the feminists' inherent weaknesses, we chauvs can't inherit the earth—again. However, once the distinction is clear between the delicate nature of the well-formed and ladylike Cheryl Tiegs and the preternature of the flinty-hard, Steinzug bulldozers, we have defined our terms and so have nailed our nemeses.

## The Ineptitude of Inaptitude

As evolution first demonstrated and Nobel laureate Konrad Lorenz conclusively showed, *leadership* is just not one of the great natural aptitudes of the female. And no matter how thick the Abzugian hide, how raucous the Brownmillerian voice, the average female has always been and always will be a follower— rarely a leader. This alone could account for the heated upsurge and the cooling down collapse of the feminists' equality soufflé.

Since that male cockroach eons ago led his harem to survival in the first kitchen cabinet, there have been only a handful of some two million species (the South African phalarope and the striped hyena, among others) ever led by a female. So after a billion years of evolution and history, it is understandable that there would be no glut of female Napoleons, Einsteins, or Wayne Hayses to bring the downtrodden female out of the wilderness. Even today the indecisiveness of the so-called feminist leaders who have bobbed to the surface is evident, as they still haggle over whether the ERA or clitoral orgasm is the movement's top priority.

Now, biologists trace this leadership role to the male aggression factor—stimulated by the hormone testosterone, secreted in the testes of the male fetus.

## As Popular as Charles Manson
## at a Girl Scout Campout

In a movement that started out about as popular as Charles Manson at a Campfire Girls' marshmallow roast, this indecisive-ness is a serious flaw. But a flaw we chauvs have always counted on. Down through the ages, when things looked particularly bad for us during those recurrent feminist flare-ups, women leaders inevitably fouled up. For instance, it got us out of hot water when President Jimmy Carter, in a political year and against his better instincts, gave lip service to the Women's Caucus (this we didn't worry about: There is no Southern gentleman alive who is not one of us). But as usual, the fems overdid it by a nagging that would have put Rosalynn to shame. So the Midges and the Bellas were bounced out of the White House with no apologies. But then, in the 1980 election, because they were mad at Carter, NOW had their followers stay neutral. By default they elected a cowboy sex object to the White House, put a *feminine* female in as first lady, elected two antifeminist senators, and just about did themselves in. In one fell pinch they cut off the life-support oxygen of their own dyspneic ERA.

## Would a Lemming Follow One?

That inherent leadership weakness in feminists has always been in our favor, and no amount of affirmative action and public laws has helped them. So, for a cause needing at the least a Churchill or a Machiavelli coming up with a Millet and a Greer was not just a poor choice. It was all they had. It was a fate determined two billion years ago by a weakness of the leadership factor in the female chromosome. So by this genetic defect alone, and without even lifting a finger, we chauvs were and always will be ahead of the game. Simply said, all we chauvinists have to contend with is a gaggle of self-appointed chief *persons* not even a down-at-the-heels lemming would follow to the water's edge.

Yet, so far, it must be acknowledged that the present liberation groupies have survived even with that dependence on a schizoid leadership. This shows a certain staying power. So we must keep up our guard and not sell the movement too short.

Admittedly, to hear all of these negative, if scientific, facts, from us of all people, a listener might be skeptical that it was all sheer chauvinist bias. Not a bit of it. The unkept promises of feminism themselves have shown those babies have not "come such a long way" after all. For instance, one of their more obvious accomplishments, which they do not care to admit, was splitting American womanhood into two armed-to-the-teeth camps—with the Schlaflyites and the Steinemesques ready to scratch each other's eyes out on every issue from abortion to the Miss America contest. Such a house divided has not been seen on a national scale since the opening shot at Fort Sumpter.

## The Grinding Gallstones

So, gentlemen, from the leadership standpoint, it appears they have a handicap even Secretariat couldn't win with. But that's not the long and short of it. Though we chauvinists are not loathe to stoop to divide and conquer, either in the backroom or boardroom, the feminists were split six ways for Sunday before we got a shot at them. Though in most revolutions few if any of the top leaders see eye to eye (Stalin couldn't stand Trotsky, and Mao was constantly looking over his shoulder at Chou En-lai)— sooner or later one or the other takes a back seat. But as we said, it is now almost fifteen long years since the women first paraded again, and still no two feminist corporals are yet marching to the same drummer. Even chimpanzees in a cage climb on each other's backs getting together to make a pyramid to reach those high-hanging bananas—but not our feminists. In this one great battle of their lifetime against the one enemy—the male oppressor—they are compulsively preoccupied with mutual mayhem that makes a Tong war look like a preteen pajama party.

Even in a simple caucus or commission meeting, they get on each other's nerves so one can almost hear the gallstones grinding. Friedan thinks Morgan a radical; Cissy Farenthold (recently out as head of Wells College)—won't acknowledge Ti-Grace Atkinson's existence; Brownmiller would not eat on the same dais with Helen Gurley Brown; Jill Ruckelshaus would not trade over-the-back-fence gossip with that awful "Total Woman" Morgan. Liz Carpenter has nothing good to say about Phyllis Schlafly; Bella Abzug has described Anita Bryant in her inimitable four-letter style. The pro-lifers and anti-lifers are out for blood (each other's). The prostitutes and the gay liberators are at each other privately; and to put it all in succinct perspective, paraphrasing professor Lionel Tiger, "Women are just too bitchy to be bonded."

Now it's being shown that there is solid research material to support these internecine battles. In a forthcoming book, *The*

*Woman That Never Evolved,* Sarah Hrdy states, "The basic dynamics of [even] the mating system depends not so much on male predilection as on the degree to which one female tolerates another."

## How to Alienate without Even Trying

Besides personal and political division among themselves, it was nothing short of suicide for a movement whose time had come to practice the fine art of alienation. That tiny group of self-seeking lady leaders did the trick, not missing one of their constituents, from the downtrodden housewife to the underpaid cafeteria worker. So in another one of their many fell swoops, the Steinzugs stridently managed to put down connubial bliss as slavery and the Mormon Church as ungodly. Then they espouse lesbianism as a way of life, and the vibrator as a surrogate for moon and June. This also did not exactly endear the movement to the Gold Star mothers or the Hadassah sisterhood. Also early on, the movement's spokes*person,* the ladylike Shulamith Firestone, described pregnancy as "barbaric," and labor pains as "sh-tting a pumpkin."

To further fragment the movement, Germaine Greer, that other Fury, wrote a book, *The Female Eunuch,* with the emetic statement that "an absolute initiating ritual into real femaledom is tasting your own menstrual blood." This stimulated a one-upsmanship catfight within the club. So as not to be upstaged, Kate Millet shouted to the rooftops, "Liberation is a demand for the abolition of wife and mother and dissolution of the family." This did not create a great surge of forty million diaper washers rushing their dues in to NOW.

## Bella's Baby—"If Mother Gets Elected I'm Moving to Hoboken"

As Lyndon Johnson would have put it, when it comes to leadership, "those ladies could f--k up a two-car funeral." But to garnish our former chief executive's opinion with happenings right in the family, it was recently brought to our attention that Betty

Friedan and Bella Abzug could not even influence their own flesh and blood. During Bella's bid for the mayoralty of New York, her insightful female offspring claimed, "If Mother gets elected, I'm moving to Hoboken!" (Thanks to an alert electorate, the young lady escaped both fates.) Then to Betty's embarrassment, her ever-loving daughter, disdaining her mother's *Mystique*, flat-footedly said, "I'm no feminist . . . I'm a person."

## Gelding the Billy

But there's much more to come. Lucky though we may be for their lack of genetic leadership, the fems also have shown a knack for self-immolation, the envy of every saffron-robed Tibetan monk. They began by slashing at the male—all of them openly flaunting their man-hate. As that more rational and rare of feminists, Diana Trilling, admitted: "Women's liberation has turned into a kind of field day for despising men. . . ."

Of course, outwardly they were not all maneaters, and as far as we know, at least one got an offer from a desperate bachelor. Germaine Greer, always on the ramparts "Gelding the Billy," took time out to fall "madly in love." She then went for the whole enchilada and indulged in that institution she had so recently despised: marriage. This change of heart was thoroughly publicized in her turnabout quote in the London *Sunday Times*. "I rage, I melt, I burn," said this high priestess of libbers. Then she went on to add, "I also simper and maunder. I'm no better than an imbecile," as she fell in love. It must have been her first shot at romance even at her ripe age. This sudden flip-flop confused and disillusioned all those dateless Nebraska State coeds and bitter divorcees who had hung on her every hate-male and antimarriage word since her first book on the subject. However, lucky for that male member of the wedding, he was able to extricate himself from his vows while the getting was good (to be exact, in just about three weeks, allegedly with all of his parts intact). Germaine did not take this short-lived romantic fling in very good grace, with the summation that "sexual politics has to do with the act of f--king—the one being f--ked is usually female and inferior." Well, she said it; we didn't.

If such self-destructive statements did not succeed in allaying confidence in the leadership, there was the added bummer of blatantly confessing every sexual kink each of them was prone to. Maybe that small hard-core of sophomore college girls, ambitious secretaries, disgruntled divorcees, and uptight spinsters would go for this. But most of *those* babies would follow a hybrid of Salome and the Marquis de Sade. However, there was no way the other ninety-eight percent would go for the antics of those feminist Gay Taleses. Anyway, it didn't do much to fire up the grassroot mothers of America.

## *Friedan—Motherhood and Matzoh Balls*

Then to make sure they left no suicidal traps unsprung, members of the Women's Political Caucus decided at their International Women's Year Conference in Houston to espouse the cause of lesbianism. Now—as is well known—we chauvinists are no prudes, and any upstanding animal, vegetable, or female leader can get her sex from any chandelier she can swing from. And we're certainly not against lesbians having as much equality as the next *gay*. But to make sure this feminist political wrist-slashing did not go unnoticed, "leaders" like Robin Morgan claimed loud and strong, "I am one," as did Rita Mae Brown [author-*person* of *Rubyfruit Jungle*, and for a while the live-in "wife" of tennis champion Martina Navratilova]. (Martina has now publicly switched to basketball star Nancy Lieberman.) Recently even their well-muscled sports leader Billie Jean came out with a TV confession of her "sport" of King's: seven years of palimonious dalliance (with husband at side, no less). Then Kate Millet again pushed front and center, bringing the situation to a boil with her own *roman à clef* on the sights, sounds, and smells of her tawdry affairs with a batch of other women. To make sure they were "all in together, girls," Florynce Kennedy, an admitted lesbian and black radical lawyer, wrapped it up on every talk show, beating the drums for legalized prostitution, while others accused women who reject lesbian love as "selling out to the male oppressors." Shirley MacLaine brought up the rear with her assertion that "we're bisexual most of our lives."

Not to be sidelined as a wallflower, even good old Jewish-mother-type Betty Friedan finally gave in on the lesbian issue, but the look in her eyes showed she would have preferred to come down on the side of motherhood and matzoh balls.

To neatly round out this movement's masochism, another best-seller in the making was recently published, *The Joys of Lesbian Sex*, with pictures imitating the original *Joy of Sex*. Well, this book has more electric gadgets than Edison ever dreamed of. And the sizes, shapes, and replicas of male organs designed for every known anatomical orifice defies imagination.

## A Fe-maelstrom of Disorganization

Having just mentioned the National Women's Conference in Houston, what better showcase for liberation leadership? Though those Furies always complain of the underhand chicanery of the male, that women's get-together (subsidized by Congress) was no different than a national political convention run by Richard Daley. Also, it was a mess of disorganization unknown even to a feminist political caucus. The Hyatt House foul-up of rooms was blamed on the sexist clerks; the lesbian liberationists claimed that the straights were responsible for the long lines at the restaurants; and the electric current was suspiciously cut off when the various vibrator booths were demonstrating their *whirring blenders*. Then, chronicled in living color, hotel flower beds were trampled, cigarette stubs were ground into lobby carpets, and sisters lurched around like Truman Capote on Saint Patrick's Day. It was reported that both political and sexual orgies were going on in the public washroom (TV cameras were forbidden there).

## Peace Writ in Bile

However, if the ladies were dedicated to anything at all in this 1977 Houston debacle, it was that "nothing" would happen. The "nothing" referred to was a repeat of the hysterio-typed New York NOW "Battle of the Bulge" in 1975. On TV, that mayhem seemed patterned after a combination of Attica, Kent State, and the Chinese Cultural Revolution. Though it was bloody, that episode luckily fell just short of a body count. From that well-televised experience, measures were taken that no one got into the Houston convention hall without either a peace pledge or an ERA blood test. This had all been worked out at the state levels and written in bile. If nothing else, these preliminary local meetings were a demonstration of democracy—as Jeffersonian as any election by Idi Amin. They had steering committees that steered Schlaflyites right out of the hall and nominating committees that nominated backers of Anita Bryant back from whence they came.

So as with any other idealistic democratic society, the majority were ruled out. With no part of that congressional five-million-dollar misunderstanding, the Schlaflyites had to pay their own way. So at their own expense fifteen thousand of them held their counter-convention. How's that for solidarity—even Polish labor did better.

## The Gavel to Gavel Grovel

To show how far they went, the official convention became a model of Gulag decorum. Any slight whiff of dissent from the (few) black women, the gays, or those looking for some signs of parliamentary procedure came a cropper. Disagreement drifting across the podium was blown away with a deadly look—a deadlier gavel—and when necessary a claquish shouting of the faithful. Bella firmly gaveled and the "girls" duly groveled as if curtsying to a prince at a Foxcroft high tea. All of the well-advertised feminists were there, from Katie to Glo-Glo (all still sweetly at each other's tender throats). Even some presidential wifely window dressing was hustled in (Rosalynn, Betty, and Lady Bird). No Jackie O—there was no chance of her getting mixed up with this tacky outfit. The nine hundred even-handed horde of female reporters sent there to record history in the making objectively were as unanimous as that true elitist salad of feminist delegates —college-bred, income-sure, young white liberals with that garnished sprinkle of blacks and Chicanos. Every resolution they could lay their hands on was passed with about as much resistance as Patty Hearst showed to the Symbionese Liberation

Army. And, other than the one little flurry when the "Dyke Vigil" was announced, and the Dubuque and Sioux City delegates fussed and fidgeted in embarrassment, everything went off like a Marine Corps drill. Chauvinistic Houston cordoned it off like a Bible belt and took it with fear and loathing.

## The Five-Million-Dollar Misunderstanding

The only real news that momentarily distracted the delegates from gossiping and admiring each other's cleverly embossed T-shirts was Betty Friedan. In a dramatic turnabout, this grand-mother of the movement, with both arms twisted behind her in a double nelson, fingers and legs crossed, reversed her field of fifteen years and came out three-square for lesbians. After this they all stood and, in a veil of tears, sang "We Shall Overcome" and "Happy Days" for the nineteenth time; and with a deep sigh of relief as when the all-clear is sounded on a bomb scare, the gavel was rapped for adjournment. The five-million-dollar misunder-standing ended just as it was arranged—"nothing happened"—with a sigh of "good riddance" from Houston's males and females alike.

These nonresults were then written up as a manifesto and later formally presented to President Carter in the Rose Garden, and immediately filed in the National Dustbin (Archives) under *F* for flopperoo. And if the fems didn't louse it up all that week, the chauvs made sure of it the final day.

By one of the most clever ruses ever, this grand saga was buried like other obituaries on page umpty-four of the *New York Times* by a pair of the most well-credentialed and highly placed chauvinists on earth. As the fems put it, obviously by prearrange-ment and malice aforethought. For on that self-same weekend, Sadat visited Begin in Jerusalem for the first time. From there on in, the Houston conference was as dead as a prehistoric drosophila preserved in amber. After threats and insults, Uncle Walter gave it a few seconds later in the week. Even Phyllis Schlafly's counter-convention, with its fifteen thousand Falwellese on their knees praying for that other convention to blow up, never made it into the living rooms. Two weeks later, by special dispensation, it was finally put on TV, getting a rating lower than Planned Parenthood would get in Vatican City.

## Chauvinist Exploitation: Who Scrubs Gloria's Kitchen?

The shortcomings of the feminist leadership seem countless, yet there is one picayune weakness that should be even more embarrassing to the fems than getting caught inviting sexual harassment. Only a chauvinist would expose this, so we do. It all came out in broad daylight at a college forum. It was a simple question brought up just after one of the Glorias or Shulamiths was going down the laundry list of ways men exploit women. A not-so-naive freshman in the audience got up and asked who made Gloria's bed; who cooked for the Friedan family; who did Bella's husband's laundry; who shopped for groceries at Cissy Farenthold's ranch; and who mopped Liz Carpenter's kitchen. This was met head-on—by a long pause and a quickly changed subject.

But Susan Brownmiller, a real homemaker and typical of lib leadership, said it all. "I never made my bed. I let dishes pile in the sink. I don't do any cooking, as food gathering takes too much time."

Now we don't deny them the little perks of celebrity life, but must those elitists at the same time enslave those they are liberating? Not that we don't see the good business sense of hiring a maid (usually black or Puerto Rican) at less than minimum wage (plus bus fare) when they themselves demand $2,000 an hour for a lecture on a variety of feminist subjects.

Then Greer piles it on the old female homebody in a statement as obtuse as it is revealing of the feelings of most of those high priestesses. As she puts it, she prefers women who are not "modern" or "liberated"—"like the woman who looks after the garden of her [equality bought] country house in Italy."

## As Negotiable as a Susan B. Anthony Dollar

Now gentlemen chauvs, all of this is in no way meant to denigrate any of the sisters but only to counteract some of the preposterous claims of their leadership. And as we said previously, this is all based on fact and figures—not just a chauvinist fancy. These captains and queens who have floated to the surface have not guided their flock to equal opportunity or equal pay, much less ERA. But that is another kettle of statistics we'll boil up in a later chapter.

So here we are, a decade later. As far as we can see and despite all the claims and pronouncements, it is the feminist honchos who have brought the movement to its zenith, high on a gibbet, swinging gently, gently in the breeze. Sure, there have been a few inroads we've allowed as only fair. But, Brothers, when in doubt, just remember as you finger your lucky beads: what the feminist leadership hath wrought is no doubt the "greatest show on earth" since Barnum, and about as negotiable as a Susan B. Anthony dollar (five for $4.50).

## CHAPTER IV

# Testosterone,
# the Hormone of Champions
# What Are Little Ladies Made of?

I would speculate . . . female hormone history will dispose one woman who is totally domestic and maternal and others disinterested in children and wanting only a career.

> Dr. Anke Ehrhardt, psychohormonal researcher and professor at the State University of New York

THOUGH IN THE PAST ten years we have shown more gallantry than good sense in having allowed ourselves to be bamboozled, we're beginning to see the light. Even Betty Friedan in her new book, *The Second Stage*, admits that the once-feisty women's movement is now showing more bags and sags than the fifth year of a face lift. But this should be no cause to allow our courtly hearts to go all mushy again and let them once more prey on our *noblesse oblige*. We repeat, keep a sharp eye out! It is not the gentle, the soft, and the beautiful who are out for our more manly parts; it is the brawny, the shrill, and the aggressive.

But any way you look at it, we hold all the cards, including the scientific ones. Yet as long as they can spit fire with their best-selling *Fear of Flying* and lucrative lecture tours, they are going to push, rattle, and roll all the way to the bank on the movement's magic carpet. Here we present the proof of what *little women* are made of.

## Delusions of Glandeur

When (not if) this liberation scam goes the way of all the others before it, those latter-day ladies will have a lot to answer for. Not only will they be accountable for the defamation of our image to their more feminine sisters (admittedly a crimp in the seduction process), but also for the outrageously unproved claims about themselves that could set science back a thousand years. We cannot let this go without setting the record straight.

## To the Moon on a Broomstick?

Though the feminist propaganda was insidious enough, how could anyone who ever slept through Biology I not have rejected hands down the idea of conditioning a sex to be what it is not? Could any of those sexy 007-Bond women be conditioned, like a laboratory rat, into a shrewd, success-oriented coronary-prone Nelson Bunker Hunt, more interested in silver than sex? Can the Yin ever be conditioned into the Yang; the tender into the tough; the intuitive into the analytical? The propaganda claimed that with us sexists out of the way, at the stroke of midnight they'd all be turned into one-hundred-thousand-dollar-a-year male corporate pumpkins and the age of miracles would be at hand.

We would never be so absurd as to distort science. We at least face the fact that you can't get to the moon on a broomstick. But that outlandish quasi-science of feminology has tried to show even evolution, genetics, and hormone power just a figment of our twisted male mentality and, what's more, that we were using science primarily for the subjugation of all womanhood.

## Scratch a Lady—and See

To get down to what is and what isn't as we males well know, scratch the *average* female—we repeat, average—you'll find a purring bundle of moving parts, amply buttocked and breasted, and thoroughly tenderized by the essence of estrogen (and the minuscule amounts of testosterone), at the ready to love and honor, bake a torte and still produce quintuplets. The fems deny this. They say women can be conditioned to be everything a man is. In all fairness, we do not say that a few of them with a tad more circulating testosterone than Terry Bradshaw can't do anything from run a jackhammer to anchor the nightly news. But as we say, they are the few and the far between—not the many nor even the average.

By contrast, we gents proudly acknowledge our own character. Scratch any nine out of ten of us, and suntan deep you have an uncontrolled raunch lusting out of our jockey shorts for those selfsame purring parts, sending her home in a cab after the "fact." Meanwhile our own high-octane testosterone is driving us to fame, fortune—and an early grave.

Then to complete the roll call, scratch an archfeminist (that Ms-inbetween, more *test* than *est*) and those taloned ladies will scratch you right back—eyeballs and all.

## Bring on the Clowns

Yet in the face of the differences, which anyone can see with just the naked eye, why in the world would the feminists take all that trouble to want to prove themselves male be-alikes? After the pains they have taken to smear and vilify everything male, from our soul to our more robust sexual proclivities—they have now got their quasi-scientific sisters (like feminologist Professor Estelle Ramey) distorting nature herself with the ridiculous idea of unisex. This new science of feminology has dragged up the shakiest theories and connected the most carefully selected evidence to produce a daisy chain of fraudulent hypotheses only an archfeminist could believe. If they are right, throw evolution, anthropology, and medical science out of the window—and "bring on the clowns."

## Feminine Alchemy—Base Females into Males

So far, thank goodness, hard science isn't Disneyland—and not even the Russian scientists ever got their spacecraft back to earth by means of a Ouija board. The initial success of the feminist movement's alchemists had, of course, encouraged the more stout-chested feminist Merlins to wave their wands and turn base females into males. And why not? Didn't they redo our language with *ms.* and *personifest destiny*, and the Bible with "Our Mother who art in heaven?"

However, to do science over in their own image, it must come out that holy water rarely cures delusions of glandeur—even at Lourdes.

## The Glands Say No to A' That

To counteract this mess of trumped-up goo which has mired the gullible American public (by our suckered male-dominated media), we chauvinists now must wade through the gummy stuff and get to rock bottom. We shall show that from the real sciences —not the Hare Krishna Yearbook of Gynecology—the glands say No!: "A man's a man and a girl's a girl for a' that." Neither conditioning nor lack of it; neither speeches, legislation, the ERA, nor NOW can make a *she* over to behave anything like a *he*—or vice versa. From the moment that wicked, wiggling sperm, carrying that tiny DNA programmer (X for female, Y for male) plunges into that shy, waiting ovum, it's all over but the christening. From there on in, it's either little girl pink or baby boy blue.

Not to get too clinical, but in pregnancy, during the first week of settling in, if it's to be a boy the little nonsexual thing, now well enwombed, will get his fill of testosterone—and that is what little boys are made of. The little *she* does not, and that lack is her problem thenceforth. A little later on in life it is that selfsame male hormone that makes him chomp at the bit to waste the bad guys with his ray gun, while the lack of it has her whining to diaper a real, honest-to-God peeing dolly. And as Professor Lionel Tiger puts it, "The DNA genetic code makes the individual not only inherit simple physical characteristics but also have a predictable social behavior according to their physiology [hormones]."

## *Hormony Is Tyranny and Foreplay Is Ecstasy*

Now this is all well-documented fact—not fancy—and there is nothing new about any of it. Though it has been proven to everyone's satisfaction but the feminist scientologists, it actually has been right before our eyes since god-given Eden—or from our more nonbiblical genesis. Whoever's game plan it was, about four billion years ago he must have decided that our earliest ancestor, the amoeba, which split down the middle (making two for one) was fine—but foreplay was better. So from there on in, sexuality reared its lovely head. Then there were two—male and female— as raunchy and aggressive or as headachy and reticent as each of their newly circulating hormones would allow. And despite the denials of the feminist prophets, Freud wasn't that wrong after all. Anatomy *is* still destiny—more accurately, hormony is tyranny.

From the opening caterwaul on the delivery table to the last rites, a female is different from the male in the way she throws a baseball or manages her bank account. A female can't buck her hormones any more than we chauvs can buck ours. She's the one so prone to splitting headaches and we to splitting atoms. And come hell or high conditioning, even the most modern of sciences shows that nothing but the glands gone haywire or a bucketful of male hormones will change this. Pavlov's conditioning bells can toll till the cows come salivating home, but he could never condition a goose to act like a gander, nor get a bull to spritz milk.

## *Femerdammerung*

These rote scientific facts have been available in any high school biology textbook for half a century. And though we will soon go into specific evidence (by female scientists only, mind you), what in effect we have said so far we repeat, only to make sure every chauvinist has it at his fingertips to help along the upcoming Femerdammerung. Zsa Zsa Gabor could have been groomed from the cradle and would still never have wanted to run IBM or pitch in the World Series. Conversely, a Skinner box would have had little effect on Muhammad Ali's preferring crocheting doilies to the give and take of the squared ring. It has been shown in a thousand experiments that if the same Zsa Zsa were to be spayed and filled to her ample bustline with testosterone, she would be ready for a proxy fight to take over Mobil Oil or in any one day gird to go a few rounds with Ali; while if "the Greatest" were neutered (with perhaps a little estrogen injected), he would probably start plucking his eyebrows and become a rock groupie. In short—testosterone is king.

## If You've Got You've Got—If You've Not You've Not

Generally behavior is cut, dried, and about ninety percent *un*conditional. There are no ands, ifs, or buts about it, with a seven-foot shelf of bibliography to prove it. Acting masculine or feminine has little to do with learning at the mother's knee. If it did, how come the male got out from under his mother's warping at her apron string, cutting the cord, then, of all things, turning the tables and oppressing not only his own mommy, but his sisters, too? How could this be if, as the Catholic Church says, "Give me a child until he's five . . ." Or then again, why didn't the little girl also rise and shine and try to be dominant?

There is about as much chance of a doting mother, a martinet father, or a Radcliffe education changing a *she* as there is of conditioning a little boy to become a Dr. Barnard or an Artur Rubinstein. Male or female behavior is like talent—if you've got, you've got; if you've not, you've not. But as our feminists repeat ad nauseum, this is all sexist theory—published by sexist scientists, in a sexist cabal, for chauvinist consumption, in chauvinist scientific journals—to keep the female in her place.

## What God Has Created—Can the Feminists Put Asunder?

From their historically hysterical point of view, one would think that every breakthrough in science from Archimedes' "eureka" to Einstein's "relatives," from Leonardo's aeroplane to Pasteur's little animalcules, was a male conspiracy to put down the ladies. Just because every scientific advance from way before

Copernicus was made by males does not mean that the world is flat. Even if Linus Pauling is a chauvinist, he might still be pretty good with a Bunsen burner, and not necessarily a sexist pig to be booted out of academe by a gaggle of NOW vigilantes.

The questions remain. Is there a secret male cabal to cheat the female of her birthright? Or is it, "what God has created the feminists are trying to put asunder." To be on the absolute up and up, we will not allow even our own chauvinist brothers to take our word for fact.

In order to get to the bottom of this with no comebacks, we have turned *only* to the work of female scientists and honest feminist writers. Could anything be more fair? Once and for all we shall try to clear up the grand delusion that conditioning can ever change the physical, emotional, or intellectual behavior of the sexes.

But it hasn't been easy. Even the few objective female scientists are being intimidated and inviting the wrath of both feminists and feminologists. Many female researchers are even carefully hedging their results. *Time* magazine cited sociologist Alice Rossi, who said, "I found myself being screamed at—by the very women I've supported" after she landed in hot water for talking about the "innate predisposition" of women for child rearing.

Women scientists are really being hounded, agrees anthropologist Sarah Hrdy of Harvard. And I'm sure Diane McGuinness of the University of California wasn't the most popular female on campus when she came out with the fact that women excel in fine motor coordination and manual dexterity, suggesting why they are better in typing and needlework—or neurosurgery. If it happens that there are more neurosurgeons than seamstresses.

## The Truth May Set Them Free

The voice of the female herself shall be heard in the land, and the truth may set her free. So here goes; just a few of a thousand pieces of evidence.

Recent research on the sex hormones suggests that . . . these hormones are not only crucial to the differentiation of (male or female) sexual organs, but they "program" the brain during fetal development, for the later display of either masculine or feminine behavior.

> Maggie Scarf, scientific and psychiatric writer, in the *New York Times*

Scarf again:

> It is presumed that higher animals and humans are not psychosexually neutral at birth. Before the onset of learning and social pressures, they are programmed to acquire specific masculine or feminine patterns of behavior.

Dr. Anke Ehrhardt, Johns Hopkins psychohormonal unit researcher and now a professor at the State University of New York (with the famous sex expert, Dr. John Money), writes in *Man and Woman, Boy and Girl*:

> A human fetus (female) whose mother has had a certain masculinizing hormone when just pregnant is born as a girl but with male-like organs [the Androgenital Syndrome]. At infancy the cases are treated surgically, removing the greatly enlarged clitoris, so that the little girl never knows that she was masculinized.

*She is thus brought up as a girl* [author's italics] by the ordinarily doting mother and father in the usual male-dominated milieu as a sex object, prepared for bedmaking and motherhood. Among many hundreds of these cases there were ten of these, ages four to fifteen, studied, with a control group, with meticulous scientific care. With the same motherly conditioning (in the usual sexist society), with dolls and training bras forced on them, each of these girls "still preferred to play with guns and insisted on football and baseball with the boys." They also didn't care for girls, and wouldn't wear skirts; all were "highly assertive and self-reliant and better in sports than their older brothers. On their minds were careers, not bridal gowns. These girls [remember this, brought up as girls in the same chauvinist society] grow up to be achievers, have fewer children, and think like men. Since this study many others have been done with similar results.

Ehrhardt gives her support to Scarf, and also to Katherina Dalton, the British scientist:

Of the ten masculinized girls, or those with Androgenital Syndrome, IQs were unusually high. Ordinarily, only twenty-two percent of females would have an IQ of 130; with these masculinized girls it was over sixty percent.

Jane Goodall, famous anthropologist and ethologist, reports:

There is no question that little boy chimpanzees have no interest in their infant chimp sisters, and little girl chimpanzees can't wait to cuddle them [like dolls] and take care of them for mother.

## T.Q.: The Testosterone Quotient

Well, gentlemen, this should be enough ammunition for the time being (with a load more, from other sources). There is not a libber in the world who can refute it. But don't think for one second that they won't try. We predict they will brush this solid scientific evidence aside. We also predict that there will eventually be a T.Q. (testosterone quotient) just like an I.Q. that will soon be able to be tested down to the $n$th power. If I were to judge by their outward behavior habits and appearance, knowing that women have a certain percentage of both male and female hormones circulating, I'd guess as follows. Let's say put ten percent as almost normal.

Among others I'd say the T.Q., in my estimation, would be eighty percent for former Congressman Bella Abzug, Indira Gandhi, Karen DeCrow (former president of NOW), Rosalynn Carter, former Congressman Patsy Mink, Barbara Walters, feminists Germaine Greer, Ti-Grace Atkinson, and Susan Brownmiller. Sixty percent for Margaret Thatcher, Kate Millet, Gloria Steinem, actress Jane Fonda, Liz Carpenter, *Washington Post* journalist Sally Quinn, associate editor Charlotte Curtis of the *New York Times*, newscaster Lynn Scherr. Forty percent, actress Marlo Thomas, Erica Jong, Betty Friedan, Eleanor Smeal (president of NOW), Estelle Ramey, political groupie Barbara Howar, Helen Gurley Brown. Normal, ten percent, Mrs. Ronald Reagan, Jackie O., *Today* show's Jane Pauley, Total Woman Marabell Morgan; less than ten percent, Sophia Loren, Raquel Welch, Bo Derek, newscaster Diane Sawyer.

What we are saying, backed by a welter of proof, is that "milk spilt can't be unspilt." Yet we must repeat again to our locker room brethren—though the conditioning myth has been nailed to the laboratory wall, this will not stop the diehard sleight-of-mind feminologists from continuing to try conjuring up a boar's ear from a silk purse. But if you study this chapter well, all of you chauvinists out there can set them straight at every turn—right from the filly's lips.

## CHAPTER V

# A Hank of Hair, a Bag of Bones, and N-E-R-V-E-S

Women display higher scores on nervousness, helplessness and anxiety than men regardless of age, social class or marital status.

*Dr. Martin Kety, National Institute of Mental Health Services*

It is anti-woman not to accept and appreciate the ebb and flow of female hormones and emotions.

*The New York Radical Feminists*

SPEAKING OF FALL GUYS, it is about time we chauvinists got out from under the most spurious rap since the Rape of the Sabines. So far we have taken our licks on this base canard as we always do—as men—without so much as a nasty word or a tearful eye. But here and now we can vouch for the fact that there is not a chauvinist among us who has ever conspired to put down females as emotional and unstable. Just because they weep at funerals and sob at weddings and bar mitzvahs, or because they go into hysterics when their thirteen-year-old daughters come home from camp pregnant, doesn't necessarily mean they have rocky temperaments. Now the brawnies claim that if it was not outright libel, it was our knowing looks, our behind-the-hand whispers and raw jokes that have impugned their temperament. Not only that, they imply that by this dirty rumor we knowingly and purposefully set out to keep them perpetually behind a mop, a typewriter, or a canning machine instead of in their rightful place at the head of General Motors.

## One Tear Is Worth a Thousand Slurs

Of course this is a low liberationist deception that will be exposed forthwith. The fact is, we chauvs are deeply sympathetic to the basic nature which may occasion lachrymose excesses in our feminine sisters. And we are as frequently embarrassed as they by the unsteadiness of their genetic heritage; but we would never gloat or take advantage of it.

We admittedly have little compassion for a tough political tomato like Gloria Steinem, especially when she broke down weeping on the floor of the 1972 Democratic Convention in Miami after losing on some minor feminist resolution. And who can sympathize with hard-boiled Bella, sniffling and dabbing away like a high school sophomore when she was hassled by a female reporter in one of her many unsuccessful campaigns?

Political males have emotions, but they don't get mad—they get even. Can you see a Mayor Daley sobbing his little heart out because one of his South Side lieutenants was caught working both sides of the street? Have you seen one Abscam "victim" exhibiting jitters, much less not brazening out his convictions to the last incriminating F.B.I. video tape? Obviously when Golda (may she rest in peace) almost flooded Jerusalem with tears at her inaugural, it was not purposeful—she just could not help herself. So if it is only natural to break down in an emotional crisis, what is there to be ashamed of? When those female glands say cry—why fight it?

### Test over Est—a Raunchy Eye or a Teary One

Gentlemen, we do not intend to grind the subject of hormones down as thin as the dime which the feminists claim is the only difference between us and them. But believe it or not, those glandular secretions alone make all the difference between a teary eye and a roving one. Those two different hormones—testosterone and estrogen—make the world go round, but—and the fems will not admit it—in opposite directions. And as we have already shown, it is not the nice gentling ovarian nectar that is the real culprit, but the absence of that wild and crazy testicular substance.

Notwithstanding these immutable precedents of history and science, the feminologists still say hormones be damned: If a girl on occasion is a little shaky it is only because of us, the male sexist society that has conditioned her so. Which is, of course, mere poppycock. A female may have Pavlov's bells ringing in her ears since birth and have had her consciousness raised into the stratosphere, and she wouldn't be any more immune to the classic blowups to which she is heir.

## Even the Way She Throws a Ball—It's Sexist Conditioning

Now we do not claim that conditioning does not have *some* influence on a few of the more superficial behavior patterns of women. But the fems' contention would wash a little better if they did not go overboard insisting that everything from monthly cramps to the way they walk is due to male oppression. Authors Barbara Ehrenreich and Deirdre English go even further in *The Sexual Politics of Sickness*, implying that female problems ranging from vaginal herpes to cystic mastitis are curable with a small dose of consciousness raising.

It is also pointed out ad nauseum that in our male society the little boy is always admonished to "be a man," and "no crying" when the fire department must pry his head loose from between the bars of the window looking into the girls' lavatory; yet the little girl is told to "go ahead and have a good cry" when her braces get caught with those of the sexist thirteen-year-old from across the street. Somehow, even if the perpetually five-o'clock-shadowed Pete Rose had been brought up in a starched pinafore and never missed his ballet lesson, it is hard to picture him banging his head against home plate when a third strike is called on a pitch destined for the press box.

## Germaine's "Sick Headaches"—No Different than Her Aardvark Sister's

What is particularly disconcerting about the feminologists' absurd catchall pronouncements is the offhanded way they dismiss factual anthropologic data. Our glands (both male and female) were not born yesterday. Betty Friedan still experiences most of the same emotional problems as her female aardvark ancestor.

And the Yogi Berra of the iguana species is just as thick-skinned, raunchy, and aggressive as the namesake he spawned. That male *Hormone of Champions* is powerful stuff, affecting every cell in our bodies from the function of that overrated puddinglike substance in our skulls to the overabundant placement of the hair follicles on our chests. And as it produces every revolting habit of our own male character, so its absence in the female dictates not only an unhairy chest but every conscious and subconscious neurotic female behavior symptom. And speaking of nerves, who ever heard of a man with anorexia nervosa.

Other than that which we so obviously see in our daily living, there is also evidence that the charming if inconsistent ways of most females are no chauvinist myth. Even the research of the bureaucratic Public Health Service shows that, from the most educated and privileged young housewives to George Price's cartoon scullery maid spouse, edginess and anxiety are quite typical. Drs. Gerard Hogarty and Martin Kety of the National Institute of Mental Health, after studying 450 specimens of both sexes, conclude that emotional bouts with embarrassing symptoms of "nerves" are just normal in women.

It's made even more evident not only in women's greater need for alcohol, which we've discussed, but also drugs, according to the National Institute on Drug Abuse. The statistics show that women have twice as many prescriptions for psychoactive drugs as do men, and women are twice as likely as men to show up in emergency rooms for drug abuse. Thirty-one million American women (or forty-two percent of the total female population) have used tranquilizers, compared with eighteen million men (or twenty-seven percent of the total male population). For sedatives and stimulants, it's almost as bad.

Of course, they'll say we chauvs have driven them to it, or male doctors are out to get them. But in return, we feel that as little as we are dependent on drugs, about ninety percent of it is caused by that implacable female weapon—deadlier than the thumbscrew—the daily nag.

## Was Hitler Less a Führer Because He Chewed Persian Rugs?

Though we chauvinists take the female's little ups and downs in gentlemanly tolerance, not so their own liberationist sisters. On the contrary, they play down each female sulk and sizzle as if they should not exist. Listening to their hard-boiled litany, you would think their more gentle sisters should have no feelings at all. Is it a national disaster for a healthy young female to dissolve in her own juices at the sights and sounds of a gyrating Mick Jagger? Was Hitler any less of a führer because he chewed an expensive Persian rug when his troops refused to counterattack barefooted in the snows of Siberia? In times of dire stress even the strongest men let it all out. So why is it a disgrace for a woman to be labeled emotionally labile when she pumps a bullet or two into her spouse as he sidles in at 4:00 A.M. sporting "lipstick round the collar"?

## As Stable as Lizzie—as Cool as Patty

Nevertheless, to the feminists any emotionalism in women is all sexist *Tammy-rot*. To them, every female from the Madwoman of Chaillot to Squeaky Fromme is as calm as a British neurosurgeon.

Women's facial appearance at the moment of truth can at times camouflage their rather unsteady nature. This makes it twice as hazardous to a male's health. Look where poor old Scarsdale Diet doctor Hi Tarnower, with his little black book, wound up when Jean Harris's hormones raged. Yet on the stand, outwardly she was as cool as a burglar as she described "accidentally" pulling the trigger five times. But that's nothing new. Statistics have shown that even the most unerring husbands are done in by their doting wives sixty percent more than erring wives are by doting husbands. The fems blatantly persist in reversing this truth, as we shall show in the battered wife myth.

Now, ordinarily, if the fems had not brought up this emotional business we would have let it lie. What reason had we to expose it when anyone can observe the collective hysteria at one of

Macy's basement January white sales? But now that we are accused of perpetrating the exposure of the true female emotions, we chauvs must defend our honor and discount the big lie. As gentlemen we are loathe to go into one of the less genteel aspects of this controversy—but we must.

## The Monthly Clockwork Orange

Over and beyond minor neurotic actions like those of Lizzie Borden with her ax, which easily could have been due to conditioning by her father—it was more likely P.M.T. (premenstrual tension)—no one would be surprised by a little shaky behavior around the time of the female's monthly clockwork orange. Remember, a jury of her peers with a compassion for the mental quirks of the females' physiology acquitted Liz. But to support the everyday observations of both males and the more objective feminine females, a report from the Center for Crime and Violence of the National Institute of Mental Health states that "a majority of shoplifting, child battering, and suicides by women happens in the week before their period." It is also cited that ten percent of premenstrual tension occurs with personality changes, uncontrolled by either hormones or psychotherapy.

With all of this, we chauvs actually try to cover for them. We certainly cover up for them in the office, rather than bruit it about that the moon has any dire effect on absenteeism or output. Of course some of those quota boys in management with their jobs on the line have a harder nose when it comes to employment or advancement possibilities.

## If It's Chicken Ice Cream She Craves—Beware the Pregnant Pause

Leave it to our ever-practical Russian brothers (not us) to come right out with it. Their official planners, according to *Pravda*, take no chances—even if it is illegal for any Soviet to discriminate against women at any time. But at that time of the month, the shop commissars prohibit lady workers from "dealing with expensive, dangerous, or delicate machinery or with instruments demanding consistent flawless performance." We are sure that even our least chauvinistic industrialist management and efficiency experts do not mind admitting that when it comes to a two-million-dollar piece of equipment, the question of female steadiness becomes more than academic. But they have more subtle ways of circumventing such delicate matters. With a little raise here and there, an occasional trip with the boss, or the shop foreman looking the other way during the half-hour bathroom break, the women are made to feel that the typewriter is as delicate and expensive as a microcomputer.

But one type of firm, to our surprise, the stockbrokers, did come right out with it on the front page of the *Wall Street Journal*. They put it right on the line, and with the scorching reaction they got from the fems, probably wish they hadn't. Merrill Lynch, among others, confessed they did not allow women to trade in commodity futures. They stated categorically that long experience shows that women get too emotional and too confused in the fast give-and-take of trading and also frequently cannot be counted on to pay up on margin or credit accounts. One executive reportedly said, "Volatile feminine emotions can lead to disasters in commodity dealings."

We also would not dare bring up the strange proclivities of the menopausal female or that other significant pause—the pregnant one. In those fertile months, during a board meeting lunch, if she orders something like chicken ice cream or begins nibbling at the lead paint on the aluminum chairs, we bury our noses in our coq au vin, look the other way, and talk about Reagan's supply-side economics.

## High Moon

Now the fems just refuse to believe that our compassionate minds are constantly thinking only of their welfare as we put our "girl Fridays" on the back burner during those periods of stress. Would we expect any human to keep on an even keel when she is having cramps that would colic a dray horse, or when she is six weeks overdue with that incipient maternal glow? How can these ungrateful liberationists accuse us, of all people, of being at the root of their own instability—we who have always been their strong right arm when the blahs were upon them? From the time of our brother Lancelots at the Round Table, we have catered to the god-given female frailties. And unless we are in the middle of an important gin game, who else has been right at their side in their worst moments, even phoning the men in the white coats when those lunar episodes got out of hand.

Still, our motives are continually misconstrued. Most of those less feminine women who would not know a case of n-e-r-v-e-s from an Excedrin headache, threaten, "Don't do our sisters any favors; all that pampering is what got them into the shape they're in in the first place." So now, since liberation, when these flare-ups occur, we men of the house have learned to take them graciously and quietly with a fifth of Black Label.

## Any Woman Treated by a Male Psychiatrist Should Have Her Head Examined

No revolution is without ailing participants; no movement can claim all healthy members. Women, prone as they naturally are to nervous conditions, are a little more so and are among psychiatry's best-paying customers (both in and out of the cuckoo's nest). Sooner or later, therefore, the male psychiatric fraternity was bound to be nailed to the feminist cross. In fact, a group of female psychologists has demanded one million dollars in reparation from the American Psychological Association "for perpetrating male superiority and contributing to female mental illness." We are especially sympathetic to those already benighted (if not slightly daft) psychiatric brethren of ours who have now come under the scattershot blunderbuss of the most scathing gunslingers of them all: those feminists with scientific degrees. Psychologist Phyllis Chesler, professor at the City University of New York and author of *Women and Madness*, came out with the blatantly wild accusation that it is the "male psychiatrist who is driving women crazy." As Samuel Goldwyn would have put it, "any female who goes to a male psychiatrist should have her head examined."

Now Chesler may need a little couch time herself, for it is no secret that over ninety-five percent of psychiatrists would not be caught dead with their couches anywhere but in the vicinity of Park Avenue or a posh suburb. So what about all those women who are "driven crazy" in Watts, Harlem, Appalachia, or Sligo, Pennsylvania, without the benefit of shrinks?

## More Like Hugh Hefner Than Sigmund Freud

This feminist Ph.D. also maintains that because women admire men as authorities, they choose to go to *male* psychiatrists. And she goes on, "if a sister is just mildly neurotic, all of her *usual* symptoms will increase with each visit, thus—more headaches, more nightmares, more fatigue, etc., etc." But the good doctor *as a female* has probably not kept up with some of the newer male creative techniques sweeping her specialty. It is calculated that over fifteen percent of our he-man healers practice a form of the mending art one would expect more from Hugh Hefner than Sigmund Freud. There is nothing new about fornication, but to our knowledge its use as a mental health tool has been somewhat overlooked ever since Hippocrates. We chauvinists have always known what miraculous therapy it is for *us*, but were never sure it could cure the heebie-jeebies. But that avant garde clique of specialists who have come up with everything from Primal Scream to est are now practicing this ancient art (older than acupuncture) with reports of phenomenal success. They insist that this unorthodox use of the couch is more effective than shock therapy and prevents more wall climbing than three Valiums and a stiff gin chaser. Of course Chesler, most likely a very chaste lady who most likely treats mainly straight non-tennis-circuit females, probably has little experience in this new miracle of the healing arts.

Admittedly, the more elderly male practitioners of the new art are actually sacrificing themselves for their profession when they have to indulge in six or eight of those fifty-minute hours a day. Not only that, but there is always the question of who gets the best treatment—Betty Friedan or Bo Derek.

Dr. Chesler also goes on to accuse the chauvinist doctor of being psychologically damaging to the female patient while bolstering his own ego by telling her "not to try emulating men and remain their true feminine selves." This therapeutic device of course makes sense to us, but according to feminist theology, the male psychiatrist is killing two birds with one stone: downing the female, while upping the male.

## It Takes One to Know One

The big question, however, is why most women take their troubles to male psychiatrists when there are so many female shrinks with empty waiting rooms. So then Chesler makes the big pitch for the female trade: "The female psychiatrist knows the female's problems better than the male because [as she unwittingly admits] women practitioners experience the same emotional compulsions, complaints, and cycles as their patients." Well, do they now? And isn't that an incriminating admission when most of her less-learned feminist colleagues claim that women are just as stoical as Gordon Liddy? These two feminist factions should get together and work it out—is she the icy type or a bundle of steam? As we have shown, she is both, blowing hot and cold.

Now there is one other rather pathetic female frailty which ordinarily we would not bring up; but recently a female did. Maggie Scarf, one of the *New York Times*'s most prestigious science writers, recently came out with a book on female depression called *Unfinished Business: Pressure Points in the Lives of Women*. She maintains that in evolution, emotional bonding developed more with females to males than vice-versa and eventually found its way into the female's genetic code.

However, whenever the feminists hear the words "genetic" or "bonding" or anything that suggests an inborn trait, other than the sexual conditioning on which they blame all of their woes, they become disturbed, abusive, and undergo a frenetic disintegration. So Maggie was bound to catch it sooner or later—and she did. But here, Ms. Scarf goes on to tell it as honestly as she always does. "This bonding, once the key to survival, is making women's lives more difficult in the feminist era; usually triggered by professional failure. They are vulnerable to depression because emotional attachment is so important to them, and mood is a function of biology, not conditioning. Some say they would rather kill themselves than live alone," which is how so many females live today. Yet as the arbiters of feminist society repeat to their sisters, "That is the hallmark of independence," even though the polls show most women want to be married and have children. And whether the fems admit to it or not, depression is something that can't be exorcised by feminologist mumbo-jumbo. It has also been shown that forty percent of the women goaded by the fems into the marketplace after years of homemaking suffered more stress and depression than those who stayed home. Though Ms. Scarf's book got general critical acclaim, the feminists, as expected, called it a "sellout," "written from a female chauvinist point of view."

## *Waiting for Godot—the Wriggler*

Well, far be it for us to argue with a top science analyst, but every chauv should at least know why *she* is what *she is* with her ups and downs.

Each and every one of our sisters has a basic function besides wanting to collect a closetful of shoes she will never wear. That function, whether she uses it or not, is built in—it is called reproduction. And bringing a little stranger into the world, believe it or not, depends on those ups and downs. That constant state of peaks and valleys (in contrast to the dull consistency of us males) means that her hormones are working day and night on every cell of her body—from brain to breast to uterus—waiting for her Godot: that wriggling devil, the pointy-headed sperm. So every day in every way, pregnant or unpregnant, there's a whole new soma and psyche. If every cell in the body and brain never knows where its next aggravation is coming from, imagine the confusion of the whole. She is lucky if she ever feels the same way two days running. But how and why did all this come about?

The male-female format foisted on us in Eden had to have some stability. How could the species survive with just the female flibbertygibbet type? So God chose the male, the cool and collected one; from the very beginning, the footloose, bemuscled, Neanderthal male. Burdened with facing the tusks of the wild boar, he either had to have nerves of steel which brought in the bacon, or he himself became it. When the time came—eyeball to eyeball—the unemotional male DNA did not blink; he trapped, hunted, and salted away the raw porker for his more flighty other half and her toddlers back in the cave.

On the other hand, while in the safety of that cave, she had only to contend with herself and her family. But to survive she had to use her every emotion (not her cool) with every manner of nasty child and moody husband. The only things which the ape man would stare at incredulously were tears, fits, and hysterical floor-pounding jags. Learning this in the bush, only those highly emotional females survived to advance to the three-bedroom, two-bathroom, air-conditioned rancher. And, by these ingrown techniques so easily evoked, she gets the living room redecorated and has her spouse take a third mortgage on the house (at nineteen percent) to make a big splash for her teenager's coming-out party. And though denigrated by her feminist sisters, the average female has lived happily ever after with her emotions, rampant and ready to explode at the slightest provocation.

For instance, who ever heard of a male acting like the ex-communicated Mormon, Sonia Johnson? She who the feminists beatified recently, said she became so enraged by the church leaders that she knelt in prayer and wished she could kill God, screaming at him for creating a religion against the ERA. Well, we thought it was a bit tasteless wishing a man dead in his own house.

## Y—Steady as a Whale; X—Fidgety as a Chipmunk

So, chauvinists, it is a rock-bottom fact that the male qualities—loving the thrill of deadly battle, on and off fornication (then the big snore), and politics—were transmitted down through the ages in that Y chromosome, steady as a whale. They are yours and yours alone. But also remember, by contrast, there is that more explosive, fragile female X chromosome carrying those fidgety-as-a-chipmunk, fly-off-the-spindle explosions still so intimidating to us sensitive males. And, from the way it looks, never the twain shall meet.

If Konrad Lorenz and the science of ethology are correct, the feminine female's emotional state is the product of her history, and not much is going to change that. And though that X substance may now be humming "We Shall Overcome," even the ERA will not ever produce a sobering of those raging hormones.

## CHAPTER VI

# The Brain That's Tame Lies Mainly in the Dame: Truth in Femming

Woman's intellectuality is paid for by the loss of valuable feminine qualities.

*Helen Deutsch (eminent psychologist)*

A woman guided by the head, not the heart, is a social pestilence: she has all the defects of the passionate and affectionate woman with none of her compensations: she is without pity, without love, without virtue, and mostly without sex.

*Honoré de Balzac*

IT'S HARDLY ANY CHAUVINIST'S AIM to upset our sexual opposites, but it's not our fault if the truth irks. From the beginning, the fems have fought the overwhelming evidence of their inborn emotional and physical plight as brought out by responsible scientists. Now it's their mental capacity that's on the line. Though it's not easy being touted as the intellectual Avis of society, there's no doubt they are trying harder. But by fighting it, all they've created is a gaping credibility that's wider than Mr. Nixon's with his tapes. In the process they've also made more male martyrs than Caesar could crowd into the Coliseum.

The latest martyr to "truth in femming" (just down from the cross) is Dr. Thorkill Vanggard, the prestigious sixty-nine-year-old chief psychiatrist at Copenhagen National Hospital and former president of the International Society of Psychoanalysts. As we know, psychiatrists have an abnormal penchant for both personal and professional masochism bordering on the suicidal. However, some choose the most peculiar methods—such as throwing themselves into a witch's cauldron. (It may be more drawn out than hara-kiri or a fistful of Seconals, but it will probably get the desired results—the author should know.)

The venerable Dr. Vanggard, expert in the ways of the brain, had the temerity to claim the truth: "Modern research has demonstrated the difference between male and female brains which explains the male's superiority in abstract thinking." He continues his suicidal course: "The average woman's desire to be a homebody is deeply rooted in human nature and has nothing to do with cultural conditioning or male suppression." Now we didn't say that—but every male with his marrow-deep ego knows this in his bones.

## *Ms. the Ramparts! Unsheathe the Hatpins!*

For some obscure reason, those few words touched the nerve roots (if not the brain cells) of most of the equalitized, affirmed Danish feminists. They went after the good doctor, dripping venom from the tongue and lightning from their bloodshot eyeballs. Their attitude was predictable: truth-schmuth; science-schmience; this Samson must be shorn. They filed formal complaints with the government's health board, the ministry of education, and medicine's board of ethics. It was like Galileo revisited or the plight of Darwin after telling the English nobility that Lord Nonesuch (that portrait above the Great Hall's fireplace) was descended from a long line of jungle baboons.

## *The Truth Irks*

The Danish hatpins were drawn for the pinking, and the sisters from Brooklyn and San Francisco joined in: "The doctor had proven himself medically incompetent, scientifically dishonest, and unfit to treat female patients." (How about treating males?) Also, he "provoked women to feel humiliated, despised, and inferior." This has been a common fem cry about every jock from the gynecologist to the stevedore. We can't help their feelings any more than we can help our own.

Like most of us, Dr. Vanggard took it—like a man. Though the highest echelons in feminist literary, scientific, and social disciplines have vilified Pope Paul, Teddy Kennedy, Dr. Spock, Norman Mailer, Joe Namath, and a host of other male notables, not a one of those suffering souls has even issued a demurrer, much less brought charges against their hang*persons*. Now a few years later, Dr. Vanggard has neither been convicted of one of these charges nor refuted in his contention by any scientist. Which says nothing of the harried life he will lead thenceforth, with the fems snapping at his heels to graveside.

## *Salivation—but Rarely Cerebration*

But enough of the present tenor of the times. It shouldn't take a Dr. Kildare to answer the big question fabled in song and story, why can't a woman *think* more like a man? Scientifically, it's elemental. As scientists have pretty much shown, she was born with a woman's brain, and everyone who ever had a mother knows there is a difference. But far be it from us to publicly cast any doubt on the state of the feminist mind or openly intimate that Dr. Vanggard isn't anything but a chauvinist sluggard of the first rank. We have no penchant for carrying crosses nor being nailed to one. We wouldn't dare voice approval of our brother's claims (as the author once did with a former congresswoman—with disastrous results). But neither can we publicly state that their brains function identically to ours. Nor can we but mention in passing that reflexes may be built to condition the female to salivate but could never make her cerebrate like a man.

But then it's not just, why can't a woman think more like a man? but rather, why does she want to? Is there any valid reason why the feminists try so hard to show their constituents that they're on the same brain wavelength as a Charles Manson or a Jack the Ripper? With a porpoise or a chimpanzee, maybe, but shouldn't they count their blessings? In itself, seeking such a dubious mental status casts doubt on female intellectuality.

However, though most feminine females don't, many of the more masculinized feminists do. Simone de Beauvoir's father and Sartre, her consort for some thirty years, both said, "Simone thinks just like a man."

## Regardless of Race, Creed, or Talent

Because of such violent attacks on the good doctor by the Steinzugs of the world, the fems are only further damaging their case. Now they've gone even further. Having launched their missiles against almost every award-giving group from Miss America to the Pulitzer, they recently dumped all out on that manly Nobel Prize jury. They're all steamed up because almost a century has passed with only the rare female awarded that greatest of intellectual recognition. They claim that the sexist Nobel jury paid entirely too much attention to brain power and not enough to female power, disregarding of all things affirmative action, female pride, and equal rights. The fems imply that achievement isn't everything, and the old system of the Crackerjack box (where everyone got a prize) wasn't so bad.

Being of democratic persuasion we can see their point, but they must understand there should still be shown a semblance of some talent in competing for the award. Talent or no talent, B.L. (before liberation) we chauvs always tried to bolster the image females had of their own mentality—but subtly, under the table. We allowed them a few kudos, and even a few shekels. For instance, in the fixed TV shows of the 50s, which supposedly tested America's best brains, we arranged it (cutting a few legal corners) so that a female or two answered the $64,000 question. Even since then, the few modern female painters, usually of secondary or tertiary status (like Frankenthaler or Hartigan), were always accorded a showing here and there, getting the usual secondary and tertiary prizes. And before that, when the rare female talent popped up in literature, like a George Sand or a Virginia Woolf, we were always soft on them, showing respect and critical acclaim no matter how androgynous they were.

## Something Rotten in Stockholm

We have never said that there aren't some brilliant women around, but as in politics or boardrooms they are few and far between. However, since the equality binge, they not only inti-

mate their brains' smilarity to the male's, but also that there are
as many of them. And the grating thing is that they rub in this
Goebbels's-like "big lie" to bosses, live-ins, and husbands as if it
came from the "Mount." Now we have taken their push for equality of opportunity and equal pay with grace, but to have them
even suggest a similar intellectual bent was too much.

I'm not sure what they expect, but so far the only aftermath
we've seen to this sort of verbal daydreaming has been a greater
impetus to wife battering, a thirty-five percent increase in divorce, and rampant female alcoholism. If they would only face up
to the facts and admit their differences, we would go even further
out on a limb to make up for those inherent dissimilarities and
possibly put even a better face on the few aptitudes they do
have.

But we must admit, taking the female at her best, there seemed
to be something rotten in Stockholm—at least in one category.
There has been only one female Nobelist in literature. We, of
course, are not surprised that the physics prize would be out of
their ken, what with their difficulties in opening cans or unclog-
ging sinks. Their checkbook balancing naturally proscribes economics. But we do believe in aptitude tests, tests which have
shown that though women may be inferior in spatial arrange-
ments, abstract thought, mathematics, and other disciplines, they
*do* show verbal skills. So if they have those skills, how was it that
Solzhenitsyn and Saul Bellow got the Nobel Prize in literature,
and not Joyce Carol Oates, Doris Lessing, or even the feminist
literary heroine Erica Jong (of Zipless F--k fame)?

## Why Not Needlepoint?

Though the fems still gloss over the incidentals of talent and
performance, there have been five or six women in those hundred
Nobel years (among a couple of thousand men) who have shown
they have both. But then the females carp that, yes, the jury has
shown some slight empathy for the cause, but that in over seventy years not one woman has become a Nobel laureate on her
own. Even Marie Curie had to share it with her husband and
another male. As Freud implied, "Are they never satisfied?" I

don't say those accusers are paranoid, but when recently those gentlemen from Stockholm chose a woman in medicine for the first time in some thirty years, the fems acrimoniously indicted them for rubbing their noses in it: that particular female Nobel laureate had to share the prize with not one but two males (and if her own male partner hadn't died—she'd be one in four).

## Total War for the Peace Prize

As is their wont, the fems didn't let up. Since the movement has become politicized, the libs have unashamedly put on an all-out campaign to get their share of national and international prizes whether they stack up or not. The 1979 peace award reflected one of the most flagrant of those campaigns. It was run as if Boss Tweed and Mayor Daley had teamed up with the Politburo. Through supporting marches, chanting mobs, and threats of a boycott of Swedish diet toast and Bergman movies, the famed feminist clout of the 70s finally did it. The prize—a first in history —went to two (as usual), women who tried to bring peace to embattled Ireland. Yet not unlike the $64,000 question, this back-fired too, giving even the white dove of peace a black eye.

Those genteel, dovelike ladies from Belfast not only soon broke up (in a less than peaceful way), but in the process produced another first for women they'll never live down. Ordinarily the peace prize money is generously given up to a good and unwar-like cause. Schweitzer gave his to build a leper hospital; even Kissinger gave his to a worthy institution. But these two biddies not only wouldn't let go of a kroner for the cause of harmony and conciliation in Ireland, but in a bloody front-page battle those peacemakers ferociously fought the peace organization they them-selves started.

## In Black and White—It's Gray That Counts

Still, as the Nobel (and the Pulitzer) gentlemen proclaim their innocence of all bias, rubbing even more raw the synapses in the feminist brain, scientific research supports them. As we said, we don't deny that there are a passel of smart women in the world, but according to the new brain scientists it's a matter of quantity. It seems that there are just not enough of them. As science and history have now shown in black and white, it's the gray matter that counts—and it seems to be stacked in the male's favor, which is understandably very upsetting to the fems. For when we get right down to it, the mental terrain is the ultimate Armageddon of the feminist forces and if they lose there, what else is left? As novelist Françoise Sagan said, "There is no such thing as winning the battle of the sexes." Now if they had just a bit more cool they'd lay back and live happily ever after. You can show the ladies every bit of historical or anthropological evidence that not only the battle but their war was lost hundreds of millions of years ago. However, they just won't face it that way back in the murky Pleistocene period the powers-that-be decided once and for all which sex would get most of the beauty and which the bulk of the brains. What's done can't be undone.

## Vive La . . .

Prior to the now-waning feminist era, we knew just by living with them that woman's brain was different from ours. Strindberg obviously knew it a hundred years ago when one of the male characters in his play said to the female, "If we were descended from the ape it must have been from two different species. There's no likeness between us at all."

But it has taken sound, twentieth-century scientific investigation to determine what a great difference there really is. That same old hormone leads the male to experience life differently, to be sensitive in different ways to all of the many and varied stimuli: sight, touch, hearing, smelling, and even loving. It's shown that we even figure our problems differently than the female and use different parts of our brain doing it.

Since the study of brain damage in humans we have known that on the whole, women are more dominated by the left hemisphere of the brain (the verbal one) and men by the right or visual one. Men's hemispheres don't compete with each other and can thus concentrate on specific problem solving, creativity, and mathematics; while women's coordinate the hemispheres which may be the seat of their intuition.

Not only that, we can see under the electron microscope that we have different sizes and kinds of brain cells. This has recently become so obvious that the usually cautious weekly journals *Time* and *Newsweek*, and the BBC, braving feminist ire, have courageously come out with cover stories of the characteristic dissimilarities governed by their hormones—even if five years late. It's no longer just theory, since both male and female scientists alike have reached the same conclusions.

## Aggression: The Endearing Lack

Far be it for us to title this chapter, "the brain that's tame . . ." as just a putdown—it's a fact of female thinking. A real feminine woman (quite apart from the feminist) was never the aggressive one in thought or action. And if she would be true to her nature, this enduring, and endearing, lack of mental aggressiveness— stemming of course from birth, not conditioning—should be counted as a virtue. Yet the feminists are ashamed of it and try to downplay it in their more gentle sisters. But as far back as our porcine ancestors, one can watch their litters demonstrate this. From the moment of birth it's the male who knows what he's after and strikes out for the fullest teat. It's the female follower who winds up with the poor hind tit. So even the big front that some females have now adopted (they call it assertiveness) is as out of character as a rabbit attacking a president.

## Ms-sion Improbable

As the evidence piles up on the separate and unequal intellectual powers of male and female, even the feminists admit that the male mind is more vigorous and ambitious. Nevertheless, they refuse to accept a recent report from the prestigious National Assessment of Educational Progress (NAEP). This group, financed by the federal government, had the nerve (according to NOW) to release a terrible report that just about put the intellect of women on a par with some of her more turtle-brained ancestors. The report showed that in all-around intellectuality, men did much better than women. The group even tested the sexes at different ages. And though we ourselves have no ready proof of this, a recent case does seem to substantiate the thesis of the report. In 1978, Oxford University, for the first time in 542 years, allowed women to apply for All Souls College. It took three years in a worldwide search to find even *one* woman who could qualify at the lowest possible level: a junior research fellowship.

## The Sexist Bermuda Triangle

That NAEP report also seems to be supported in the brainy games people play. How about chess? Only two percent of some eighty million players are women. Now there may be a Siberia for the only two picketing Soviet feminists but never for a Soviet chess player, male or female. Any topnotch Russian chess*person* has as much prestige as a commissar. It goes without saying that had a female champion or even a female master surfaced, a Russian father (chauvinist that he is) would hardly hold his prodigy daughter back—knowing what it means in rubles and dachas.

Not only chess but the game of bridge also supports the NAEP report—in spades. We all know in the West that bridge in the afternoon has been a national female pastime for over a half century, and though it's not weight lifting, there must be a reason that there is still a men's and women's championship (as there is in chess). In more than thirty years of the Bermuda International Bridge Contest where women are allowed, only a handful of them have been qualified among those millions of day-in-day-out lady bridge club addicts. Most don't survive the opening rounds. Could there be a sort of sexist Bermuda Triangle dulling the brains of female bridge players, letting the male get through?

## Relax and Accept It

But feminists, with their own research feminologists working overtime, will no doubt try to show even the NAEP tests as fixed, distorted, biased. And why not? They'll still not admit that a male brain put another male on the moon and also thought up the Whopper Burger.

As Johns Hopkins researcher Camilla Benbow said, many women "can't bring themselves to accept sexual differences in aptitudes. But the difference in math [two males to one female in math scores over 500] is a fact. The best way to help girls is to accept it and go from there."

## Libber-gate

But not NOW. They wanted the NAEP report suppressed because it blows away their equality party line. Well, this kind of feminist coercion smacks not only of quota systems but of a cover-up tantamount to our own male Watergate. Of course in our jockish world it's taken for granted that cover-ups are a part of American industrial life. We know that the lifetime light bulb has been under wraps for fifty years and that there is a perpetual motion machine hidden away in some conglomerate warehouse. But that is good old U.S.A. corporate ethics, not the forthright, unbiased, impartial organization which NOW and other liblike groups lay claim to.

Not only did the female brain amateurishly practice the skills of intellectual cover-up but even the fine art of bribery. Here they committed the cardinal sin—they got caught. The ERA girls were exposed redhandedly offering an Illinois legislator money for his yea vote on the amendment. Of course the ERA didn't stand a chance once this bit of Abscam hit the headlines. It's appalling, but the feminists' cerebral cortexes can't seem to get it straight that they, like Wilbur Mills, Wayne Hayes, and Caesar's wife, must be above suspicion even if below on test scores.

## That Sour Smell of Success

Since the NAEP report has been proved undoctored, there are other more incriminating reports on the state of their mentality, such as Dr. Matina Horner's. As a psychologist and the president of Radcliffe College (not bad credentials), she recently stated that "competition, independence, confidence, and intellectual achievement are in conflict with feminity." Well, what's so new about that? We've been saying all along that really successful women are masculinized—more or less—which science has now proved.

Then Dr. Horner goes on to say, "There is a natural fear of success by women." Well, we can't buy that for all women. After seeing those few of the androgynous jugular-type females clawing their way toward the top, their aggression shows no "fear of success." If they could make it—by hook, crook, or brain—they would. But again, feminist must not be confused with feminine.

## Damn the Cum Laude—Full Speed Abed

However, Horner is saying that if the bright female wants to date she must hide her smarts. She's way off base. If Sophia Loren had the brain of George Bernard Shaw, she'd still be drooled over by stevedores and sophomores alike.

It's true that men are more attracted by breasts than brains, but it's also sad but true that the masculinized brainy women are usually not that breasty. So it's not that the female "brain" intimidates; it's just that usually their sexual wherewithal is lacking. But whichever way it's figured, when a man comes home from a long day at the office, he's not so much in the mood to discuss the fourth law of thermodynamics as he is in seeing his sweetheart of Sigma Chi in a Saran wrap. Also, when he goggles at those beauties jiggling at a "live show," Chaucer is not foremost on his mind.

Now we are not alone in our feeling on which type of female has the gray matter. The eminent psychologist Helen Deutsch puts it right on the line: "The intellectual woman is so because she is masculinized." Naturally if that chemistry makes the brain more male, it obviously would make the breasts, buttocks, and bottoms less female. This of course is the real problem in the sexual attractiveness of brilliant women. So Horner is way out in left field as to why Burt Reynolds wasn't nuts over Hannah Arendt.

## The Kinky IQ

Though we chauvs have always been intrigued by a pretty face, we're chagrined to admit we've been fooled. We don't even know what we're missing if we write off those brainy ones arbitrarily. If we can overlook some of their masculine traits we're in for a treat. As Professor William Simon says, the female brain works itself up to a strange magic. He maintains that the female intellectuals—the Margaret Meads and Susan Sontags—to our amazement are "less hung up by sex, are more orgasmic and more varied in their sexual activity" than their Phyllis George sisters. In other words, they are the real sexpots: "They not only want sex more often, but enjoy it more." This thesis undoubtedly held up in history. The brainy Catherine the Great of Russia divided her time equally between running the government and running her courtiers ragged—sometimes six a day. Cigar-smoking (hardly a feminine habit) George Sand would romp in her special sleigh bed till all hours—then get up and write until dawn.

As Kinsey showed, fifty percent of graduate school women had had sexual play before the age of nine (Wow!) and orgasms by eleven (Wow! Wow!). Not only that, but most single women who were getting their Ph.D.s had coitus at least five times in any single week (Wow! Wow! Wow!)—when they could snare a partner. Also, according to Kinsey, they were much more kinky in their sexual practices—We-e-e-o-o-o-o-w! So behind those hornrimmed specs, Dr. Horner to the contrary, lurks a woman of sexual spirit who shouldn't have to hide any of her prowess under a bushel. They just need that equal opportunity.

## Testosterone, Where Is Thy Sting?

Neither the beautiful nor the smart need accept this next piece of scientific evidence. There has been data already reported that could throw the most intelligent feminist into a lifelong slump. Most objective female investigators are intimating (what we knew all along) that the influence of the male hormone testosterone generally determines the level of intelligence and achievement of the female. Though Helen Deutsch mentions it, Dr. Corrine Hutt in her book *Males and Females* states categorically: "To be an achiever in any discipline calls for single-mindedness. ... The male hormone is what contributes to this success. Furthermore, from experiments and observations, "as the masculinity of the female rises, so does her IQ." This, of course, could account for some of the shrewdness of some of those he-man feminists.

Now does this mean that if we come across a young girl who loves to hang around poolrooms, pitches a no-hitter for her high school, and admires Jimmy Hoffa more than Robert Redford, that she'll someday be the head of AT&T? Well, it looks that way. This has been substantiated (see chapter IV) by Dr. Anke Ehrhardt, formerly of Johns Hopkins University (and a host of other female researchers). To repeat only to emphasize: A meticulous study of ten girls who were masculinized in utero and brought up in the same sexist society as any other female, all were achievers of the *worst* male kind. They had unusually high IQs: sixty percent had IQs over 130 (while random samples of feminine girls showed IQs of that level amounted to about twenty-two percent). All of these testosteronized girls were more interested in fantasizing about achievement than in listening for wedding bells. They also scored twice as high in aggressive activities. Dr. June Reinesch of Rutgers states, "The male hormone by its presence or absence sets a potential in females for . . . intellect."

## Those Female Turncoats

Without a stiff double vodka chaser, this of course is tough to take for the average feminist. Nor does it make a host of honest female scientists any heroines of the feminists. In fact most are given short shrift by the hard core of consciousness raisers and are considered as some kind of female Benedict Arnold. For instance, Jane Levy, a top brain researcher at the University of Chicago, was blasted by hostile feminist letters and threatening phone calls. Harvard's Professor Hrdy, a feminist who published on "math superiority" was stunned when another female scientist sitting beside her at a meeting hissed, "Don't you know it's evil to do studies like that?"

## Women's World—Survival of the Fetus

At the risk of being a bore and relating all of man's (*person's*) habits, vices, and virtues (as I have done before) to those dark doubtful forces such as history, evolution, genes, and hormones so unacceptable to feminists, I shall only cite anthropologists who have studied male and female before Peking man.

With the coming of the Ice Age, when our vegetation-eating ancestors had to come down from the trees to hunt, only the most intelligent, the most wily, and the most devious could survive. The female couldn't have, for she was too busy with things like cooking, pregnancy, and keeping the kids from winding up as python rations. So for ten thousand generations it was up to only the most testosteronized male brains to devise an ambush, build a fort or an alliance, and think up a thousand ways to kill and not be killed. Thus only those best at it survived. They then naturally passed along those brainy qualities via the male hormones—naturally—to their male offspring. If the male were any less than this, he could never have outsmarted either his lesser-brained predators nor trap the red-meated animals he so loved to crunch.

## *P.M.T. = Q.E.D.*

As for the Paleolithic woman, she had excellent excuses even then. How could she have made it on her own, going to bed for three days with an Excedrin migraine or premenstrual tension; or when in labor, leaving her kiddies with nothing to eat and at the mercy of roving bands of pygmies or leopards? In those perilous times, her survival, her insurance policy, was only the protection her man gave. And thus she depended more upon her charm to the male eye and her childbearing success to the male ego than her brain power.

According to laureates Tinbergen and Lorenz, even today one can see that a female robin seeks security (no less than the modern female on the make), not looking twice at an unintelligent potential mate who didn't have the brains to stake out a territory for her. So, as the male animal has said for eons, "take care of the cave and leave the hunting to us."

However, if the libs want to revise history, change genetics, and fly in the face of Darwin just to be like us—all is not lost. We hesitate to bring practical science into such a discussion; however, it has been sort of proved that it's only a matter of removing the ovaries and taking a few shots a day to keep femaleness away. If the male hormone can make the East German females gold-medal swimmers, why shouldn't this potent stuff make Nobel laureates? But, as Dr. Faustus reminds her, there is always that day of reckoning. And as she puts Mozart to shame and invents perpetual motion, she'll also grow hairier, become more arrogant and sexually compulsive, work harder, and die younger. "The paths of male glory lead but to the grave"—quicker.

## CHAPTER VII

# Fathers Are the Mothers of Invention Sans Genes: Sans Genius

I would not agree that there are a lot of female geniuses waiting to burst through providing all obstacles are removed. If there were, they would be.

*Professor Alice Heim, Cambridge University, England*

Germaine Greer, in writing her last feminist opus, *The Obstacle Race: The Fortunes of Women Painters,* was quoted that she "originally planned a study on women and creativity but could find no research material."

*Carol Kleiman, Baltimore Sun*

In the male, intellect frequently overlaps with talent and talent with intellect to produce something creative. It seems in the female, neither overlaps with either. The simplest proof of that pudding is in the invention of the soufflé—a man-made creation. If after a couple of million years on her own turf (the kitchens of history) women still don't have the wherewithal to come up with at least a creation like a coq au vin or a Baked Alaska, why should we ever expect a female Einstein to come up with a theory of relativity?

Yet the feminists insist on extolling their hidden creative talents as if full equality with the male will make them blossom. After fifteen years of at least the opportunity, there is little more blossoming than in the past 2,000 winters of their discontent.

But if she's so unhappy with her lot and is only seeking some super achievement to make her look good in those new ersatz books on female history, she has one original creation right under her nose and can't see it.

Here she is, dredging up every sparse tidbit to add some luster to her dismal record in originality and she overlooks her one great creation, never duplicated by anyone else—anywhere. She did what no male has ever done. She created the creator in all of *his* glory. From her very pith and pelvis comes that philosopher, artist, writer, scientist, all rolled into one—the most imaginative wonder of the world. So why should she worry and fret that she's left not one monument, neither in classic marble and stone, à la Christopher Wren and Stanford White, nor in steel and concrete, as would Le Corbusier and Frank Lloyd Wright. Why should she worry about those who beat her out to invent electricity, penicillin, television, and Money Market Mutual Funds? She invented the inventors—the male.

## A Tough Act to Follow

Though she has shown little other originality, even during her more liberated recent past she's still producing the male. That should be enough for any woman, if not for the freed female leaders of the world. They still constantly goad their sisters to do more, more—trying to squeeze ideas out of every female turnip that comes down the pike. But it seems that her one marvel of creation drained her of every ounce of originality. We pity the poor dears, afflicted not only with iron-poor blood from the physiological mechanisms that produced *him*, but a lack of brain fertility to match. Yet though that marvelous male may soon duplicate her achievement with cloning, gene splicing, and all of that—we admit it's a tough act to follow.

Of course some female skeptics will say, "Okay, if our creativeness was so great, why wasn't it also passed down to art or math?" Well, that's easy; it's again a matter of genes. It's like hemophilia, or other hereditary diseases transmitted only through the female to the male. But in some ways even the lack is a godsend. The female DNA no doubt knows in its protoplasmic bones the anguish, soul-searching, and early demise of those male creators—so it just passed. We are afflicted and she isn't—and yet she's unhappy with that kindly sterility!

## Who's in the Kitchen with Dinah?

Her demanding sisters insist it is not enough for her to create the creators, that she herself must also produce a *Guernica*, a

Sistine Chapel, or the Porsche 1600. And then to really heat her up, they keep insisting she has it in her and only our male sexist obstruction and harassment shackles her originality.

Well, we personally feel she's done a bang-up job producing us, and she has every right to rest on her laurels. As we've been telling her for years, you can't fight your chromosomes. If it were at all possible that they could have done anything original in the last few thousand years, it should at the very least have been in something they've been doing since fire was invented. Certainly she who has had a hammerlock on the family cuisine (if you can call family cooking cuisine) can't say that we've kept her out of the kitchen or thwarted her from coming up with veal scallopine or even the hot dog. How could we possibly have stifled her initiative on her own turf, learned her trade, then gone on to become the great chefs of the world if she really had the *stuffing* to do it? Why did the Borgia girls, Joan of Arc, and Cleopatra have male chefs? And didn't *Time* just pick nine males out of ten chefs as the world's greatest gastronomic innovators, on a par in their field with Newton, Galileo, and Marconi? Even the mundane sandwich was created by an earl.

## Out of the Frying Pan

If the last best hope to lead them out of that wilderness is Julia Child, who went public with her "love of cheeseburgers and hot dogs," forget it. When the average housewife watches that zucchini-shaped Prima Boilerina (as one female author described her) morning after morning, copying every recipe and buying each of her exotic ingredients but still unable to boil a three-minute egg, how could she originate Oysters Rockefeller? Worse yet, madam homemaker's record for charring toast to a cinder is attested to by every Maalox-chewing commuter account executive. Actually, if it weren't for the male chefs of today, who else could have saved the sensitive palate from degenerating into just another vestigial organ like the appendix or the tonsil?

## . . . Into the Beauty Shop

Another outlandish example of the male filling the vacuum of female talent is in hairdressing. Even here we had to originate that sanctum sanctorum of gossip shops, along with the driers and curlers in the world of Princess Daisies. Since the exotic coifs of Madam Pompadour, there has not been one distaff Vidal Sassoon. How did he, not Mrs. Sassoon, get up there? Go into any middle-class beauty shop in Pottstown, Pennsylvania, or Des Moines, Iowa, and practically every coiffurer in charge is male (at least in appearance). Females are hired to do the more mechanical work of shampooing and blow-drying the tresses—of females only, mind you—and of course under male direction.

Or take dress designing. Who else wears them? How did we break into their game one hundred thousand years after that first lady couturier hemmed the first tigerskin for her daughter's nuptials? As advertised in *Women's Wear Daily*, as seen at the fashion shows in New York and Paris or in the shops on Rodeo Drive, there are ten Halstons for every Molly Parnis, eight Cardins for every Chanel.

Now we don't mean to harangue this bit ad nauseum, but taking a leaf from the feminists' handbook of "nag tactics," we just want to make our point clear: When male talent excels in those all-female worlds, women can hardly come up with the excuse that we shut them out. If the female mind can't create in her own backyard of coif and cookery, how can she possibly do it in ours of space and psychiatry?

## You Can't Teach a Poodle to Run a Rabbit

This of course is not to say that minor creative talents may not overlap with a minor intellect. As Fran Lebowitz, best-selling author of *Metropolitan Life* says, "Oppressed women brought us real coffee and well-kept fingernails, whereas the liberated women came up with chairperson and Erica Jong." A brain of some mediocrity, even female, can be molded into a good dentist, a $100-an-hour lawyer, or even an insurance salesman in the "million dollar club." But real talent? Creativity? It isn't made or fabricated: it's born. Conditioning, sexism or otherwise, has little to do with it. A poodle can never be conditioned to hunt a rabbit, just as a beagle naturally runs the scented trail from birth.

An Isaac Stern, an Albert Schweitzer, or that chess genius, Bobby Fischer, did not learn at his mother's knee. Their talent was there from delivery on. Institutions and teachers could only bring it out and polish it up—no more. By the same token it's a rare real talent that can be bottled up, cut off, or buried, as the feminists so grossly accuse us of doing. If this be so, it must be even more impossible for a sexist society to gang up on it. So where are the female Horowitzes, Flemings, or Eli Whitneys of yesteryear—and where the de Koonings, Oppenheimers, or Salks of liberation?

Ordinarily we wouldn't go to such lengths to prove a point, but we do so here for two reasons. The women know as well as we that aptitude tests, especially for talent, rarely lie. And those tests have shown for years that females are just not strong in the abstract thought processes, and for good reason. Creation comes from the right hemisphere of the brain, and feminine women are usually left-brained. It seems that women just have no biological credentials as the mothers of invention.

## A Vast Wasteland

Actually it wasn't we who brought up the embarrassing lack of female originality. It was at *their* insistence on "women's studies" that we just had to see for ourselves and not that we are unreconstructed misogynists. We were perfectly willing to let this touchy subject be "a mouldering" in its grave. But no! the brawnies had to disinter their old talentless skeleton and, to their own chagrin, hang its meatless bones up for all to see. We didn't mind the smokescreen of "women's studies" or any other gimmick put over on the caponized male academics to engender female pride. Those veneer-thin courses (in every institution dependent on government funds) were created to buck up the young females' ego. Also to unearth wherever possible the marvelous contributions women had made which our sexist society supposedly had cruelly buried. Well, that's fair enough.

So they dug deep and long. However, even at the "rock" bottom, the barrel was bare. It was not only difficult to find much worthwhile, but there was hardly a record to find it in. For instance, the Schlesinger Library of Womanhood at Radcliffe College (which culls books by women from all over the world) could only gather about twenty thousand volumes in toto, dating from Genesis to NOW. About three thousand of those were mediocre cookbooks. On the other hand, that library in Alexandria, Egypt, before it burned down 1500 years ago, had more than two hundred thousand volumes—without even a female recipe.

It also didn't help that youthful Vassar and Wellesley pride much to find not one Socrates, Shakespeare, Descartes, Luther, or Van Gogh hidden even in the cracks at the bottom of that barrel. The second and third echelon were also bare of a Henry Ford, a Mark Rothko, a T. S. Eliot, or a Buckminster Fuller. Of course we give them full credit in the last hundred years for occasionally producing a Jane Austin, a Marie Laurencin, or a Mary Cassatt. Yet those bare few ladies who produced creatively back then came through under a much more sexist, less educated, less free society than the Bennington class of 1981. But if today there is even a pittance of creative women in our now-liberated times, why haven't we heard more from those free-swinging Goucher and "Cliffy" geniuses? During this same period, among hundreds of others, a Princeton junior (with no such thing as male studies) showed how he could build an atomic bomb out of spare parts and a little leftover uranium.

With all of this, the pressure was still on for women's studies, and even Yale succumbed, covering a B.A. in that dubious melange of nonsubjects with legitimate ivy.

## A Little "Test" Will Do It

Of course we can't deny that a small percentage of talented females (and even a rare great one) with the right hormonal mix will pop up here and there. But the big question was whether liberation of the female from sexist conditioning has or will ever bring out an equal share of greatness in creativity. As we've shown, if we had to take over even in their own bailiwicks, the outlook couldn't be particularly bright.

As we have repeated over and over: In physique, in intellect, and even in girlness or boyness, our genes also program us. It's no different with genius. That selfsame DNA that handed down to us males baldness, raunchiness, and our love for mayhem also determines originality and ingenuity. The male who invented the bidet, the Concorde, and the three-button suit comes from the same strain of male who invented the wheel and the flute. To them the works of Mendel and Darwin are part of the sexist plot. Heredity and evolutionary frailties, as with any of their deficiencies, is stuff for high school biology texts. They even try to blast their honest scientific sisters with screeds such as, "What has happened in the past two billion years has little to do with woman's creativity today." But it's not so easy to blow away all of anthropology with just a hurricane of words. The frog became a rat, and the rat which became a baboon was the same baboon who became Mozart or Leonardo da Vinci, not Mrs. Mozart or Mrs. da Vinci.

## Ars Gratia Feminist

Speaking of Mozart, there should really be no more difference in talent among the sexes in the fine arts of music, painting, or literature than in the grosser arts of hairdressing or dress designing. Let's compare women and men in those fine arts, where talent supposedly reigns supreme. But as we said, because the feminists hold no truths of male genius to be self-evident, as long as there was sexism, it's no use bringing up Wagner, Schumann, Verdi, or a dozen others. And if it's so embarrassing that there was not one female composer in that ancient era to compare with any of those male giants, let's play only in the nonsexist time period, since liberation. But before the feminists can cry "sexist judges," Joan Tower of the National Endowment of Arts' panel on composers says she has never seen a woman's work discriminated against.

What female composers of today are even known, much less have the stature of Copeland, Menotti, or Virgil Thomson? Ever since their consciousnesses have been raised, in any facet of music the best they can produce even in interpretation or conducting is the voluminous Sarah Caldwell. Yes, they did have one great music teacher, Boulanger—but as we said, teaching is the female bag. According to music critics and historians alike, Caldwell's talent can't approach her diameter in girth. They say the cost of her publicity campaign to put her in the news as a great female conductor could never be earned in the concert halls, much less elevate her to the podium of even the minor-league maestros.

As for literature, we only have to peruse the *New York Times* Sunday book review section and, aside from an occasional Didion, Tuchman, or de Beauvoir, the authors are ninety percent male in whatever category or rank you choose, either in books reviewed or advertised. In just one Sunday edition taken at random in 1981, there were only two females out of thirty authors on the best-seller list: one of them with a Hollywood diet book and the other with the story of Maria Callas.

But as with Mary Cunningham in business, the feminist bitchiness even comes out in writing, and there is not room for any two literati to stand on the same pedestal. Ms. Lillian Hellman now has a suit against Ms. Mary McCarthy for damages of 1.75 million dollars for mental pain and anguish, plus another $500,000 punitive damages. And all Ms. McCarthy said on TV was that Ms. Hellman was "a bad and dishonest writer and every word she writes is a lie, including *and* and *the*." And all Ms. Hellman did was describe Ms. McCarthy as a "lady magazine writer." Recently, novelist Martha Gellhorn came down on McCarthy's side. Irving Howe, of the male literati, said, "It's not just two old ladies engaged in a cat fight." But it is—it is. Did anyone ever see T. S. Eliot act that way to George Bernard Shaw, or even that harpoon-tongued Gore Vidal go that far after Norman Mailer punched him in the nose?

But that is only part of the tacky goings-on in the female literary world. Because of their low pay scale (blamed on us chauvs), female editors are in abundance. They get their licks in by equalizing reading matter for the public, with the likes of the penis-envy stuff of the Jongists, as they turn down good chauvinist books. Or they push those "perils of Pauline": the weepings and wailings of the Brownmillers, Greers, or Frenches, who expound on the intellectual subjects of female pride and the beauty of androgyny, or rape and the evils of sexism *ad regurgitatum.* But not unlike hemlines and hairdos, women's literary efforts (unlike males') go in fads. Presently it's not just sexism but sex itself. Just recently (as if they invented this, too), the female hard-core sex books came flooding into the market. Among others: *The Joy of Lesbian Sex* (with drawings); *The Kahn Report* (on sexual performances); *Night Thoughts: Reflections of a Sex Therapist; Sex and Birth Control for the Young;* and *How to Make Love to a Man,* among others. Closely following these literary gems comes the new kiss-and-tell era: *Shelley,* by Shelley Winters; *Scarlett O'Hara's Younger Sister; Actress,* by Elizabeth Ashley; *Bittersweet,* by Susan Strasberg; and a host of other disenchanted pillow-talk sagas. As Ann Taylor Fleming put it, women writers "emphasize their sexual performance and seem more swaggering and macho than their male counterparts."

## Nary a Rembrandt or Pollock in Skirts

We're not going to dog this arts thing to death—but just to be complete and put it away once and for all, we must discuss the graphic arts. The fems have been unusually quiet about their past in painting and sculpting—and no wonder. Their talent was almost exclusively recorded in nude modeling for male artists. But Germaine Greer, in a book on female artists, *The Obstacle Race,* gives it to us right from the horse's mouth. She tries desperately to make a case that female works of art were lost by deliberate neglect, and female artistic talent put down by the male guilds. She then bolsters these accusations with those well-worn feminist clichés from "fulltime motherhood" to "sexist societies' strictures." Then, without being aware, she lets it out of the bag: "Women didn't dare to experiment or challenge." We've said that a thousand times, it's just part of their lack of aggressiveness.

She then goes on, "So they became imitators or did detail work or copies for their masters [men]." She even admits, "Women generally abandoned art when they fell in love." Did Rembrandt or Pollock abandon their art with every affair they had? And as she says of Berthe Morisot (another third-rater, 1841–1895), "She was happy to coexist with music, conversation, and children. She just didn't work hard enough at her art." Well, scientists have been talking of the females' lack of concentrated effort for years.

Then Greer, putting one foot in after the other, remarks on the "unevenness of work, execution, and quality," then even quotes Pliny. "Women are as salamanders in a fire. They burn out quickly." So, in trying to defend the defenseless (women, as creators), Greer actually echoed everything we chauvs have known and already said. This longtime feminist activist then tries to sell some *great* female artists: Gentileschi, Adélaide Labille-Guiard, Nora Carrington, Mary Beale, and others. Has anyone anywhere ever heard of any of these forgotten imitators? She finally wraps it all up and it all comes out in her final confession. She "originally planned a study on women and creativity, but she could find no research material."

Greer never got to modern art, obviously seeing another creative desert on the horizon. Her lesser artistic sisters, however, go into ecstasy about their recent "liberated breakthrough." However, we know that in the past—from the Renaissance up to liberation—like cuisine or music, the graphic arts of watercolor and oil were taught only to genteel parlor ladies and virginal girls. Yet we know that history is as meaningless to the egalitarians in art as in music. So let's discount the early Italian church period, where not a nun showed among the Caravaggios or the Tintorettos. And later, not a Rembrandt nor a Rubens in skirts. Then we also skip the period of Matisse, Mondrian, Cézanne, and Renoir in their impressionistic creativity, or of Picasso, with his multiplicity of styles ranging from cubism up and down. But what about 1982? What have women done for art lately?

Taking it entirely out of the realm of the sexist excuses, we shall limit our comparisons only to the era of equality, from 1968 to 1982. Of course, knowing art dealers as we do, there is really no reason to even do this. If any art could sell, those mavens would have put on a show and publicized a hermaphroditic patas monkey. And as in any other of the art forms, from the Pavarottis to the Picassos, the modern criteria of living greatness is their price. So let's get a true comparison by taking a look at female artists, even those who married great male artists who then pushed the works of their wives as far as they could go.

The work of Helen Frankenthaler, the top female artist of today, sells for about one-fifth the price of that of her former husband, Robert Motherwell's, works. And for good reason—originality, or lack of it. From a recent show of hers in 1981, Hilton Kramer says, "In the present exhibition her watercolors . . . are very close to Marin and Kandinsky. Later, much was still owed to Pollock or Gorky." Then there is Elaine de Kooning who doesn't even get one-hundredth the price her former husband, the colorful Willem, does; and Lee Krasner Pollock not one-thousandth of her deceased genius husband, Jackson. The recent Pop and Op art of the 70s has not a single female name artist in sight. The male chimpanzee finger painter in the Baltimore Zoo had better press and got more for *his* paintings.

## If the Widows Won't, Who Will?

But when we get right down to it, it's not fully the fault of the second-rate female artists, but the female buyers as well. Where are the female Mellons, Rockefellers, Hammers, or Hirschhorns? If all of that "widow money" would only show loyalty instead of just good taste, it might help. It's the male who has the eye or the feeling in his guts and thus is the collector and the museum-giver. But as we know, he is short-lived and his wife usually takes over. Here in the U.S., seventy percent of private money is owned by widows who overwhelmingly still buy only the first-rate male artists. The latest painting donated to the Metropolitan Museum, a Willem, not an Elaine de Kooning, valued at 1.7 million dollars, was given by Mrs. Muriel Newman, a widow from Chicago.

So here we are, the twentieth century fading fast with a good fourteen years of equality, and creatively the female is still a midget among the male giants. There are now female architects, scientists, painters, and engineers in droves—but little creative has happened. So far, no Parthenons; no Mona Lisas; no fuel-saving car. Our predictions for women have held up since the battle with Patsy Mink. We still hold the scientific truths of sexual evolution and genetics dear and true. But if they still insist on butting their brains against the stone wall of history, we can't help but feel they'll be worse off. If they had the resilient and practical mentality of the male whom they've produced, they'd be satisfied with just creating with pride that originator of everything original.

## CHAPTER VIII

# Unidentified Sexual Objects— a Male Phallacy

Women are more cunning than prurient in refusing us admittance to their closets—before they are painted and tricked up for public view.
*Montaigne*

The loudest complainers about sex objects rarely look the part.
*Harriet Van Horne, syndicated columnist*

ONE THING we chauvinists in good standing can never deny: We are born and will die the noble lechers—true sons of de Sade, prurient knights of the chase. We can't help it, and what's more, don't want to. Day and night, consciously and subconsciously, the sight, smell, taste, and touch of a beautiful female (with or without love or affection) is with us in sickness and in health, till death do us part. And no one can convince us that what was *under* Eve's fig leaf wasn't what enticed us to bite the apple. Since then it's been up, up and away to that "last tango," *Hustler* porn, and Lolita.

Believe it or not, Lolita, that precursor to the nymphet Brooke Shields, is the culprit—the spider, not the fly. It is that prepubertal "she" starting early in her trade as temptress and *agent-person provocateur*, following closely in Eve's devious ways.

## It Began with the Tsetse Fly

The liberators may not like it, but even before Adam, as far back as the tsetse fly, sex was always the female's bag. So whether by the scent of the female cockroach, the eyeshadow of the new girl in the typing pool, or the sensuously undulating antennae of the outer-space floozy, sex is the name of the female game, and all the world's males are her lovers. As the early Christians put it, she was "the devil's gateway" (and what a gateway). Robert Ardrey in his *African Genesis* scientifically records it, "from asp to zebra, the female of the species is the sex specialist." Even that great feminist Simone de Beauvoir disagrees with her feminist sisters: "Women's eroticism and sexual world have a special form of their own and cannot fail to engender a sensuality and sensitivity of a special nature." And how special it is!

## Cherchez la Phlegm

It may not be sour grapes, but it does sound fishy when a motherly type like Betty Friedan and a lanky, natural-born tight end like Germaine Greer constantly knock Raquel Welch and the *Playboy* centerfold. To our mind, better "cherchez la phlegm." It is doubtful that any of the feminist ladies could ever qualify in the Atlantic City tryouts or in the Miss Nude America contest. Yet give any of them the chance and they'd grab it. The whole gaggle—*to a man*—would rather be sashaying bikini-bound down that boardwalk ramp on their way to becoming America's "Sex Object" (S.O.) than marching in cap and gown to pick up their B.S. degrees in female studies. Deep down, they would all rather listen to the strains of "Here She Comes" than to "Gaudeamus Igitur." When the French sex objects are told they must be liberated, they say, "From what?"

## Sour Gripes

There is nothing new about archfeminists condemning the Garbo face or the Harlow figure, and wishing that all sex objects be *un*identified. From our experience, Harriet Van Horne was right on the money: "The complainers rarely look the part." With all of those affirmative action-minded ladies, we agree: It is unfair to have the kind of head start Brigitte Bardot had. It smacks of the worst kind of inequality. It is just not right for those naturally flaunting females to be followed, ogled, and whistled at (enjoying every minute of it) by homburg-sporting gentlemen and hard-hatted construction workers—while most feminists could walk down Fifth Avenue stark naked in the Easter Parade and get no more attention than the bunny rabbit.

Certainly one cannot fault the feminists for trying to even it up. However, the age-old ploy of putting down and handicapping their better-endowed sisters in the ancient art of man-snaring has never gone over big. Since Jezebel, we know it was the less-attractive orthodox sisters who conned the Jewish beauties into shaving their heads (covering their bare scalp with something that looks like a swallow's nest—a *sheitel*) and banning all that aphrodisiacal myrrh and frankincense. And rumors to the contrary, it was not the freewheeling Muhammad (a harem man himself) who veiled the comeliest of Muslim ladies into purdah—it was one of his preordained dowdy wives. Similarly, it was hardly the God-fearing Christian males but the warty Sisters Superior who prescribed *habits* (both moral and dress) for the nuns, leaving all things carnal to the imagination only. (It is rumored, however, that many of the more pious men of God "got *into* the habit," humming "Nearer, My God, to Thee.")

Even today to the fems—as Gay Talese mentions—"nymphomaniac" is a pejorative term, while "jock," "womanizer," "flesh hound" is a proud badge of virility.

Regardless of the specifics, the results throughout history remain the same: There was no way those devious feminist strictures could any more bottle up the sex objects than put muu-muus on a Dallas Cowgirl. Could the fems have gotten Cleopatra to hide her sexual light under a bushel? If Grace Kelly had been draped in a gunnysack, her skull Brynner-ed, and her perfect features veiled as her tougher sisters might have wished, she never would have made it with a pauper, much less a prince.

## Summa Cum Laude vs. Summa Cum Monroe

Still the feminists continue to harangue their constituency. "Don't give in to being a cheap S.O.; your natural heritage is mousy hair, woolly armpits, and a sallow complexion—stay with it. Keep your pride intact, be fulfilled with a double crostic at home rather than humiliation at Regine's or on the Waldorf roof with a Gregory Peck. Hold your heads high, get to bed early (climbing the wall) rather than just be orgasmized in some de-grading male pad."

We males, of course, take all of this with a knowing smile. It seems even in the souls of the most summa of cum laude feminists (or First Ladies) there is that secret ache to be All Sex Object to All Men. If not, why did the 1977 committee for Woman of the Year nominate Farrah Fawcett (without success) rather than Erica Jong to be their mistress of ceremonies? They certainly did not choose her because she could expound on the "Myth of the Vaginal Orgasm." This hottest of American sex symbols since Theda Bara was chosen because in the cockles of their hearts she is the dream girl they would all like to be.

Even our former First Lady gave it a real go. Leaving no wrinkle unsmoothed and no stretch marks unsanded, Rosalynn had her eyes plasticized and her hair turned a reddish blond, and took to wearing contact lenses. She wouldn't have dreamed of setting foot on Air Force One without her hairdresser in tow. Well versed in the sexual history of presidents from Warren Harding to JFK (besides having a husband with an admitted lusting heart), she knew she had to be a twice-born sex object if she was to keep that presidential eye from roaming in the gloam-ing. Of course our present number one, Nancy, was a beauty queen, and in her heart will always be one. She is the best thing that's happened to the cause of sex objects since Frederick of Hol-lywood's glittering garter belts.

## The Sexual Survival Tool

Contrary to popular opinion, sex objects have not always been just for fun and games, or a weekend in Las Vegas. And it's no wonder there is that instinctual female longing to be one—that is, if one is not beyond the skills of Helena Rubinstein. From time immemorial, sexual attractiveness was a basic survival tool for the species—not just for the go-go female with her eye on a new mink. It was serious business. Even now the skintight jeans, the nipple see-through, the buttock roll, and the braless bounce—with malice aforethought—is for men only.

As modern anthropology proves, if the *Australopithecus* female was not a sex object, she became maleless, childless, and useless. If she could not propagate her own, what good was she? For a while it was touch and go whether the female could outbreed the predators who were so particularly fond of tender human flesh. At that time those animals were a more effective means of human population control than the IUD. So this sex object thing became the *sine qua non* not only of female survival but survival of the species.

But the human female was then number two and had to try harder. At that time she came in heat only a couple of times a year, like her anthropoid ancestors. Something had to be done to make sure she bred faster than the saber tooth's digestion could handle her output. So to keep up with production, woman *had* to become a year-round sex object. Her raunchy pinheaded lover had to be accepted night and day, 365 days a year (not just when she was in heat), always ready and waiting, just like now. Actually, as it turns out, our present-day lechery, no different than before, but for which we are now excoriated, is at least put to more frequent use—for the species of course.

## Hope Lies Eternal in Both Female Breasts

In the process of becoming an all-year-round girl, it was even more important for the human female to have swivel hips, ample breasts, and the fur you love to touch, because males then were not loathe to cast an eye at some of those lovely cousins lower in the scale. She had to compete with those closer primate cousins, whose tails were primarily to swing from. The human breasts alone are proof positive that the modern female had to become more an S.O. than her orangutan sister. Today, if as fallow as a panda in captivity, our women have larger breasts than those on a nursing dray horse. So they were not exclusively for suckling. Then dress designers, massage parlors, and Las Vegas got into the act, catering to our chauvinist instincts, and breasts became a bigger and bigger thing—a blue chip, an all-around better money-maker than IBM. It's even a frequent issue on the Donahue show. In fact, since 1974, when San Diego's nude beach was sanctioned, breasts have outdrawn that city's famous zoo. Over a million people came out to ogle them in 1980; ninety-eight percent of the voyeurs were males.

## Covet Thy Neighbor's Wife—but Please Don't Eat Her Husband

The sex object female of the species had yet another survival souvenir in her Pandora's box, which even Gay Talese did not discuss in his *scientific* treatise. No doubt without the ever-ready, huge-breasted, smooth-skinned early female, the average male might have gone on to extinction by his own hand. The wondrous wiles the feminists are now trying to put down are the exact sights and smells which have distracted the males from swilling and killing each other to eventual species oblivion. Before sex-on-demand became operative (as we said, not just twice a year like the elephant or the kudu) the male cannibal was so busy, exhausted, or dead from eating or being eaten by his butchering brethren, he never would have made it to 3,000,000 B.C., much less A.D. 2000. So, as preoccupied as he still is today in doing in his fellow man, civilization should give orchids on special Sex Objects Days—certainly as important as Mother's Day. For now, he does take more than enough time out from mayhem for the seduction process, fantasizing, and sexual exercise, so that the body count on the battlefield does not overcome the population growth rate. Which shows that, even for posterity, S.O.s aren't all bad.

## In Lust We Trust

It must be admitted, however, that on and off in history's survival game, the sex object business was not all sugar and spice. A beauty like Helen of Troy started a thirty-year war. Genghis Khan in his travels south did not help much by looking for Semitic S.O.s, and Hannibal on the prowl for blond northern Italians vandalized everything in his path. Henry the Eighth gave the Pope his comeuppance for the body he could not resist, not to forget the Duke of Windsor who gave up a kingdom for the "woman he loved."

Profumo, Wayne Hayes, *et al.*, attest to the role of the female's wiles in shaking up modern governments. And to bring it down to everyday street level, harassment is the busiest *two-way* street in town. What office has not been turned inside out by a sweet young wriggler using her charms in that quest for a night on the town in the luxury of the boss's Cadillac?

## Germaine Contemplating the "Bust" of Farrah

From the nubbin-breasted Lolitas to the Merry Widow waltzers, woman has always used everything she was endowed with to wangle her way into the hearts and wallets of man. As Harvard anthropologist Irven De Vere put it, "A female chimp in heat will use every sexual come-on she has to get more than her share of bananas from the male provider." (Do the feminists ever wonder why only female prostitution has been an indestructible institution since the Essenes?) But as natural as it has been in the past, the modern miracles of science have produced add-ons, building even better mantraps. Most of the more seductive and titillating cues come directly from the animal world. Revlon, Rubinstein, Arden, and Avon are not unknowing of the scent that attracts the male cockroach. And the substitutes for the sweet musky smell of success are plagiarized right from our curly-tailed cousins. Even the colors of lipstick, rouge, and eyeshadow take a page from the success of the baboon in heat as she displays her electric blue and crimson *derriere* to lure every simian jock who swaggers down the jungle trail. The beauty shops, the hairdresser, and those super deluxe female spas (the Golden Door at $3,000 per week) are just feminine extensions of the patas monkeys as they groom and delouse each other for the sexual hunt.

## The Way to a Man's Heart—through His Penis

And as Montaigne said, "she has more reason than any other animal to cover (or cleverly uncover) herself." The female gilds her own lily with a $5,000 Halston décolletage to show a beautiful cleavage, or opts for an ankle-low St. Laurent hemline to hide a piano leg, because not only life—but the good life—is at stake. Even those spiked heels, rhinestone garter belts, and now so-popular black lace negligees and "Teddies" put out by Frederick's and Kent are only the most basic accouterments of the come-on. They are just frosting on the female cake. It is no secret today that most women at sixteen or thirty-six will gladly risk life and fortune in four- and five-hour operations to get their man. Talk about being totaled—they have their noses Loren-ed, their breasts Bardot-ed, their legs Dietrich-ed, their eyes pinched, their "shifting sands" fanny perked, and their striae sanded—and it's worth every nickel of the investment.

## I Dream of Cyclops with the Light Brown Hair

All of these S.O. gimmicks are readily understandable to both male and female, and the cause commendable, but the trip some of them take to the *lifters* may not be necessary. We are not talking about those over forty who have undergone the ravages of six pregnancies. They, of course, should use everything they can lay their hands on to tighten the sags, lift the droops, or bolster the framework. But for the rest—they needn't go that extra mile. When the male's gonads are stirring, which is about as constant as his heartbeat (except for the ten minutes during his post-sexual nap), he is vulnerable to just about anything female—human, animal, or vegetable. But it is, of course, a matter of supply and demand.

During the World War II campaigns in Africa and the Pacific, for instance, the chaplains had to fend off hordes of GIs madly in love with females who would have been the pride of Barnum and Bailey. Two GIs in New Guinea had a shootout over a very attractive Cyclops, and one Princeton lad sent the picture of his intended microcephalic back home to the *New York Times* society column. So it does not always take the Total Woman technique of greeting him at the door with a cellophane G-string or drooling into his ear between the soup and the baked beans.

## Sex—It's Not by Bread Alone

No doubt the Cosmo Woman of Helen Gurley Brown has been a big shot in the arm to the fine art of the Sex Object, and by the same token has really shaken up the feminist hierarchy. For not only can't the brawnies stem this tide, but even since the recent inception of the present feminist *putsch* in the early 70s, preteens are décolletaging lower and lower. So we can understand how, in desperation, the fems have resorted to all kinds of counter-insurgency moves. Now, instead of just knocking beauty contests (nude and otherwise), movie queens, Beautiful People, and lacy brassieres, they are not so subtly going in for guerrilla warfare. For instance, even after these past ten years of exhorting their sisters to abandon the evils of kitchenhood, they are now trying the tricky business of luring them back—via cuisine. The party line is no longer the "slavery of the kitchen" but "the way to a man's heart is through his stomach." Betty Friedan, according to her confessions in the *New York Times*, rediscovered the romance of the kitchen with her live-in boyfriend. And that tough-bitten radical female, Robin Morgan, now says that after a long layoff, she too is going back to the pot roast. But this "back to the kitchen" movement to get their man (bound to fail—another feminist mis-judgment) is less of a ruse than an instinct. They just cannot help it. Even the most militant feminists are like sleepwalkers drawn by some sort of innate magnetism to the sink and the disposal. As we said before, Golda Meir, while positioning troops and ordering air strikes at a cabinet meeting in the middle of the Six-Day War, sighed openly for the peaceful sizzle of fried matzoh in the skillet. Margaret Thatcher admits she is lured by the smell of the gravy and the whirr of the Cuisinart.

## All Roads Lead to Roam

But alas, as any anatomist will tell you, those feminists are off on the wrong nerve pathway. It is not from stomach to brain; it is all routed through the senses directly to the penis. Since the dawn of time, the way to a man's heart races along the same tried and true synapses. It will be the rare man who will be turned on by a leg of lamb rather than a silk-sheathed thigh. And the scent of cherry pie wafting in from the kitchen cannot draw like the aroma of My Sin from the boudoir. All roads lead to roam.

## In the "Pink" of Perdition

*Hustler* magazine brings to mind one of the feminists' pet peeves—raw sex as a commodity to be bought, traded, or hustled over the counter. Though they inveigh against it and put it all on our chauvinist shoulders, they are in on it up to their raised consciousnesses. Curiously enough, even some of the holier-than-thou leaders of the movement dabbled in it at one time or another (with the most trumped-up excuses money can buy). Gloria Steinem, of all the liberated liberators who now rails against females plying the sexual scam, was once (in her more feminine years) a bunny—a disciple of no less than Hugh Hefner. As she now tries to explain, it was to get a story for a paper. That is her story. Others say she almost gave up reporting after just a few lusty weeks on the job. The money was better and the fringe benefits more exciting. Notwithstanding her denials, the classified ads in her *Ms.* magazine (she was a founding mother) show there is some pretty hot porno stuff—but for women only. They advertise everything from condoms with 126 extra ribs which "guarantee ecstasy or your money back" to three different kinds of vibrators and "Eve's Garden—a place where women can have access to sexual products (send twenty-five cents for catalog)." There are also ads galore for females "desiring *compatible friends.*"

## The Male Phallacy

As a highly exciting combination of softly curved protrusions and indentations inviting our most lurid imaginations, there is no way of undoing our chauvinist vision of the ideal sex companion. And it's a rare female that does not try to live up to that male phallacy. After all, there are at least three million years of evolution in this male and female give-and-take. At this stage of the game, S.O.-ism is no less an industry than shipbuilding. It is a healthy part of the gross national product, and to abolish it is to invite another '29 crash. Doing away with the S.O. would be disastrous. Just think of the world of finance without fashions, perfumes, contact lenses, cosmetics, furs, bikinis, panty-hose, shoes, et cetera, which must total near the gross of the national debt. Cosmetics alone account for a billion dollars a year. It would take the world at least ten years of depression and another ten of retooling to adjust to a non-sex-object world.

For France and Italy, the national homelands of sex objects, governments would fall at the first hint of abolition. *Women's Wear Daily* would not last a week, and Gucci, Pucci, and Bloom-ingdale's would be reduced to selling health food. It would lead to a global revolution that would make the Bolsheviks look like the Camellia Society. The masses, all the masses, from the most prurient pubertal boys to the dirtiest old men and from nubile acned girls to three-time losers in the lift parade, would be manning the barricades.

## *Is There Life Beyond Revlon?*

The psychological and social impact would bring added disaster. What would females do without their basic morale boosters? Even now they go into a catatonic depression if by some quirk of fate their bedmates catch them in the face-cream stage of nightly rehab. What would happen if all the world saw her without her Tangerine Kissable Lips by Revlon or her Lover's Blush by Estée Lauder. How could she face the day without the uplift of Maidenform, the batting of the Mabelline eye, or the containment into slimdom by Playtex? Could she stand herself in the morning without legs satined by a Princess shaver, after freshening with her hygienic strawberry spray and stepping into her Bergdorf's lace undies? Withholding these bare necessities of life would not only treble the suicide rate (now so rampant) and fill our female mental wards (now overflowing), but also would force those sexist psychiatrists to deal in twenty-minute hours just to fit in this flood of female patients.

If it isn't bad enough that this S.O. liberation could take the fun out of life for the well-endowed females, pity the hordes of those not-so-well endowed. It is only by dint of every cosmetic camouflage, come-on, or misrepresentation that money can buy that H. L. Mencken's death wish is satisfied, and "some homely girl is winked at." She may even attain the status of being loved, honored, and having her bills paid without benefit of typewriter or welding torch. We have no wish for cruel and unusual punishment for a vast army of dowdies whose only hope is a cover-up larger than Watergate.

## Sex Objects Über Alles

If the female militants had any sense they would not waste too much time on this sex object kick; it's a losing proposition. Even if the Health and Welfare department allowed affirmative action to go all the way—beyond just jobs—guaranteeing dates and marriage to all qualified sexless objects, it would be tough sledding. When one sees a dyed-in-the-wool nonfeminist haggling over a pound of coffee at three dollars per—but not batting an eye at shelling out a one-hundred-dollar note for an ounce of Joy or two thousand dollars to get her breasts minimized or maximized—it is time their feminist sisters gave up the ghost. Can't they see it is instinct when an Israeli army sergeant succumbed to high heels and bikini to become Miss Universe? Is it any different to sit for hours being coiffed, shampooed, and rubbed with hormones for the April in Paris Ball, just as her counterpart in the Dark Ages anointed herself with yak fat to catch the local swineherd?

## The Death of a Tailsman

As for the effects on the run-of-the-mill office lecher, wolf-whistling construction worker, henpecked husband, and singles bar regular, the demise of the S.O. would be the "death of a tailsman." Better at home with "Kojak" or "M*A*S*H" than being turned off by a mousy-haired, pale-lipped, droopy female in sandals and granny dresses, even in the liveliest of singles haunts. After all, even Squeaky Fromme used lipstick.

With the female unenticing and unadorned, he and all of his parts would be subject to a state of permanent hangdog dejection. His depressions would be deeper, his football mania greater, and after his then-monthly sexual duties, and duties they'd be, he would roll over quicker and snore louder. This status of women could only lead to an increase in battered wives and children and an increase of husbands "on the road" in a drab world not worth saving for democracy.

Even as it stands now, a good sex object is hard to find. And for any male animal who is at all appreciative of the basic *ins* and *outs* of womankind, living with only unidentified sexual objects is not living at all. But brother chauvinists, worry not. Though the feminists may knock it, ban it, or heap shame on it, it appears that seducing the male by using the sum of her parts is psychologically grooved on the convolutions of the female cortex. And pity her not—she is no wilted violet, as attested to by Samson, Aristotle, Virgil, and Wilbur Mills. As Schopenhauer described the sex object everlasting: "Beauty, fascination and fullness cloaks an innate cunning and duplicity which have beguiled and debased the mightiest of man." But what a debasement.

## CHAPTER IX

# The Curse: A Period Piece
# Meno: The Pause That Depresses

Menstruation is an emblem of celebration.

> *Janice Delaney, et al.*, The Curse

Menopause is a "liberation," a more "joyful" time than in the preceding twenty years.

> *Feminist Woman's Workshop of California*

> Yesterday upon the stair
> I had a cramp that wasn't there
> It wasn't there again today.
> Gee, I wish it'd go away.
> *E.B.*

ORDINARILY, no gentleman in polite society would ever bring up such indelicate subjects. But from the feminists' recent spate of morbid interest in the phenomena of menstruation and menopause, one would think they had invented them—if the Russians hadn't already laid claim, as they did with baseball.

However, since the feminists have now taken these taboo subjects out of the closet to revere as some sort of celebrated infertility rite, it's incumbent on us more realistic gentlemen to set the matter straight. It also impugns their credibility to insist that the mental and physical aberrations of these conditions are figments of the female imagination brought on by sexist conditioning.

During the recent, semicentennial revival of liberation, all manner of female beliefs and natural happenings have had an attempted sanitization. No question, over the years female pride has been tattered beyond description by some few insensitive male clods—but we would have hoped not to the point of dredging up, of all things, the Curse (they named it—we didn't) or that latter-day pause that depresses. During more genteel times a woman would no more talk about her period or her flushes and flashes than about an orgy at Plato's Retreat or her most recent face lift. Today, though, it is almost as celebrated and frequent a subject on the daily talk show as the clitoral orgasm.

## *The Opiate of the Menses*

Though we shall begrudgingly discuss these squeamish subjects (in the order of their appearance), this is not to say the average feminine woman appreciates her monthly physiological phenomenon of blood, sweat, and cramps any more than the seven-year itch. The fems' attempt to convince any sane female that menstruation is "love in bloom" is like persuading Larry Flint of Xavier Hollander's virginity.

## *Fem-Think*

The way the feminists in the heyday of the 70s portrayed this unpleasant, though necessary, buildup to reproduction, you'd think it were some brand-new cure for cellulite.

There has been a flood (now subsiding) of books and articles on this physiological nuisance by liberated authors, each trying to paint a prettier picture than the other. Some have tinted the lily so rosily, a ten-year-old might dream of its possible surprises as she would a visit from the tooth fairy. But like so many other promises held out by the fems, it goeth before the fact. There is no known type of suggestive power, brainwashing or consciousness-raising that can alleviate the misery of the lunar cycle half as well as Midol. There is even one book simply entitled *The Curse,* which describes the menarche (or panicky period in the lives of the twelve- and thirteen-year-olds) as a "treasured moment." Another book, *The Red Flag,* goes on about this blessing in disguise as if Burt Reynolds doesn't know what he's been missing all these years.

Though we chauvinists have not been blessed with this monthly occurrence nor the dubious pleasure of its ultimate cessation, we have heard enough complaints about the symptoms and inconveniences from our wives, daughters, and sleep-ins to know that we are truly the chosen sex. The absence of the Curse for males should make the worst of us faithful believers and regular churchgoers.

## The Pink Badge of Scourage

Not that the Curse is as bad in some women as the chauvinist jokes portray it; yet it could hardly be as divine as the feminists describe it. In the context of feminist dialectics, anything totally female (except the Total Woman) is now good, and anything even remotely male is now evil. Even in that skin-deep field of Women's Studies, there is this kind of Orwellian fem-think from Big Sister. It puts everything (not only the Curse) in proper feminist perspective. It makes splitting headaches a sign of intelligence, and pregnancy (if one gets caught) a reaffirmation of motherhood. The way all things feminine are being embellished, it would surprise no one if vaginal shingles becomes a pink badge of courage and a hysterectomy a prerequisite of beatification.

The Curse, as the new feminist liturgy puts it, "is used as an emblem of celebration." Which just goes to show, what is New Year's Eve to one female may be another's Yom Kippur. To sip Mouton Rothschild in a toast to backache, blinding headaches, hair-trigger temper, and bloating is a euphemistic mountaintop. The only time the onset of the period could elicit even a call for a six-pack is by the college sophomore who had forgotten to take her pill.

## The Bind That Ties

Some of the more clubby moderns describe the Curse as a "common bond." Well, if this is the female tie that binds—it's a strangler. For though it may be a symbolic bond to some of those androgynous sorts like the masculinized Joan of Arcs (who naturally skip it eleven times out of twelve), for the majority of the sufferers it's more bondage than bond. Regardless of the maxi- or mini-pad advertisements showing a happy young menstruating woman climbing Mount Everest in a snowstorm, or down there with Cousteau on the ocean floor (smilingly emitting bubbles), what they don't show are those millions of sufferers climbing the ceiling. In history this aggravating bond has even been blamed for Salome's serving up the Baptist's head on a platter, and Lizzie Borden's giving her mother forty whacks.

Since the beginning, the Curse has gotten a bad name, so we can't fault women for trying to garnish it a bit. But just as they've overdone it, we admittedly have attempted to show it up in the worst possible light. Even New Guinea tribesmen, born chauvinists like the rest of us, warn that contact with a woman during that period can "kill his blood, waste his flesh, darken his skin, and dull his wits"—which I think may be overdoing it a bit.

In France, the wine producers of the Rhine Valley still prohibit women from crushing grapes with their feet during their cycle. And the Talmud, the book of Jewish law, had similar strictures against females baking bread at that time of the month. Well, all of this seemed sort of silly until one of the grand old men of pharmacology, Dr. David Macht, proved there to be a definite toxin in the sweat of the palms of menstruating women.

## It's Easier Than Laying Eggs

Regardless of old men's tales and new Ms.'s embellishments, the Curse from the very beginning had a definite purpose. It has always been part and parcel of the complicated human system to propagate itself. All it is is a buildup of very vascular and nutritious tissue in the womb each month to welcome the coming of the fertilized egg. If all of this comes to naught, all of that nutritious material is expelled in hopes it may be better luck next time.

In any event, whichever god brainstormed this one and came up with a plan, he had no doubt as to which sex should be the bearer. In his infinite wisdom he knew it would wear better on the female. Naturally, *she* was the only candidate who had the leisure, the disposition, and the thoracic and pelvic measurements to be given this Hobson's choice. And what a choice: three achy, crampy, swollen days a month, or the alternative of being bloated and stretched out of all reasonable human shape for three-quarters of the year, finally winding up with the pain and hazards of labor. We men accepted this decision from on high with grateful appreciation.

Though the method could have been arranged in a neater and less complicated fashion, it could also have been worse. Though the kangaroo and the aardvark may have managed to avoid the Curse altogether, some of their predecessors prepared for pregnancy in ways yet worse. Splitting oneself in half every twenty minutes, like the one-celled amoeba, is no cup of tea. Nor is the Curse any more anguishing than laying an egg every twenty-four hours—especially with all the clucking and carrying on that goes with it. Moreover, to the male, with his usual thrashing about, an egg in the connubial bed each morning would not only be a terrible inconvenience, but a formidable sexual block (and according to Masters and Johnson, he has enough of those).

## Not All Things to All Ladies—or Jocks

While it is understandable for the libbers to try to make the best of a tough deal, "Eve's blessing" is not all things to all ladies. As we said, regardless of sex education and pills, to an eleven-year-old it is still a hemorrhagic terror. To a college sophomore around exam time, according to Katherina Dalton, a distinguished physiologist, dysmenorrhea means a *B* instead of an *A*, and Miss Porter's School (for well-bred young ladies) serves breakfast in bed during that time of affliction. Of course, to those seniors who have loved and lost (a period), it reappears with a gush of relief; and to the female hurdler, it means four-tenths of a second added to her best time. To the women on the assembly line it comes as a heavenly few days at home without that efficiency expert breathing down their necks; and to the housewife, a restful night without a pawing, panting bedmate. To the nymphomaniac it's a bloody nuisance, and to the male singles jock, a waste of dinner, theater, and cab fare. . . .

## Ms. Harvey Wallclimber of the Premenstrual Tension Set

Still, the Steinems and the Greers insist that a woman is the same before, during, and after those monthly seizures. As one of them put it, "It's no worse than having the sniffles." Obviously

these celebrated ladies of the movement don't sniffle like other
ladies. They should interview Ms. Harvey Wallclimber of the
premenstrual tension set, who must be prepared every twenty-
eight days for either a lunar fix or a lobotomy.

It's certainly not all that bad with all women, but at best
dysmenorrhea is no weekend at the Waldorf. If the archfeminists
want references, they should just consult any one of the 75,000
gynecologists or 20,000 psychiatrists, the acupuncturists—
and when cramp comes to shriek, even the reverend clergy are
summoned.

Those blasé feminist leaders who shrug it off and claim that
only the role-playing sex objects complain of it may be interested
in the findings of Dr. Salem Shah of the National Institute of
Mental Health. He categorically states that these hormonal ups
and downs affect every cell in the body including the brain; but
more, it is as much a cause of violence in women as her childhood
phobias or a drunken father. The feminists, of course, put those
findings down as just another biased report from a chauvinist
male psychiatrist. However, despite this feminist whitewash, a
host of other government and scientific statistics show that a
woman wrecks more cars, loses more time at work, makes more
mistakes, steals more, attempts more suicides, and batters more
children when this "love is in bloom." Another piece of research
by the same professor Dalton shows that around that time of the
month a husband is less safe from his wife in their kitchen than in
a hijacked 747. Even the legal defense for women murderers uses
those mental changes during that period—pleading temporary
insanity.

## He Ain't Got Rhythm

On balance, an ordinary male thanks his lucky stars that he
"doesn't have rhythm." But at least one ordinary scientific feminist,
Dr. Estelle Ramey, is making a career of trying to saddle the
Norman Mailers of this world with "female troubles." It seems
that she has some sort of illusionary vision (if not evidence)
explained by a convoluted theory that men also have cycles. This
lady is a Ph.D. (not an M.D.) from Washington, D.C., who deals

more in laboratory rats than in humans. But even so, she either has an extraordinary breed of male rodents or she's just seeing red. And if she keeps coming up with these neo-feminologist phenomenons, she may yet have Dan Rather coming down with a false pregnancy.

Another feminologist, Karen Page, even claims those monthly bouts including dysmenorrhea, backache, sluggishness, and the excessive flow of a period are due to male conditioning. If this is so, our sexist society will also be blamed for bunions and tennis elbow.

## Coping Out

Most women have their own way of coping with the Curse, whether on the Avenue Foch in Paris or in the Casbah in Marrakesh. For instance, the more affluent and utterly feminine Camilles don't fight it; they join it. The more introverted types hole up with a bottle, a book, and a heating pad for their "R and R." However, at the other extreme of this menstrual rainbow, there are those few androgynous, cigar-smoking insurance-executive females who hardly know they have it (if they do at all), and if they do, no nausea, cramps, or ankle edema ever keeps them from their appointed rounds.

Lately the feminologists have even conjured up a theory to explain this last hardy breed—their kind of woman. They think it works as in any other meritocracy. If the female achieves, then by divine rights she's rewarded with a reprieve from her monthly anguish. It is like earning a gold-filled watch for thirty years of service. (In the female lexicon, an achiever is any woman who refuses to make beds or wipe a kid's runny nose.) As they put it, it is because a female garbage*person* or police*person* who gets out of the house and into the mainstream is so happy and busy that this normal physiological problem ceases (however, it's peculiar that other uncontrolled functions like sweating, thirst, hunger, and evacuation still occur). So the liberators assure us the Curse couldn't possibly interfere with the real working female's efficiency. The male management isn't convinced, especially when those afflicted spend more time in the bathroom than on the assembly line.

## The Period—a Question Mark???

Of course the more logical and scientific reason for the amenstrual female is never mentioned. It's too simple, and anyway it doesn't fit the feminist propaganda. Yet everyone knows that if she is one of the few female achievers, it's usually because she's lucky enough to have a goodly level of that circulating hormone of champions—testosterone—which from the beginning makes her more male than female. And it's a known scientific fact that that hormone in no way, shape, or form would be caught dead implicated in any which way with anything feminine, pregnant, or menstrual.

So most likely the stay-at-home women do suffer from being more female. On the other hand their masculinized sisters who make it in the male world would naturally have less female trouble. I would think it highly unnatural, if not phenomenal, for some of those high-strung "network" media women I have known to have a period at all. Period.

## The Curse, from Saint Joan to the Soviet Astropersons

As far as I'm concerned, this theory has an irrefutable history. According to unimpeachable sources, Queen Elizabeth I of England, a real "can do" woman who even beheaded her uppity half-sister Mary Queen of Scots (not a very feminine act), supposedly never had a period at all. At one time she remonstrated to one of her counselors, "You have advised me as a Queen; now advise me as a woman." Then the Maid, the virgin Joan of Arc (no mean superdoer in her own right) stymied us all with bloody achievements in politics and on the field of battle, which even most macho males couldn't accomplish. The Vatican was embarrassed, having to sanctify a male-ish female five-star general— even if she did have visions of Mary. It might be noted in passing that in the archives, she is recorded as having an infantile womb (sometimes the size of a walnut), which of course made her curseless. (The chauvinist wags, of course, jumped on this one: "gussied up with a hundred pounds of impenetrable armor plate, how would her gynecologist even know?")

The new feminology claims that the achieving woman's cycle (if she has one) has no effect on her performance. But the pragmatic Russians don't buy that theory. They aren't betting a hundred-million-dollar spaceship on it. Though they too (like the feminists) have a long-standing habit of changing science to fit their propaganda, when it comes to allowing their female cosmonauts to guide a space shuttle during "that time of the month," it's a big *nyet*. What's more, Ms. Cosmonaut, with no feminist ax to grind, thoroughly agrees.

## Don't Tamper with Tampons

Though menstruation may be a big problem to most women, it's big business to most men. Any national movement for amenorrhea such as some feminists suggest would be disastrous. If the billions of napkins, sprays, drugs, tampons, and a thousand other feminine-oriented products were ever withdrawn from the drugstore shelves, Wall Street would quake. The advertising alone is worth a sheik's harem. As with the Sex Object industry, the feminine hygiene business would have its lobbyist breathing down congressional necks and giving forth more unburnt cash offerings than the Korean CIA. And you can bet on it, the word would go out from the Council of Economic Advisors: "Don't tamper with tampons."

## Someone Up There Is a Male Sexist

Now we go from the dismal to the abject; from the "Curse" to the "Pause." One would naturally think that menopause would be a change for the better. Yet "unmenstruating" turns out to be little more inviting than its predecessor. To have looked forward to finally finishing a lifetime of bloodletting and the panic of pregnancy, only to become frenetic, flushed, and fatigued, with a loss of appetite, weight, and libido, is double jeopardy at its worst. As Dr. Robert Butler, director of the National Institute of Aging, said, "Aging is a women's issue."

If ever it was imagined that there is a benign power watching over the female, the menopause shows that someone up there is a male sexist. For Yahweh to have sentenced woman to thirty or forty years of the flow, then to turn around and cut it off but only to wither her like some kind of desert prune, gives the lie to all those feminists who say that God is a female.

## "Bring Back My Menses to Me!"

No one has ever disputed the fact that most of the young and healthy can muddle through the Curse. But is it not cruel and unusual punishment for woman to be only a shadow of her former self in her declining years, through the desiccation of sagging bodily tissues and the brittleness of bones? And in this state, where did anyone ever come up with the myth of the "merry widow"? There are twelve million widows in America; their median age is fifty-two. How could they be anywhere near that "merry" as they slow down and wrinkle up? Even the simple pleasure of smoking is now denied those aging women, because it has become known that cigarettes bring on this menopausal state earlier than necessary. And just to make sure she gets the full measure of aggravation, the unluckiest female elderly are further frustrated, having that lucky good-for-nothing spouse with his roving eye still on the lookout for more tender stuff at even a later age provided he is not yet defunct from a coronary occlusion.

Robin Morgan, one of the more radical mothers of feminism, spouts off the top of her head that for most women "menopause is a snap." (Of course she has not gone through it as yet.) If so, however, according to Robert A. Wilson (in his book *Forever Feminine*), it's a pretty cold snap. He epitomizes this mellowing period of female life as a combination of "breast flab, stiff and unyielding vaginas, aching joints, hirsute-ism, frequent urination, itching skin, and loss of memory"—not to mention the high incidence of cancer, particularly of the female organs. Now, isn't this just an adorable condition to look forward to in those mellowing years?

## The Cure Is Worse Than the "Pause"

But isn't it ironic that these ravages of this fate should be visited on the feminine woman at a time when most people are looking forward to those Golden years? If it is as depicted in the movies, where Margo changes from a ravishing beauty to a wrinkled crone as she comes out of the perennial youth of Shangri-la in *Lost Horizons,* it's more like the leaden years. Then to compound this affliction she can't even assuage her mental state with tobacco or alcohol because statistics show it only leads her into real trouble with lung cancer and cirrhosis.

Naturally the male's libido—at any stage—is not too enchanted with aging females, as proved in every romantic affair. As ridiculous as it may sound, the fems, in trying to put a bloom on our faded rose, fabricated a new myth—that of the young raunchy jock preferring the senior Mrs. Robinson to sweet young things. Katie Hepburn had a few words for this fairy tale: "I think it's fine—if the younger man is some sort of a sap."

Yet in all chivalry, from the time of Cleopatra to Queen Victoria, though we chauvs didn't lust for them, we at least showed compassion for the benighted menopausee. For instance, in the Middle Ages, we Johnny-on-the-spot helpmates provided a sure cure for flashes and flushes: We had our woman bled to a bleachy white. For those symptoms of drenching sweats we concocted diabolic purges that would shrink the considerable bulk of Sarah Caldwell to reasonable proportions. Frequently as a last resort the gentlemen pukers were called in to try their hands at those blinding headaches. Their concoctions could nauseate and de-appetite Henry VIII. There were also those little specialty home remedies tried and tested for centuries: a dozen leeches behind the ear for wrinkles; or a passel of those little bloodsuckers at the anus for those palling depressions (even the psychiatrists agree that this Rx could bring a catatonic out of a depression faster than electric shock).

## Work and Gray the Feminist Way

But to get at the cause rather than just use those noxious hit-or-miss cures, it has always been thought that unwomanly occupations caused the premature onset of aging and menopause. All the evidence seems to bear this out, though the feminists take exactly the opposite view. By observation alone, one has only to contrast the equality-ridden female worker in Russia with the average U.S. housewife or mother. In that perfect workers' paradise—as advanced as they are in the medical sciences—their chunky thirty- and thirty-five-year-old women truck drivers and girder welders speak for themselves. They look as lined, sagging, and harassed as one of those ancient Uzbek centenarians that the yogurt industry claim as their very own. By contrast, the average U.S. housewife (considered a drudge by the Steinzugs) seems younger than springtime even compared to some of her own graying, taut-as-a-bowstring American executive sisters. And you must be myopic if you can't see the difference after five years between a coffee-sipping telephone-gossiping, luncheon-prone, shopping housewife and a female insurance agent or pole-sliding female fire*person*.

## The Rebirth of a Nature—Making the Deserted Bloom

So they may say life begins at fifty—but for whom? Not for any woman in her right mind. It would take a twenty-four-hour day of the power of positive thinking, plus a brainload of superassertiveness, to take this latter-day change in stride. But again we male benefactors have come to her rescue. This time the answer to the aging maiden's prayer was her illusionary dreamboat and savior: the gynecologist. He came up with that magic youthifier—the female hormone. So—a great leap backward; a new lease on life.

It was as if the lost legion found the fountain of youth spritzing nothing but ice-cold holy water in the burning desert. It was the perfect oasis to the parched *Pausee*. And good to the last drop, it made the *deserted* bloom. Talk about reborn Baptists—this was the rebirth of a nature. And believe you me, those forgotten ladies took their salvation any way they could get it. Besides pills and shots, they rubbed it into their faces for wrinkles, into their breasts for firmness, and into their buttocks for those shifting sands. They gargled it to bring back the dulcet tones and swished it around their mouths for that nondentured look. They douched it for sexual potency and enema-ed it for regularity. They took it before and after dinner to ward off the usual circulatory ups and downs, and took it with their Wheaties to prevent the heebie-jeebies.

## Between the Devil and the Deep Blue Funk

And then even that great big dream bubble burst, adding more evidence that God is no female—at least not a graying one. For just when we thought he was trying so hard to right the terrible wrong he had perpetrated on femininity, he who gave—snatched away. If anything, it was a trick only a disgruntled chauvinist would do. Through his watchdog, the Food and Drug Administration, in headlines an inch high, he thundered: "Estrogen—a Cancer Risk." That's all they needed. Again, they were caught between the devil and the deep blue funk. It was a choice that Hobson would quail at, a no-win proposition. They either took a shot of cancer every day and kept themselves glowing on a relatively even keel, or reverted back to a mass of depressing (and cancer-free) sags. It was an early grave or the chronic blahs. So again she was back to only the biblical comfort of the twenty-third psalm—or regular and hopeful prayer meetings, transplanted monkey ovaries, or procaine injections at one hundred dollars per wrinkle.

## In Males—Cycles Are for Riding

There they were again, back to square one. It was a pity, however, that the feminists wouldn't let it go at that. Though there are certain things that one wouldn't wish on the devil himself—the fems even tried to stick us with that plague. Of all the loaded slings and arrows the feminists have tossed at us compassionate and loving males, this was the worst. Imagine trying to pin the menopause on our permanently priapic curse-free carcasses. It was that same rat specialist, Estelle Ramey, who, unsuccessful in pinning rhythm on us, now tried to give us "pause." Though it got pretty far in the antimale consciousness-raising circles, it died in the scientific ones. As any sixth-grader who ever dissected a frog knows, there can't be a *pause* without a *Curse*, and so far a maxi-pad has never been a must in a shaving kit. Again, it took a real female scientist, Katherina Dalton, who had been studying humans and their hormonal relations for twenty-five years, to finally put this myth to rest with the argument that there is no more evidence for male "pauses" of any kind than there is of male pregnancy.

## No Gifts from the Sea

So here we are in the miracle age of uppers, downers, and nuclear medicine; and no matter how the feminists slice it, euphemize it, or try to foist it on the male, the Curse is the Curse is the Curse, and the Pause is the Pause is the Pause. And, poor soul, our heart's delight is stuck with both of them. So let's all bow our heads, and with hands over hearts stand for one minute in silent prayer each time the moon is full—and make it two minutes when the sun sets in her West.

CHAPTER X

# Her Mother Was a Fullback
## for the Baltimore Colts—
## There Is No Joy in Maudville

My mother isn't too thrilled about this.

> *Lori Wasserburger, University of Wisconsin,*
> *after deadlifting 325 pounds*

My star quarter-miler wore bangles the length of each arm . . . I could hear her jingling clear across the track. Between races the girls work on one another's hairdos.

> *Dick Lacy, coach, New Rochelle, New York*

When a college starts to take its women's sports seriously, it puts a man in charge.

> *Ann Uhler, Executive Director, Association for*
> *Intercollegiate Athletics for Women*

ON ONE SUPER BOWL SUNDAY, there she was, just a wee tot, wan, undernourished, and shivering, standing pathetically outside of the Astrodome selling souvenir pennants. I was shocked. "Little girl," I said, "why are you here; why aren't you in Sunday School or out on a playground?" She cast down her eyes and clenched and unclenched her tiny fists, tears rolling down her cheeks as she sobbed, "Sir, my mother was a fullback for the Baltimore Colts." Then, in a burst of anguish: "The doctors say she'll never be the same."

## The Kamikaze Feminists

If the fems have their way, the athletic slaughter of the innocents will get worse, not better. It is up to us chauvinists to call a halt to it—for their own good. Though we males have admitted openly there could be an honest (if farfetched) difference of opinion when it comes to similarities in emotions or intellect between the sexes—are the libbers not mad to think of comparing the two in bone and brawn? Now mind you, we chauvs are fully cognizant that women have won the legal right to rub elbows with sweaty undershirted steamfitters at McSorley's all-male bar, and been granted the privilege of getting the bends one hundred fathoms deep like any other sandhog. So with this kind of legal (if misguided) support, how can we stop them from being ful-filled, slugging it out with a stevedore welterweight in the Golden Gloves? Yet the very thought of one of our clean-cut American girl wrestlers locked in a half nelson by a hairy mass of male Albanian muscle in the Olympics gives even the toughest of us jocks the shudders.

Sure, through the years we may have dug a few sandtraps here and there to bury some of those affirmative action incompetents, but we've certainly allowed that one female in a hundred who is capable of competing for some of our more lucrative spots in the professional or business world. However, in sports they should thank us on bended knee for keeping them out: it could be a matter of life and death. When it comes to boxing, ice hockey, or lacrosse—females against males—well, it's suicidal. We are just not a nation of bloodthirsty men who condone permitting future mothers of the world to become kamikaze sacrifices, even to satisfy the monomaniacal goals of the movement. We do draw the line somewhere.

## That's What They Want, Dr. Freud

Then again, perhaps we chauvs, whose lust for tender feminine flesh knows no bounds, just do not understand the psyche of the more bemuscled branch of the female sex. The melon-biceped Billie Jean King and the bar-brawling Rosemary Casals seem to feel that "man to man combat" is the answer to Freud's immortal question, "In God's name, what do they want?" And even more mystifying to us, some of the other brawnies are out for the same kicks as any red-blooded American boy (with a doubtful IQ); the satisfying crunch of a fractured fibula and those heady concus-sions on the playing fields of Eton and the Houston Astrodome. Every day we see where another hefty lass, like Renee Marino in

Massachusetts, made defensive guard on her high school football squad (as her teammates say, "she's just one of the guys"). Other young things are going to court to get their fair share of the knocks on Dartmouth's ice hockey team. If this kind of suicidal equality urge is so strong, no one can tell us that there is not some sort of spontaneous self-destruct button deep in the feminist psyche—maybe in that lower reptilian level of her brain. Now many of us are as muscle-bound and fearless as a maverick mustang, but still we do not sky dive with a parasol or hang glide over the Mount Saint Helens volcano to demonstrate our manhood.

Even female reporters are not up to the give and take of the brawling professional locker rooms. Rosemary Ross, a ten-year veteran of the *Philadelphia Journal*, fled from the Pittsburgh locker room in tears. Jane Gross of the *New York Times* was physically thrown out in San Diego. And talk about indecent exposure! The athletes love to sidle up to the female reporters without the benefit of even Jim Palmer's jockey shorts and have them back off confused, embarrassed, and with unprintable remarks.

## The Delilah Complex

According to psychologists, the real challenge (or death wish) in competing body to body with the male is the subsconscious urge to get even. It is the old Delilah complex. What could be more satisfying to one of those man-eating fems than the realization of their fantasy—bringing another Samson to his knees? Of course the odds are no better than those of the Christians versus the lions. As ridiculous as all of this must sound, if those libbers get their way on unisex sports, the female athlete may become as extinct as the brontosaurus. But as in other competitive areas such as bullfighting or the rodeo, the feminist leaders will not budge. It's all the way—down to the death rattle of the last female blocking back.

## The Broad—and the Tough and the Tall

To show that we are not reflex misogynists—just antifeminist— we go all out for one of the female athlete's more legitimate and more life-supporting aims—money. Many women are well aware of the pot at the end of the World Series rainbow and of the Rolls Roycers like Reggie Jackson, Pelé, Gerulaitis, and the richest jock of them all, Dave Winfield, the new twenty-three million dollar Yankee ( $7,500 a game).

Sure, the girls want a piece of the action; it's only natural in either sex. Though many are still female enough to be satisfied with just outdoing Gussie Moran in the lacy shorts department, or even the lesser women-against-women purses in softball and field hockey, it's not enough for the huskies. The latter lot still want to get to that new free agent status and play the big boys in the big time for the big money. Granted that some born athletes of the female gender could work up to beating the paunchy Howard Cosell in the one-hundred-meter dash or pin Liberace in two out of three falls; but coming up against the average Pete Rose, Terry Bradshaw, or Yogi Berra would be an invitation to an intensive care unit. We can understand the weight-lifting Billie Jean King taking on the aging hustler Bobby Riggs, but why so many female athletes must have that gutsy *je ne sais quoi* of a three-hundred-pound body check by Bubba Smith is a mystery—even if it were for Super Bowl shekels. Last year the only woman who got signed in the big league was a female basketballer, Ann Meyers, at fifty thousand dollars a year. After the publicity had died down she never got off the bench and was soon relegated to slam-dunk P.R. handouts rather than snatch rebounds. Still and all, to the broad and the tough and the tall, Wimbledon alone just won't do—it is Shea Stadium or bust, and from where we sit the latter seems much more probable.

## Here Comes That Rub Again

But then here comes that rub again. Relentlessly, just as they blamed us for their emotional binges, so they are back with the same tired excuse, pinning their smallness and flab on sexist conditioning. Again we are the culprits. Imagine their coming up with the absurd notion that lack of build, strength, and coordination is due to their suppression and, get this, *overprotection* by us for a million years. We are even blamed for their inability to kick a forty-yard field goal. And because we have enough feeling for their frailty of build and lack of musculature, and try to help by hauling a fifty-pound garbage can out to the alley, we have oppressed them. So it is we who have made her unfit to slide thirty feet on her stomach into home plate.

## The Origin of the Species—or Specious Origins

This bit of feminist fraud is put out with the certitude of the Sermon on the Mount, shucking off such minor differences of opinion as *The Origin of Species* and the laws of general genetics. Even after it's been proved that every female ancestor for twenty million years, from the rat to the thoroughbred filly, has been smaller, less muscled, and more fragile than her male counterpart, it's meaningless to them.

The fems also maintain that it is chauvinist medical science that has convinced the world that the female was boned, muscled, and strung together more to bear children than to block a punt. Well, that may be, but from the obvious alone, we do not see how a wider pelvis, an elastic orifice, and two pendulous mammary glands could be more suited to punt blocking than childbearing. But to make this bit of feminist self-delusion totally absurd, there is no doubt in their minds that the ERA will right all of these wrongs.

## More Hernias Than Medals

There is no male or female medical expert alive who can prove that the female is built for contact sport. And no Jimmy the Greek in his right mind would put up a nickel even at bookmaker odds that the best of the heavyweight female boxers could handle even a flyweight sparring partner. Though some of the toughest female athletes, such as the once-great Babe Didrikson (with her almost-male buttonlike breasts and her scrawnily padded frame) hardly seem female, we must admit that most modern female athletes are much better endowed in heft, if not exactly of the Suzanne Somers ilk. Still, Lloyds of London will not cover either type for major medical when it comes to contact sports.

And why should they? Any female trying to beat the five-hundred-pound knee and jerk of the Russian champion, Vasily Alexeyev, must wind up with more hernias than medals. We would bet even money that Nadia Comaneci and Olga Korbut, those two nearly perfect ninety-pound gymnastic geniuses, will undoubtedly come down with prolapsed wombs from too many upside-down hours on the bars.

## Multiple Choice—Bats, Barbells, or Babies

Speaking of hernias and wombs, the big question for society is not whether today's woman can totter in (legitimately) among the first 190 in the Boston Marathon (which the 1981 lady runner did), but can she fulfill her god-given biological destiny? Is she physically that strong (or mentally that weak) to take on the best of the musclemen and still be the mother of us all? And notwithstanding padding, helmets, and aluminum athletic supporters, do too many rabbit punches, too many body blocks, and too many contusions and abrasions of vulnerable parts make her less fruitful to multiply? Well, we are not sure, although the medical profession says they cannot see where a ruptured spleen or a hematoma of the mammaries favorably affects the conception or nursing of a child.

Generally, most of the top (especially track and field) female athletes are indifferent to this problem. From the record, the more masculinized a female, the less maternal she is. So though we do not know for sure, we suspect a nonfertile breeding record from one of those mastadons such as the 250-pound Hungarian javelin thrower (who was banned from the Olympics when her tests showed her less than a true female). And even in the non-contact sports, most of the big names are childless (Helen Wills, Nancy Lieberman, Stella Walsh, Babe Didrikson, Martina Navratilova, Billie Jean King, Kathy Kusner, et cetera). If an occasional one such as the likes of one of those East German Brunhildas of swimming fame did become in the family way, nothing less than a veterinarian trained in the obstetrical maneuvers of delivering a hippo could do the job without a block and tackle.

## The Player Draft versus the Marriage Market

That the more jockish liberators are going all out to show us up by building and training hardier, heftier (if afertile) female youths is not going over well with the League of American Mothers. They are still old-fashioned enough to presume that one of the prerequisites for making babies (at least for the time being) is marriage. They outnumber the fems about ten thousand to one. These practical homemaker-type mothers dream more of daughters drawing one man to the altar than fifty thousand to the Garden. To them it is not whether their little girls will ever play tight end for the Green Bay Packers, but whether a cauliflower ear is an asset in the marriage market. They question whether the Big Man on Campus is panting and proud to escort one great hunk of a charley horse with fresh facial cleat marks to the junior prom after a bruising Saturday afternoon in the College Bowl.

## Fear and Loathing at the Virginia Slims

Now mind you, we chauvs are not out to dissuade the real fem jock from being what she naturally is; we just want those more feminine sporting types (or borderliners) to know what they are actually getting into. For besides the connubial dilemma of the female athlete, she has special worries once she has made it. She may be the best double-play shortstop the Oakland A's ever fielded, but what does she do for relaxation once the locker room is emptied—go catting with Vida Blue? Carol Mann, former U.S. women's golf champion, complained of the lonely nights spent crying herself to sleep on the professional circuit. One young lady on the pro tennis circuit complained she used more energy warding off her romantic female colleagues than a three-setter with that most feminine of tennisers, Chrissy Evert Lloyd. (By the way, I've heard Chrissy admits she couldn't win a set from her 305th computer-ranked husband.)

But the tour must have also gotten on Pam Shriver's nerves when she had her winning opponent, Tracy Austin, in tears with a barrage of four-letter words a Marine sergeant wouldn't use.

The rigors of the tour must get to their sportsmanship, too. Then to top this off, imagine the chagrin of even some of those tough babies like tennis star Rosie Casals subjected to a chromosome test to prove she's a lady. In the 1976 Olympics that chromosome business was a real problem.

## Queen Kong

Olympic committees still have that same dilemma. I'm sure it's embarrassing for those gentlemen, when just by looking they can't tell a woman from a man. It seems you just can't be that sure. Take poor Stella Walsh, for example. It took an autopsy to know that that great female Olympian of the 30s was really one of us. And some of those Eastern Bloc babies in 1980, shot full of anabolic (male) steroids, were more like "Queen Kongs" than the weaker sex. For instance, one shot-putter from Kiev tossed a twenty-five-pound weight around like a spitball, and an East German swimmer had thighs which would have been the envy of the Empire State Building's foundation.

Though most of them may have tested out female (seven didn't), no one can convince us that a test tube was not involved somewhere in their hardly divine conception, or at least that their childhood bath water was not laced with the Hormone of Champions.

## You Can't Tell a Player without a Chromosome Test

I know it is a sore subject with the fems, but in the 1972 Olympic games, Danuta Dosani of Poland was banned for taking shots of the male hormone. Many others were suspected of it, including Evelin Jahl (East Germany) who, in 1980 for the first time ever, threw the discus farther than a male. No question, it does the trick—especially among some of the naturally inclined, more beefy females. Experimentally, we know that a series of those shots could convert the most pampered of female poodles into a bitch that would take on a Doberman. But when a female athlete goes so far as to take the male hormone just to have a Gold pinned on her ample chest as her national anthem is being played, where is that female pride they are always boasting about? Actually, it is a rank admission of the superiority of that golden male testosterone and also a confession as to what lengths they will go to be like us. Yet some experts ask why those Olympic committees should be so queasy about female athletes? We breed a bigger and better Angus bull by giving him steroids just to get the prize at the country fair; so why not a quasi-female champion welterweight who could give Sugar Ray a tussle?

## A New Ball (or Ball-less) Game

So today, with drugs and needles floating around the Olympic villages like a South Bronx street corner, and with all the talk about sex changes, it's a whole new ball (or ball-less) game. It has gotten so bad that a sports committee must have a gynecologist, a geneticist, and a sexologist palpating, photographing, and probing every body orifice. Maybe at birth we should treat potential female athletes like thoroughbred horses—just tattoo their sex under their upper lip. Then there would be no mistakes and no ringers.

## A Myth Is as Good as a Miler

Putting aside the physical equality myths which the fems spread about for the purpose of recruiting more women into men's sports, there is more evidence to back an opposing theory that "females are naturally not team players." Zubin Mehta, the great symphonic conductor, allowed no women in his Los Angeles orchestra as it was bruited around, because they were too troublesome in a team effort. The great von Karajan thinks so, too, and many coaches agree. We tracked down this canard, and though there may be much truth in it, the liberationists scorn the research, as always. It was done by a male, wasn't it? The eminent Rutgers sociologist, Lionel Tiger, states that history proves that females just never had the team spirit—no urge to work together—even with other women. He claims in his book, *Men in Groups,* that males have been "bonded" ("a deep instinct comprising loyalty, mutual respect, and collaboration") to other males ever since their hunting days. As he documents it, if men were not working as a team, they never could have made it on their own against bigger, more vicious predators. Today it is not just a chauvinist myth that she has neither the instinct nor the experience to play together in an orchestra or on a basketball team. Maggie Scarf, the science writer, as we've mentioned, even blames a female's depressions (six to one over the male) on that biological lack of bonding.

## *As Coordinated as Jerry Ford and His Shoelaces*

Other common putdowns are attributed to us chauvs which even we are not sure of. Does the female have a lack of co-ordination—especially in how she throws a ball? Again, as the male anthropologists explain it, the Neanderthal lady had no need to throw for her supper. Only those males who could drop an oncoming tiger with a spear or a rock at one hundred yards— before the cat dropped him—lived to throw another day. Those who performed best survived and passed along that Phil Rizzuto throwing-arm gene—to men only. That is what the experts say. But one could doubt this evidence according to the reputed accuracy of some women with crockery aimed at a weaving husband target at three o'clock in the morning. And it must also be acknowledged that a female in her natural habitat, at the sewing machine, with foot and hand acting as one, certainly couldn't do worse than that supposedly all-American Michigan footballer, Jerry Ford, with his gum-chewing and lace-tying problems.

## *The Tenderness of a Hangman*

We also know that another piece of propaganda attributed to us (which we hotly deny) is certainly not true: that females have no killer instinct. Could a Bobby Orr on the ice in the Boston Garden, or a Muhammad Ali with a Spinks on the ropes compare in this department with Jean Harris or one of the Borgia girls? One only has to look at the wifely record in marital combat to see who is usually on the wrong end of a .45 slug or a kitchen knife. As Strindberg said of his wife, "She is sometimes seized with the tenderness of a hangman for his victims."

## *Double Indemnity—the Pregnant Pole Vaulter*

Of course the most malicious rumor fraudulently attributed to us chauvs is that "raging hormones" are a tremendous burden to the female athlete. It's taken for granted that if the curse each month can keep a cafeteria worker in bed for a couple of days it's certainly not going to enhance the prospects of a female Olympian's breaking the record in the one-hundred-meter hurdle. In female against female, this problem would be canceled out by the law of averages. Even with an Olga Korbut, it could be bad. At that time of the month, missing the bar in a triple somersault could be disastrous.

Anyway, the less masculine of the female jocks rarely looks forward to the lunar calendar with its attendant nervousness, pain, and fluid retention. One thing for sure, when they have it, it certainly doesn't help their performance. But as the saying goes about "the heat and the kitchen," any real musclewoman who cannot bear the bone-crushing scissors grip of a mustachioed Turk wrestler as she stifles the pain of those abdominal cramps should be back home with her needlepoint.

Now, pregnancy in athletes poses even more problems. (As we said, luckily most heavyweight sportswomen are about as fertile as whooping cranes.) At the Munich games, it was rumored around the village that a female pole vaulter suddenly found herself three months gone right before her team left from Bratislavia. She kept it a secret. According to observers, she not only had trouble dragging that little stranger over the first bar, but if she competed any time before twelve noon, she had to keep the little brown bag handy.

## *The Pill and Her*

The safer female athlete on the pill is not much better off. She carries three to five pounds of extra fluid in her body, which would be like taking the high jump with a lead dumbbell in each sock. If the egalitarian ladies were smarter, they would demand the Olympic committees give weight handicaps for males as they do at Pimlico and Churchill Downs.

The females have an overwhelming bit of catching up to do when they go against the male athlete. Though they've made a point and now compete against us, they seem to last only as long as the publicity lingers on. Ms. Guthrie broke into the Indy 500 with great fanfare but did not stay long enough to test her rubber for more than a few turns. In 1980 she did not even qualify, and in 1981 she could get no backers. Jockey Kathy Kusner has been around the track at Laurel and Pimlico a thousand times and has not brought home enough winners to keep her mounts in oats. (Steve Cauthen at sixteen won a fortune in one year.) Robyn Smith, of course, saw the handwriting on the wall and took the easy way out by marrying Fred Astaire. And to date there is no one on the female horizon threatening either Sugar Ray Leonard or Jack Watson; and you know what Rosie Ruiz had to do to come in fifty-ninth in the Boston Marathon. From the looks of the 1980 Olympic records alone, it appears it would take another Ice Age, a turn of evolution, a gene combination of Jack Dempsey and Bronco Nagursky and/or enough testosterone to float the *Queen Elizabeth 2* to do the trick. Right now, neither Bruce Jenner nor Reggie Jackson needs look to his laurels.

Here is an example of how far the ladies have to go in Olympic competition.

## 1980

|  | Women | Men |
|---|---|---|
| 100-Meter Run | 11.6 | 10.25 |
| 200-Meter Run | 22.03 | 20.19 |
| 400-Meter Run | 48.88 | 44.60 |
| 800-Meter Run | 1:45.40 | 1:35.5 |
| High Jump | 6 ft. 5½ in. | 7 ft. 8¾ in. |
| Discus Throw | 229 ft. 6 in. | 218 ft. 8 in. |
| Javelin Throw | 224 ft. 4¾ in. | 229 ft. 2⅜ in. |
| Swimming: |  |  |
| 100 Meters Freestyle | 54.79 | 50.40 |
| 400 Meters Freestyle | 4:08.76 | 3:51.31 |
| 100 Meters Backstroke | 1:00.86 | 56.53 |
| 100 Meters Breaststroke | 1:10.22 | 1:03.34 |

All of this just goes to show: The male did better in the one-hundred-yard dash fifty years ago than the female does today. In the four-hundred-meter hurdles, when you are dealing with records broken by split seconds, Bruce Jenner could probably eat six matzoh balls at the starting line and still beat the best East German female by a country mile.

## From Bean Bags to Bean Balls

But as the liberationists say, if a female athlete (like a female consciousness) does not break out of the oppressive male conditioning at a tender age, a potential female tackle will never have the thrill of clutching that fumble, buried under a thousand pounds of flesh, cloth, and leather. It is said that Nadia Comaneci was swinging on a trapeze bar before she was toilet trained.

This brings us to that big Little League brouhaha—should little girls be allowed to play hard ball with the little boys (even if they throw funny)? Well, it was finally decided by the courts that if a little girl would abide by all the boys' rules, even to wearing an aluminum crotch cup (protecting something that isn't there) she was equal and could play. (Mothers are still confused whether you wash a supporter like lingerie, put it in the washer-dryer, or boil it in lye.) The rationale behind the Little League decision was that if a female athlete wanted to expose herself later on in life to a concussion by a Jim Palmer bean ball at ninety mph, she should get started early.

## Multiple Choice: Baton or Blocking Back

Here in the United States the Little League is, of course, only the beginning. The courts went along with the fems and have come up with rulings encouraging every girl in high school to turn in her baton and go all out for the helmets and shoulder pads just as the boys do. This of course has caused a big problem with male athletes; they bring in the money and now have to share it. You could not get a scalper ticket for under two hundred dollars for the last NCAA basketball tournament even if held in a civic center in Wahoo, Nebraska, while the counterpart female championship could not fill a garden club tearoom in New York City. But court rulings and all, with the glory road now open to them, there somehow have been a paucity of feminine takers. But the Billie Jeans of femaledom still can't understand how any girl would choose to shiver in a mini skirt, braless, with their T and A routine, leading the cheers of their male oglers, rather than take their lumps on the field of battle.

## *There Is No Joy in Maudville*

So, as we have always known (though the fems cannot be convinced of it), regardless of female pride, drugs, or androgyny, nature will never let nurture beat men on the playing fields. There is no way a ball*person* can leapfrog millions of years of genetic culling and—either by perseverance, the Pill, or even a few varied and sundry hormones—consistently make it. Though feminist leaders will brook no interference from Darwin, Mendel, or Pete Rozelle, they will never win out—even down to the maimed and crippled bodies of thousands of their sisters. They truly believe there is no more noble cause than breaching the sanctum sanctorum of the all-male locker room, or providing every housewife the opportunity of hefting a forty-ounce Louisville slugger, or being knocked senseless by a right cross. But it will be a long time before there is joy in Maudville. And we are dedicated to using everything in our power to keep it that way— doing them a favor, as it were.

## CHAPTER XI

# Spouse Beating, a Contact Sport— Saturday Night Fervor

The most unreported crime is not wife beating—it's husband beating.

*Professor Suzanne Steinmetz, sociologist, University of Delaware*

Acts of violence are committed by women almost as frequently as by men.

*Congressperson Barbara Mikulski*

IN THIS DAY of the physique beautiful, the once-popular body-building fad of spouse beating\* seems to have caught up with jogging and racquetball. All over the world, according to Mrs. Erin Pizzy, an English expert on the art, "There is every evidence that it is growing by leaps and bounds." Strangely enough, though it is a sport of ancient tradition and at least as healthful as boxing or push-ups, it has never been encouraged by the President's Commission on Physical Fitness. From the number of court cases alone, it seems to have a broad general appeal. And though the feminists have finally gotten a marathon accepted by the Olympic committee, those sexists still seem to have little interest in bringing this bangup sport out of the closet.

From all indications, the international surge of interest in the

---

\* It is in no way to be construed that this chapter either condones (or condemns) this ancient sport, though for over thirty thousand years it has been indulged in by caveman, king, and congressman.

The author, though generally content with the joys of marital existence, confesses that (with due provocation) there comes a great inclination to indulge in this venerable action. However, he professes no authority (or expertise) other than some spectator recollections, as practiced in an uncle's household, usually on Saturday night.

This chapter is presented here solely to inform the sports-minded public on the fine points of a game that may one day take the place of baseball.

sport paralleled the push of the women's movement. Germaine Greer's publicized lectures in Europe, women's quest for job equality, and the general raising of female consciousness seem to have enhanced the male's attraction to it. The game has always had a loose tie-in with the worldwide rise and fall in the consumption of bourbon and gin.

However, the sudden resurgence of this game in which even the feminist movement has taken an interest (though not a very sporting one) has been an enigma. According to government statistics, it has become no less popular than backgammon and is right on the heels of tennis. Congress*person* Barbara Mikulski of Maryland warns that "from ten to fifteen million persons in the U.S. now participate."

Until the late 60s, spouse beating in the U.S.A. was strictly a beer-and-hotdog, blue-collar affair; more recently it has climbed, from East Scranton to East Hampton. Reports of its popularity in Palm Beach and Grosse Pointe as well as in the older sporting spas of Deauville and Antibes have not been exaggerated. But as Congress*person* Mikulski says, it's a people's pastime, "affecting adults in all socio-economic groups in all areas of our country"— no different than disco or wife swapping. It would be no surprise to hear of more of those "Chowder, Marching, and Spouse Beating Societies" springing up in the sporting clubs of Europe with their individual club colors (purplish black, and blue).

## Jimmy and Rosalynn and Anwar and Jihan

Spouse beating is certainly not unpopular in political circles. In the recent past, during a visit by President Anwar Sadat of Egypt in Jimmy Carter's regime, it was the principal (if not entirely candid) topic of conversation between the two first ladies. The Steel Magnolia, Rosalynn, hardly a parasoled Gone-with-the-Wind type, put it on pretty thick—she talked about it as if Jimmy had never laid a glove on her.

The gentle Madame Sadat, from the most advanced nation in the Arab world, gave her a fishy eye but in turn also played it straight, saying, "In Egypt, work is being done with husbands to teach them how to treat their wives better." It has obviously had results, for it is alleged that any man caught using more than one wife at a time as a beast of burden or for other than strictly agricultural purposes is fined seventy dinars, or about six cents, by the local affirmative action agent.

## A Shiner Example

From the passionate interest these first ladies showed in this sport, it is obviously as important in the White Houses of the world as budgets and MIRV missiles. Though not usually publicized at his press conferences, it was well known that Canadian Prime Minister Trudeau's former wife Margaret used to come out of her house of a morning with a shiner or two and a few well-camouflaged contusions after newspaper accounts of her prolonged *musical* jaunts with Mick Jagger. The front-page picture one post-bout morning, showing Madame Trudeau with a nice broad smile, was only to assure her subjects that not a tooth was missing. This was all before their separation, but a subtle political warning for all uppity first ladies everywhere.

## True to the Colors—Black and Blue

Lately the press has given the *sport of queens* a lot of front page coverage, though little of it still gets anywhere near the racing or football results. We think it is mainly because the more bleeding heart feminists are protesting it as unfair and much more risky for the wife than for the husband. And though the usual semiliterate sports editors, conditioned by years in the locker rooms, are as chauvinistic as any of us, they too have been rolling over for the libbers. They obviously believe the unfounded rumors by peeping Tom neighbors or the cop on the beat that it can be as gory and one-sided as bullfighting. Gory, yes. But one-sided? That is pure poppycock, as shown at the Orlando, Florida, *Spouse* Center (not "battered wife" center, but "spouse" center). The counselors there weren't shocked at all by a twenty-six-year-old husband staggering in bleeding, claiming his wife attacked him with a hammer and also hit him with a full-length picture frame. It was routine for them, but that poor husband didn't have a fanatic organization to publicize it, stand up for it, or to promote halfway "Houses of Abel" (not Ruth) for him. That spouse center's records show that for about every ten women abused there are six men who catch it even worse. Nationwide, records show it's more like fifty-fifty. As Professor Murray Straus of the University of New Hampshire concludes in a national survey, "About two million husbands and the same number of wives commit at least one serious attack on their mates each year." Even then husbands are less likely to report it than women. But also, men weather the rough ones better—usually without hospitalization, and thus they're not likely to get on the police blotter.

## Mix and Match

As in all other sporting events, everything depends on the matching. You wouldn't match Sugar Ray Leonard with "WKRP"'s Loni Anderson. With more even skills the outcome of these bouts could never be as one-sided as people used to think. Then again, today, both sides take advantage of every little handicap they can lay hold of. Though one would think that the usually obtuse male would not be so farsighted, the statistics show that he always takes a wife smaller, lighter, and less aggressive than himself. If she has bad eyesight, is a little deaf, and can't handle a kitchen knife, all the better. It is hardly believable to what extent each will go. One woman at a conference on spouse beating at Trenton State College claimed gross unfair advantage by her husband, a well-to-do engineer. She gave testimony that he beat her while her arm was in a cast (from a previous bout), then he called a doctor who placed her in a straitjacket and had her "voluntarily" committed to a New Jersey state mental institution. That of course was hardly cricket. But on the other hand, would even the healthiest male specimen in his right mind chance a go-round, married to twenty-year-old Lori Wasserburger of Wisconsin, who deadlifted 325 pounds?

Though the feminists complain of the discrepancy in size, it's not always brawn and bulk. Never forget, as in lacrosse or ice hockey, one uses not only ploys and stratagems but also lethal weapons. So not only skill and tactics, but the choice of weapons is highly important. For instance, in Camden County, New Jersey, a Mrs. Roxanne Gay, only five feet two inches, weighing 100 pounds, was obviously no match in sheer bulk for her six-foot-five 265-pound Philadelphia Eagles husband Blenda. Yet, by clever maneuvering and psyching, she did him in—with a little help from an ice pick hidden in her cleavage.

## The Feminist Pearl Harbor

It's especially intriguing when one gets down to some of the fine (or even blunt) points of the game, other than the physical gamesmanship. Psychology is at its very core. In this vein the sport can be as challenging and complex in its subtle gambits as English cricket or Japanese go. The element of surprise, for instance, is always an advantage and can be the winning margin. Francine Hughes, in the dead of night, as stealthy as the attack on Pearl Harbor, doused her batterer husband with kerosene and tossed him a lighted match. He never knew what singed him. She of course was acquitted—temporary insanity—of the feminist kind, and has since become as famous as other sports*persons* like Reggie Jackson or Bobby Orr on the talk shows.

The adventures of Mrs. Gay and Francine Hughes have shown us that analyzing some of the special tactics, feints, and maneuvers are as fascinating as Monday morning quarterbacking the Green Bay Packers.

## A Face on the Kitchen Floor

Women contestants have other little ruses and are not loathe to use them. They always try to sucker their opponents into *their* own turf where, of course, they have the best of it. By any known ruse from food to sex, the female frequently tries to manipulate this hand-to-hand combat phase into the kitchen area. Here she is on familiar ground—and even in the dark she'd know the exact location of every cleaver and knife. This often works out not only to the male's disadvantage, but frequently to his last rites.

Another equalizing factor in offsetting the male's advantage in heft and reach is his well-accepted sportsman's code. By tradition, all of his prebout limbering up is at the corner bar. The most popular conditioner has been found to be gin, and the quantity depends on just how much mental and physical priming is necessary. He usually gets oiled to the point of instability and lack of coordination so that neither his uppercut nor his left jab has that old zip. Can a gentleman give more of a handicap than that?

## Salome's Daughters

Looking back into the history of the sport shows that the odds are not particularly weighted to the male. The best example is that of the physically tough John the Baptist competing with the sylphlike ballerina Salome. Whose head was handed by whom at whose instigation on that platter?

And today, as women get out of the home and more and more into the masculine fields of crime their skills will sharpen accordingly. Even on television there are subtle hints and how-tos for the underphysiqued female. The young women frequently take a page from our modern-day police*persons* (like Angie Dickinson), grasping their .38s with both hands and yelling "freeze," then blowing him away with a bullet between his sexist eyes. And that Charlie's Angels Mafia in tight short-shorts and jiggly bras. Has anyone ever seen any of them come out on the short end as they mangle the Incredible Hulk with every nasty karate trick they're so adept at?

We have only to look at international terrorists to see how long a way women have come in equality of mayhem. To cite only a few successes: What husband would think of knocking around a Susan Albrecht, that famous machine gun-*person* in Hamburg, Germany; or Marie Torres, the FALN Puerto Rican terrorist so handy with her homemade bombs? But the woman to be most ardently  avoided in a spouse-beating contest would be the once notorious Ulrike Meinhof, the female leader of that murderous group (mostly female) of German anarchists. So let's not put this male-female contest down as some kind of a pushover for the average married jock.

## A Grand Old Game

Still, one can't appeal to the fairness or logic of a feminist. She still complains all the way to the emergency room that the dice are loaded. Here she is, pushing for equality of opportunity in all sports, while right under her bloodied nose there exists a male-female contest readymade—with absolutely no sexist bias. In fact, by definition, this game cannot exclude females. Yet she's still knocking it.

As any real student of this grand old game knows, though it is not tiddlywinks, it's still this side of the mangling that goes on in boxing or ice hockey. Though it may be deadly at times, the death rate is no higher than in football. And not unlike those other games, when tempers get short and fists begin to fly, the police may have to step in.

## Not Exactly Marquis of Queensbury

There is, of course, a fair and mutual protection guaranteed by the rules and regulations of spouse beating. In a very complete book on the subject, *The Silent Crisis*, by two sportsminded gentlemen, Langley and Levy, police intervention goes strictly by the rules: Right off, "police will not step in until after the first contest," which is sound policy because the opening bout is usually just a warmup and may lead no further. This avoids a lot of amateurish "cry wolf" kinds of thing. According to those authors, in some areas there is a strict regulation that "a certain number of stitches must be required before they call a penalty." This is considered unfair by some women's groups where the husbands are clever blunt-kidney-and-body punchers. Even as far back as 1971, the state of Alabama (probably through its athletic commission) came up with some tough provisions, making illegal "beating her with a stick, pulling her hair, choking her, spitting in her face, or kicking her about the floor," during the bout.

In different states and nations the culture may necessitate totally different regulations. For instance, in Utah, what chance does any male have against the low blows of seven wives? Yet not one law has been passed, even after the most recent gang-up murder of a well-known polygamist by his wives. Also recently, due to changing times, the game has opened up to practically any type of male and female couple. One doesn't even have to be married to receive all the healthful benefits of the sport. As steady dating gets younger and younger, the sport has burgeoned. At Arizona State University, Professor Mary Laner reported that sixty percent of the students during dating, courtship, and live-in had, in one way or another, battered each other. Live-ins, especially if they last more than a month, have taken to the sport in a big way, and as lawyer Marvin Mitchelson has shown in palimony cases, it can now involve big money just as in football and other contact sports.

## *A Brief Encounter of the Psychiatric Kind*

Even some of our noted psychiatrists ( always ready to get into the act) have announced that the female enjoys it as much as the male—starting with the foreplay of a few four-letter words to the final brief encounter of the turbulent kind. We have never gone along with the idea that deep in her subconscious the woman invites, even does, on her punching-bag role. But why not? Not everyone enjoys every sport for the same reason. Doesn't the male enjoy the sheer joy and competitiveness of the take as well as the give?

This not only shows the mental health aspects of the sport, but it explains to some of the knockers that there is a different psychology to every athletic contest. Some hate jogging; others think racquetball just a sweatbox with a paddle, involving no skill at all. A well-known psychiatrist, Dr. Brownhouse, claims that over fifty percent of the women who participate in the battering before marriage—before, mind you—still can't wait to lead this hard-knocking man of her dreams to the altar. Some people still can't understand this. But Dr. Brownhouse cites chapter and verse on women wanting it, liking it, and needing it; without it, he says, paranoid symptoms and depressions set in. So subconsciously the ever-ready, helpful male may be doing his ever-loving wife a big favor.

Well, we aren't sure of any of this—especially putting that much credence in what any psychiatrist says. However, NOW (National Organization of Women) backs Brownhouse up. They cite police reports that support the doctor's claim. They show that there are usually a half-dozen attempts on a woman's life by a loving spouse—before she's finally done in. This brings up the question of why the little woman didn't get out while the getting was good—at least before the third or fourth try. The usual female response is, "If I reported him, he'd leave me." Well, she has her option—but if it were I, I'd take my leave above rather than below ground.

However, we think we have some nonpsychiatric answers as to why a constant loser doesn't go for help. Like any other athlete, she may well enjoy the heat of the battle every bruise of the way; according to the old cliché, "it's not whether you win or lose . . ."

## The Baiting Game

In our own brief experience, knowing that women for some subtle sports*person*like reason get a big kick (and occasionally a concussion) out of this game, we go Brownhouse one better. We have seen the cunning and craftiness of some sly females who may use only one buzzword or phrase to start the action. Yet we are always accused of throwing the first punch. Now I ask, would any woman not spoiling for a real mix-it-up contest greet her disheveled, besotted, lipstick-plastered husband at the door at 3:00 A.M. with, "Where have you been all night?" Is that the time for small talk? Or what could she expect when the spouse comes home from a hard day at the office, only to be confronted by his charmer still in curlers and housecoat with a half-pint of Black Label peeking out from behind the sugar bowl? Worse yet, what better provocation for a bout than pulling into the garage, only to see one side of his new Mercedes accordion-pleated?

## As American as Mugging

As we said, the gentle art of the battered spouse is certainly not confined to the U.S.A. Actually, we are a Johnny-come-lately to the sport. As Langley and Levy say in their book, though it is a family tradition in America, and though some tender hearts only began to look down on it just recently, it is solidly founded in our Anglo-Saxon roots. Under British common law, a man "had the right to fisticuffs with his wife." So, as is the wont of men, they took the law at its word. It had always been long respected in pub circles (Henry VIII did overdo it a bit with Anne Boleyn). Tales to the contrary, England would never have won a war on the playing fields of Eton without the nationwide postgraduate training in this venerable sport, especially in the early formative years of marriage (the marriage vows should have read, "Love, honor, come out fighting, and may the best *person* win).

## The Wide Wide World of Spouse Sports

In other lands, one hears little of the sport. Though the Japanese usually copy everything American such as baseball and automobile production, one hears little of it there (other than the case of Prime Minister Fukuda, an admitted fanatic of the game, as described in his one bout which made the papers) or, for that matter, anywhere in Asia. As Confucious say, "Never pick wife or concubine large, strong, or handy with ax." Which is a more practical suggestion than any I've ever seen in fortune cookies. As we know, the Oriental male is rarely bigger than his spouse—and another thing, he has much too short a reach to score well enough to win even by a decision.

In other nations, as in darkest Africa, it seems to be more of an economic problem. According to one of the sources in *Roots*, in the marketplaces of Uganda and Burundi, where wives are a commodity, women who have broken bones or who are otherwise maimed are put in the used-car category and bring only bargain basement prices.

## More Fractures Than Trophies

No one questions the fact that with or without certain handicaps, U.S. wives, who usually pay only lip service to the Marquis of *Doonsbury* rules (no sharp, blunt, or explosive instruments), are the underdogs in these matches. They frequently come out of it with more fractures than trophies. But that doesn't hold for the rest of the world, especially for some of the East German women swimmers or Bulgarian female weightlifters (on anabolic steroids). Here, any manner of male spouse must be an odds-on loser. In those countries, the males are trying to make it mandatory that one marries only in one's own weight class.

## Even in Eden

But the beginnings of spouse beating go back much further than the contusions and lacerations of the Western world. The archaeological digs of the Leakey family's famous Olduvai Gorge are rife with evidence of this ancient sport. However, in those early days it was hardly as even-steven, well matched, and regulated a sport as it is today. The broken bones found on the cave room floor were practically all female. But what could one expect from the uncivilized with no equality or affirmative action, or anything even approaching the family love of today? One can easily imagine the reaction of a Neanderthal male coming back after a tough day on the tundra to face a hysterical mate with a report that one of the kids was taken off by an eagle; that the cave roof leaked, which had put out their only fire; or that all she had for supper was cold brontosaurus cuts. If she weren't as agile as a Nadia Comaneci and didn't dodge and backpedal like an Ali with his ropa-dopa, she might find herself hanging on a wall hook like a smoked pastrami in a Sixth Avenue deli.

## A Game the Whole Family Can Play

But enough of history; today, spouse beating is an ongoing sport whose time has come. First, it's a game the whole family can play—especially if the kids have the nerve to interfere. From infancy on, even if they only occasionally see the action over a transom or hear it through a keyhole, they feel the excitement of the give and take. It also has more educational (and survival) value for later life than Sesame Street. And every little male (more so than the little female) seems to yearn for the day he can play it on his own.

## Love in Boom

But spouse beating is not all breaks, stabs, and bruises; there's also a romantic side. The morning-after-the-night-before routines are usually ultratender in that kiss-and-make-up-let-bygones-be-bygones sporting attitude. And, according to government statistics, there are no hard feelings, for in forty-nine out of fifty cases they are all good losers and don't report any of it, unless the emergency room does. Frequently, when the kiddies visit their mother in the hospital on her first day of hospitalization, there is a sort of teary-eyed nostalgia about the whole thing as they autograph her cast.

Even at its ultimate there can be a certain passion to it. Francine Hughes, the acquitted husband-burner we spoke of, accepted a bouquet of flowers from an admirer with a card "to a battered rose that blooms again." And as was seen on the Phil Donahue show before millions of women viewers, there was no bitterness. She pleasantly explained how she sprinkled the kerosene around, then the romantic excitement of that moment of ignition. It obviously was a vicarious thrill for the two hundred wildly applauding women in the studio audience who had never had that "one night of *love.*"

## It's Not Whether You Play the Game—But If You Win or Lose

Sports*person*ship is a big part of the game. Without it there would probably be no return bouts. Some cases coming to court are on their twelfth rematch. Even the law is set up to make sure it's an ongoing thing. A wife can't press charges against a husband in a criminal court, and the family court is only there to get people back together again.

In New Hampshire, the Governor's Commission on the Status of Women refused to endorse or finance programs to aid either contestant, stating, "It would be an invasion of privacy."

## A Cottage Industry

However, because of all the carping and nasty publicity, this sport still hasn't emerged into the big money with the Bjorn Borgs and Dave Winfields. It's still kept mostly on the home turf and occasionally at a bar. When compared to football or even soccer, it is just another cottage industry. The real spouse-beater superstars (unpaid) come by their skills naturally as they would the family-type skills handed down from father to son, such as cabinetmaking or horseshoeing. There are no tickets, no peanuts and popcorn, and not even a World Series in sight. It's just good healthy exercise with everything usually confined right in the home. On occasion it may start rather spontaneously, as during a boozy weekend at the Concord.

It's also a simple sort of sport, more like stickball or mumblety-peg, with no need for expensive clubs, racquets, or uniforms. The participants usually come dressed just as they are, at any time of the day or night. There are no twenty-dollar-an-hour instructors, and up to now, not even paperback "how to" manuals.

But recently, as the sport has been publicized and has become more important to family life, everyone seems to be getting into the act. There have been indications that there are small groups pushing to have it played formally in a ring, strictly by Marquis of Queensbury rules, with shin guards, face masks, and referees with whistles and stopwatches. If it ever comes down to that, it will lose all of its devil-may-care, catch-as-catch-can appeal, and maybe even some of its exciting morbidity.

Some feminists have raised such a ruckus, one would think spouse beating was illegal, like cockfighting. But would the government get in on the act more and more to really try to help the game if it were at all shady? In the congressional hopper are funds to the tune of sixty or so million dollars, as the Mikulski congressional bill puts it, "to provide information, train volunteers to assist in local programs, and provide assistants for organizing, managing, or operating proposed programs." This legislation is supported by both sexes of the American public.

There are also all sorts of Health and Human Services grants for the asking, many of which are somewhat discriminating. (Though they provide shelters and hotlines for women, no consideration has been given to that forty percent of bruised and broken male losers who not only have to suffer physical and ego damage, but worse, the scorn of fellow jocks besides.)

## Saturday Night Fervor

In our good old U.S.A., it's a shame that a bout between two mature adults of the opposite sex on an otherwise dull Saturday night is anybody's business but their own. It should be understood once and for all that this is no child's play, but something for consenting adults only. If do-gooders would stay out of it and let the sport develop naturally, there is no doubt this simple in-house game could catch the fancy of the public and truly become the great American pastime. With baseball and basketball on the decline (due to the dullness and the strikes by one and the high cost of Earl the Pearls to the other), these dying sports are desperately trying to keep the game of spouse beating uncompetitive, bottled up behind closed doors. Even the feminist TV announcers knock it—but I'd bet these sportswriters could see the beauty of it. Yet there is no way anyone can stop the groundswell of sportsminded Americans when the concussion, abrasion, and fracture quotas of this most popular sport are all there—still with a lower mortality than skiing or the Indianapolis 500.

Spouse beating is not yet a spectator sport (especially when the shades are drawn), but there's no question that there is a gold mine ready to be tapped here by any TV tycoon like Roone Arledge who wants to get in on the ground floor.

Besides its barroom-brawl tradition spiced by the battle of the sexes, it has the additional thrill of the unknown ending—will it wind up in police court? a hospital? or the morgue? In the next ten years, if it is handled right with no fix scandals, it has all the ingredients of the old Christian versus lion contests, and you couldn't ask for better action than that.

*CHAPTER XII*

# Women in Labor: A False Pregnancy

Though Queen Elizabeth II and Prime Minister Margaret Thatcher may have no cause for complaint, the situation of the working woman in Britain is grim.

*Susan Anderson,* New York Times, *1981*

JUST A HUNDRED YEARS or so ago it was a tossup whether a husband would hitch his wife or his mule to the plow. She's come a long, long way (the mule—not the wife). Now, in 1981, the ladies, with their horse collar calluses long gone, have opted for new ones on their bellies. Slithering along a coal mine shaft five miles deep under a West Virginia mountain may be no cinch—but it's liberated. And at the end of the day, those females can now proudly stand shoulder to shoulder with equally sooty men, over equally grimy wash basins, scrubbing an equal amount of black coal dust out of equally clogged pores. And when the mine disasters come, women no longer have to wait it out above ground like the poor pitiful dependent creatures they once were; they are now down there trapped with the best of them (let the husbands do the worrying).

## *This Year a Garbageperson—Next Year the World*

And a thousand miles away there are equally liberated, T-shirted entrepreneurs, also freed from home and even from their true out-of-the-house domain, the secretarial desk. Rain or shine or one hundred degrees in the shade, you can see her on the sidewalks of New York, dragging a five-hundred-pound hot dog cart (mulelike), competing with all those mustachioed Greek and

Slav vendors. There is no doubt any more that the feminists have finally broken the back of the last tycoon. More and more, they no longer are mere waitresses, seamstresses, or secretaries. This year, sanitation and garbage collecting; next year the world—of sewers, gas works, and Fuller Brush *persons*. Equality of opportunity has now pervaded every aspect of the world of dollars, francs, and marks, and each year another male bastion is penetrated.

Even the crack in the door of the giant industries of chauvinist Germany and Italy is widening. After all, if the Krupps and the Agnellis could make the Hitler and Mussolini war machines "run on time" through slave labor, why shouldn't they see the shining light of gold in "that thar" equality. They've found that those nimble fingers, so instinctually adept with thimble and needle, can also drop a spot of solder on an electronic circuit twenty times a minute, eight hours a day, five days a week, year in, year out, without the usual alcoholic jitters on hangover Monday morn and other breakdowns of maledom. So Liberation *über alles*.

And to that freedom-loving female who has finally gotten out of the house, it shows that she too can be muddling her way via minimum wage to a ten-year pin and a twenty-year duly inscribed, gold-filled watch.

It may still be worth it, even if she's hoisting those fifty-pound sacks, and her mind is busy with, "Is baby Linda catching a cold? Can I get to the store, buy the hamburger, and still get all that laundry done before midnight?" But on the other hand, there are rewards at the end of the rainbow. If she lives that long, at retirement maybe she'll again be able to enjoy her first love and natural state of full-time *"kinder, küchen, and kirche."*

As strange as it seems, and as much as the feminists have claimed they've done for their sisters, a 1980 exhibit at the Smithsonian shows that the status of women in labor has not changed in one hundred years. Curator Deborah Warner innocently lets the cat out of the bag as to women's place in the workers' world then and now: "If you see any decorated valentines or painstakingly sewn garment involving careful close work, you can be sure it was done by a woman."

## *I Love My Job—But, Oh, You Kid*

Since liberation, by government legal pressure we chauvinists have been presented with an ultimatum to give them a break in more manly jobs—or else. So we did. We really didn't need legislation or arm twisting. We've always been generous to a fault. So, gentlemen that we are, without reluctance, we even let them in on some of the higher paying, shorter-hour sinecures.

But as we told them before they started, there was already a precedent for our largesse. As far back as the Civil War, women were assigned the job of loading powder into bullets at the Watertown arsenal. True, there were few men applying to get their fingers blown off, but for the women it was a step up. Even in World War II it enabled the U.S. to lead in the production of arms and armament, which we chauvs roundly applaud. Now, for instance, we continue the same generous precedent. We encouraged and allowed them into the unions for taste-testing saccharin and high-tar cigarettes. After all, research can't go by rats alone. And if that's what they want, we'll even smooth the way for employment as leak investigators in nuclear power plants.

## *Infirmative Action—for Males Only*

No doubt, more and more females who don't know a good thing until they lose it, are leaving their three-bedroom rancher Shangri-las. And only when they get a toehold in the male world of cheap labor do they realize that they knew not what they did.

The Gallup polls show that most women, no different from their brothers, work only because they have to. And as we've shown, the National Institute for Occupational Health and Safety, ranking 130 occupations, showed that the ones with the highest incidence of mental disease were nursing, secretarial work, and waitressing. So, with good reason, like their male comrades-in-arms they pray for an early retirement in case the lottery windfall doesn't come through. In many cases, even pregnancy is a welcome relief from the ker-puk-a, ker-puk-a, ker-puk-a, deadly rhythm of a bottling machine eight hours a day. Yet, from the way the feminists advertise it, you'd think that all females just can't wait to be pumping gas or be on the working end of a sewer rooter. No more suffering the deadly peace and quiet of a warm kitchen on a sleety morning, watching Donahue, or submerging oneself into that dissolute life of sneaking back into bed after breakfast when everyone is gone. Even those boring afternoons at Gimbel's or Weight Watchers need be tolerated no longer. Most men hustling for a buck, doing what they can (not what they want), think these agitating feminists are this side of bonkers. It's insanity for the fems to hustle their eager-beaver sisters to jump feet first into that brave new world of roaring pistons, numbing assembly lines, hourly quotas, and efficiency experts.

## Five-Foot-Two and a Mack Truck Too?

But they must want it badly if they are now going directly against Dr. Spock, the man who has been their guiding light for fifty years. He says (and the feminists hate him for it), "It is much more creative to rear and shape the personality of a child than work in an office or even carve a statue."

However, if that's what they want, you have to give them credit for their timing. They are right on the money. After all, with fifteen years of civil rights, the blacks, who are just beginning to make it in the big pay unions (electrical, plumbing, and bricklaying), aren't about to go back to that wonderful world of scut work—waxing floors or slaving on an assembly line in a shoe factory. So now the girls can stand hip to hip, chatting about shoes, Robert Redford, and the kids between coffee breaks. Now their gracile little fingers, once so clean and refined by ILGWU, button-hole making and embroidering, are calloused and grimy from work as a mechanic's helper in a truck garage.

## Primp Time—a Fringe Benefit

But they'll have to change some of their female ways if they're going to play the union game. They just haven't caught on to that fine line of where featherbedding stops and unemployment begins. There are ways, and there are ways of goofing off, but even the most cabbage-headed male steelworker quickly latches on to all the subtleties of the art. For instance, one study showed that women made 509 visits to the lavatory during working hours, to a man's 230, and spent an average of 10.7 minutes—the man, 2.5 minutes. Well, it didn't take management long to catch on to that. Not enchanted by those "primp time" lapses, they immediately called in the shop foremen, threatening a TV camera in every washroom. The embarrassed unions then had to give in and clamp down.

Though this issue has, as yet, not come up for negotiation at the National Labor Relations Board, there is no question that women are gradually making some inroads into the unions via feminist lawsuits. However, the Department of Labor, since Reagan was elected, has been plagued by much fewer court cases insisting on a shot at all those jobs of hod carrying or stevedoring like their bulky sisters in Prague or Pinsk. So, though the payoff is slowing perceptibly, the fems were heartened by a recent report. It showed that females are now firmly holding on to about one out of a hundred construction jobs and represent a whopping five out of a hundred in the craft trades, which means that equality in blue-collar job opportunity should come easily before 2050.

## The Tongue That Wags—the Togs

Yet with all the effort, time, and planning put into the task of getting women thoroughly ensconced in labor, there seems to be little room to advance. They have made no greater inroads than their higher-status sisters, who are vying at the boardroom level. Despite the unusual quasi-female who has shown she can change a washer and stop leaks with the best of her plumbing colleagues, there are few female master plumbers. And in other menial trades, no matter that female negotiators are persuading, threatening, and sobbing out their case, Meany-ful jobs are still reserved for males only. The thirty-five-man (and we mean all man) executive council of the AFL-CIO has only just elected their first and only board female, Joyce Miller. She would have as much say at thirty-four to one as the concrete-besuited Jimmy Hoffa (wherever he lies).

The International Ladies Garment Workers Union, made up of eighty to ninety percent women, had only one woman guiding something other than a buttonhole stitcher. Though that chauvinist hierarchy of garment-working men wouldn't know a treadle from a bobbin, they did recognize the nagging expertise of women and put Evelyn Dubrow in as their Washington lobbyist. And well they did, for as it was so well put in *The Beggar's Opera*, "by her we first were taught the wheedling art."

But not all unions are as open-armed to females as those for waitresses, food checkers, and seamstresses. The liberators may claim that a tractor trailer is duck soup for the average housewife, but Jimmy Hoffa's boys fight it all the way. They claim that besides their record of jack-knifing a sixteen-wheeler, women teamsters have been a big disappointment on the goon squad. Both their pistol whipping and hijack skills supposedly are much too ladylike; they also are entirely too nervous to wire up a strikebreaker's car with a pipe bomb (Union-Made).

## The Barrier Beef

Also as Baltimore Police Commissioner Pomerlau says, "Policing is no job for those balls of fluff." Well, that may be, but with a .38 calibre blazing away, that "ball of fluff" can do a lot of damage. A few months ago in Nashville, Tennessee, the police were called in on a grocery store robbery. The lady policeman killed the manager of the store and two customers. The robber escaped unscathed and she got the hook.

So to be within the law in the most jockish of all unions, but still to get rid of the ladies, the boys just tightened up their already high standards. In small print they added height and weight restrictions, whereby only a Wilt the Stilt, built chunkier than a sumo wrestler, could apply.

This kind of barrier is not common only in unions. Just recently the Mexican-American Legal Defense Fund put up a howl when a rather hefty, female border-patrol rookie was dismissed because she couldn't get over an eight-foot training wall without some such aid as a ladder or a catapult.

## That Great Leap Downward

Though the feminists have taken due credit for these great leaps in union advancement, no one had ever measured that leap (forward or backward) until recently. And by whom else? A woman, an honest one—and a feminist at that. According to Louise Howe in her book, *The Pink Collar Workers*, that leap could only be compared with Evel Knievel's attempt to span the Snake River—more P.R. than R.P. (Real Progress)—usually winding up in a heap at the bottom.

Mrs. Howe, for the first time, revealed a shocker to those pink-collared secretaries, beauticians, and even nurses. "They don't have it so good." She tells them in no uncertain terms that the feminists have done more *to* the working woman than *for* her. She shows the female worker earning a median of $3,000 to a male's $4,750 in 1957; sixteen years later, he's widened the gap: $11,000 to her $6,500.

## Consciousness Up, Salary Down—Back to the Plow

Mrs. Howe also showed in black and white (from the U.S. Department of Labor figures) that the female *who has to work* is no better off in her job today than her sweatshop sisters of 1900. Little did they know, but the *Dictionary of Occupational Titles* said it all. The usual female pink-collar job "gets exactly the same financial rating as a *dog pound guard.*"

## The Lady's Up for Burning

Mrs. Howe's truth in femming blew the whistle on those pie-in-the-sky feminist leaders. But as she pulled that wool back from the eyes of the worker liberati, she unsheathed their claws. Though those distaff critics and editors usually push their own beyond their talent, this book was put on their *best bummer* list before you could say *Rubyfruit Jungle*. They were not about to let this half-sister come on blowing their fog away like Hurricane Agnes. As they would have it, a woman who spouts such scurrilous stuff (as the truth) is just not loyal to the movement. So they put that honest lady "up for burning."

## Pink Collar versus the Housebroken

But the Steinems and the Friedans placated their sisters, in defense of poor pay at the bottom, suggesting, "Don't think only of yourselves. Look where your other sisters are." But the *working stiff* woman began to scream back to the effect that pink-collar ladies didn't care about those in "the womb at the top." Those beleaguered, low-level ladies warned their B.S.- and M.A.-degree'd leaders to "stop nudging their split-level housebroken sisters to come out, competing with them for jobs. They don't really need to work, and it's tough enough going for the males' positions without bumping heads against our own." (This was even before the-later-to-be-canned Secretary Califano of HEW, whose heart bled for the women's movement, came out with new affirmative guidelines that even the fems raged against: "Alcoholics and dope addicts can't be discriminated against, either."

## Barking Feminists Also Bite

Yet with all of the goodwill exhibited by that tight clique of unionist chauvs who helped bring a few women into the pavement-pounding world of picket lines, leave it to those barking feminist workers to bite the hand that collects their monthly dues. No sooner did they wedge their nyloned thighs into that all-male closed shop than they're pushing for paid-up pregnancy leaves, makeup kits in every washroom, and even their own female union within the union.

This undercutting of the unions stung to the quick, but it also brings up another sore spot with us men. While there is always open season on our jobs, theirs are a protected species. They'd be hanging us in effigy in every pink-collar monopoly in the land if we ever tried breaking into their world of kindergartens and typewriters. Those occupations are beyond the pale—have been off-limits to male intrusion for centuries, and still are. Women may talk about union bias and sexism keeping the women from the lathe, yet they're not about to let a gent (even if he wanted to) break into that sacrosanct receptionist sinecure or even wangle his way into the bottom rung of the char*person* echelon. On the other hand, the chauvs let Linda Eaton in as a fire*person* in Council Bluffs, Iowa, and what does she do but sue us and win $2,000 because she couldn't breastfeed her baby between bells.

## *The Medal of Stalin—or a Hemorrhoidectomy*

In the field of labor relations, we chauvs are naturally management tilted, and between labor and women we are at best probably on the side of righteousness and almost equal opportunity. But we're getting a little tired of the female leaders always pointing to their role model, the Soviet and Soviet-satellite woman worker. Few of them have ever been anywhere near Russia or Bulgaria, but on hearsay alone they extoll the virtues of those babushka'd huskies who can administrate a cement mixer or install a clutch in an earthmover. They keep reminding the U.S. housewife, for instance, that seventy percent of all Russian doctors are female. Of course, they don't level and tell their pigeons that those M.D.'s work for a wage that an unemployed U.S. gravedigger wouldn't sniff at (about $135 a month, the same as a Soviet sewer pipe worker). And, even though this female doctor usually winds up treating only diaper rash and colic, just like an ordinary mother, or being sent out by the male chiefs to buck house-high snowdrifts by foot on night calls, that's just for openers. She's got even more low-level responsibility: Those upwardly mobile, equality-plagued lady doctors coming in from all-night deliveries must still queue up an hour or two for a peck of beets, still scrub the apartment floor, cook, and clean, just like their grandmothers did under Czar Nicholas.

## *The Minsk to Pinsk Study*

Now if our feminist leaders think that the liberated Soviet sisters in that grand army of the worker's paradise are so great, why don't they tell their protégés of the Minsk study. This report shows that the average "liberated" Soviet woman, after working in the textile mill of Breznevogorsk forty hours a week, has another forty keeping the home samovars burning. However, the one saving grace is that she has none of those U.S. worries about complicated machinery—such as the vacuum cleaner (one in fifty has one), or the dishwasher (Olga Korbut is one of the few Russian ladies without dishpan hands).

Our lady leaders are also a little shy on explaining the marvelous bonuses for the Soviet working mother—unheard of here in America. For instance, after the birth of a baby, she gets fifty-six days nursing leave. After going back to work, greasing the Dnieper dynamos, she also gets an added mini-bonus: one half hour, twice a day, to nurse the child in the dam's *crèche*. Then, after a production quota of ten pregnancies, that Nobel Prize of Soviet fertility, the Stalin Medal of the Working Mother, is hers. She'd probably like to trade that medal in to get her pipe-stem varicose veins taken care of.

## Chicken Soup Liberation

Another model of liberation that U.S. feminists insist on throwing up to their sisters is the Israeli female working women. But in this case too, freedom seems to ring more for the downtrodden Jewish father than the celebrated Jewish mother. The Sabra may be shown glamorously posed with a submachine gun over shoulder, protecting the borders; but, in reality, the nearest a female GI comes to a weapon is in a factory, loading a machine gun belt at 120 shells a minute. Much to Betty Friedan's chagrin, she found on a visit to Israel that the real liberated Israeli sister turned out to be the one with skin parched to a saddle-leather consistency from hoeing three acres of sugar beets a day. One who, like her working sisters everywhere, still runs to the kitchen every hour to make sure the knishes aren't burned. Yet even these hardy females, true to their sex, are wrinkle fighters if not freedom fighters. It's a rare kibbutz without a beauty parlor.

According to Professor Harry Krantz of American University, the author of a book on female liberation, ninety-six percent of Israeli working women are in the lowest pay scale, with only six percent working out of the home. Less than seven percent are in management roles (and only two percent are professors and one percent engineers)—not that different from the females of Abu Dhabi or Uganda. And with the passage of the Israeli equivalent of the ERA (the Israeli Pay Law of 1964), they still earn only forty percent of what the men do (the Israeli chauvs show no heart at all). Even in that idealized lifestyle in the kibbutz, it's not the men who do the laundry and wash the dishes, and still produce the pilots to bomb a nuclear plant in Iraq. No South Bronx mother on welfare would trade places with that workhorse. In fact (no matter what the Israeli minister of propaganda says), according to Moshe Dayan's liberated novelist daughter, the Israeli working woman is a helluva lot less equal than an Iowa hog farmer's wife.

## The Secretaries—of Labor

Getting back to the good old U.S.A., life isn't all that tough for all working females. Take the cream of the run-of-the-mill female job holders, the office secretaries. The bosses unashamedly tell barefaced lies to them on that one great day of the year, National Secretaries Day, and flatter them as "the backbone of the male business world." On that day there is "lunch on the boss," and the mayors proclaim: "This day bespeaks our respect for their vital role in the American businesses and professions. They've done themselves handsomely proud." Of course not a word is mentioned about a better salary, hospitalization, or vacations like those grubby union girls have. But as we constantly remind them, where else can they get the intellectual stimulation and the prestige and recognition of working *intimately* with a boss.

## The Joy of Harassment

There also are hidden and forbidden bonuses, one of which is that great intangible benefit: harassment. Though the libs may rave, rant, and sue over it, there has never been a peep out of a real feminine woman of spirit. It's been said that eighty-five percent of all extramarital affairs start not with the oft-accused housewife and the Fuller Brush man, but with the working woman and her boss. And if that's why they got out of the house, it's the best reason we've heard so far.

Then there are even those few thousand female coal miners screaming harassment. This couldn't but be a phoney. Just from the looks of them coming up to the surface, it's a mystery how anyone less than clairvoyant could guess the sex of those black-smudged, overalled, steel-shod carcasses. And if so, who needs it that bad? Then in those two-and-a-half-foot-high tunnels, there are complaints of rape—which is even harder to account for. Five miles under Harlan County, Kentucky, is not even close to a backseat, much less a Beverly Hills boudoir.

But besides the fun and games it's no secret that a secretary has an eighteen percent better chance of snaring the boss than either a laundress or a spot welder—if not in actual marriage, at least in some other rewarding role. Secretaries in the hospitals fall only a little behind the nurses in snatching a doctor—or at least a lab technician. Isn't just that extra chance worth more than a fringe benefit?

## To Bed or to Boot

But, as with that ungrateful female union member who strikes even at her leaders, the "boss's best friend"—mainly the older one—shows little gratitude. Besides the routine complaints of having to run out for coffee at odd hours, or to pick out the wife's anniversary bauble, recent interviews in the Washington *Post* posed complaints of other petty harassment, such as her "having to fix his zipper"—without his taking his pants off; or "taking before and after pictures when he shaved his mustache off." Who else is going to do those little things in life that need doing?

Recently *Ms.* magazine, with grand inquisitor Steinem officiating, actually held a seminar on "Sexual Harassment in the Office." Is it sexual harassment when a compassionate boss takes his beautiful "right arm" to a cozy, dimly lit, out-of-the-way place for filet mignon and a little relaxation (on his late nights at the office)? Should he allow her to go home night after night to the depression of an empty apartment and canned spaghetti, letting her next day's work suffer the consequences?

## Homework or Harassment

It seems to us it's all a matter of interpretation. What's one woman's harassment is another's ecstasy. And the younger and prettier the secretary, the less interpretation is needed and the fewer complaints are heard. Still and all, this harassment scam has caught on like a venereal disease in a fraternity house. But just because a new lass in the office needs the care and attention of a mature male, is no reason for some older, less attractive girls to gang up and convince her to bring it up to the local human rights commission. In Texas, the Bell Telephone Company was sued for $29.2 million when thirteen (count them, thirteen) secretaries sued two (only two) company officials for sexual harassment and "breach of promise"—of advancement. This case is not yet settled. The government has already paid out $189 million for identical stings in public offices.

At Yale, six coeds sued, claiming they got low marks because they wouldn't do "homework" with the professor. Now this type of individual attention could be very educational. Five of the six claims were thrown out by the judge; the other got her grade honestly adjusted from a *C* to an *A*.

## Ms.—Male-nthropes

But at the "Steinem Harassment Clinic," where a proposition here or an assignation there was divulged, not one of those disgruntled or long-in-the-tooth raised consciousnesses told of the fun side of secretarial life. Did just one mention those weekend "business trips" to Las Vegas or Hilton Head, or those monthly "out of pocket" cash bonuses? The feminists even got the U.S. Court of Appeals in Washington, D.C., to hold "on the job harassment as sexual *discrimination*" under Title VII of the 1964 Civil Rights Act. But what should an efficient boss be, if not discriminating? He's not about to "harass" just any broken-down typewriter jockey because she can take shorthand and type one hundred words a minute.

## Caveat Temptor

So, before any of you sisters set your minds to rushing out of the house for "the good and bountiful life in labor," again be aware of Margaret Mead's warning that you make sure you know what you're getting into: "the same dull work that husbands are always complaining about—greasing engines, carrying out the factory trash, or, not unlike home, making salads and cleaning bathrooms." To make doubly sure, we urge all liberatees to ask the nine-to-five sorority what it's like out there trying to make a buck. After this, ask yourselves where you'd rather be: changing sheets on your kids' beds on Mondays at a nice, even seventy degrees Fahrenheit, or changing a flat tire on a Mack truck in the darkness of a winter night on lonely Highway 40 in New Castle, Pennsylvania. And remember, what's good for a female bulldozer operator in Nyetotogorsk may not be good for a female on the assembly line in Detroit.

Yet having said all of this, if they still persist, and if everything goes as well as it's been going for all those liberated doctors and plumbers' assistants in Free Russia and for the female auto mechanics in Israel, every woman in the world may get just what the Bulgarian ladies have—and they'll wish they were dead.

## CHAPTER XIII

# A Womb at the Top—
# Withering Heights

Women who gain power have an obligation to their sisters.
*Joyce D. Miller, AFL-CIO*

I have never met a man who would upset his work for love, nor a woman who wouldn't mess up her work for it.
*Author Doris Lessing*

IF THE LADIES thought it difficult to breathe in the stultifying air of labor's lowlands, the rarified atmosphere of management and the boardroom will have them gasping like a catfish out of water. Those heights are as perilous to an aggressive lady's health as three packs of Gaulloises a day, the pill, and the monthly tampon combined. But according to medical authorities, even when they are nearing the top, they go through a deterioration that makes Dorian Gray's metamorphosis look like a Cinderella switch. Yet the feminist leaders still push those happy pink-collar girls toward the pin-striped Olympus of anxiety and depression, which they'll never reach anyway.

When the feminists talk about their dreams of getting to the top, it always reminds me of a *New Yorker* cartoon of the 60s. There, standing in front of the Kremlin, are two five-by-five, dowdy Soviet lady snow sweepers leaning on their brooms of twigs, gazing at the moon. The caption reads: "And I guess when they get up there we'll be sweeping that, too." So far it's been as prophetic as all the depressing statistics on advancement brought out by the feminists at Senate hearings.

But if they think that "labor's love was lost" down below at the bottling plant and the glass factory, they're in for a shocker in the uplands—even with the recent Supreme Court decision on equal pay. Up there, the petty laments of harassment, raging hormones, and the weight of carrying that heavy homemaking incubus on their backs cuts no ice at all. In that big league, there is no complaint department. It's pure power, money, production—and let the ladies take the hindmost. One woman, Jane Cahill Pfeiffer, who did tolerably well as a vice-president at IBM, got to the peak —for the first time a female chief—at NBC and had to abdicate in six months—a flop at the top. And as for the Fortune 500— that's a club that in fifty years only one woman has wheeled herself into.

Still, the siren song led the poor dears on, with more wishful thinking and frustration than success. Yet at times there is some short-lived triumph. But if you think it spoiled Rock Hunter, wait till you hear what it does to Linda Tycoon! When the feminists prod their ambitious sisters to head for the top, they forget to mention that on the way to Godfather's penthouse on the hill, Little Red Sisterhood has both male and female wolves coming at her from every nook of the woods.

## The Quest of Doriana Gray

According to Professor Ivor Mills, an endocrine expert at Cambridge University, England, the eager-beaver females who carry their oval wombs up the ladder are plagued by more "boils" than were ever visited on Job by a testing God. As Mills put it, it could literally be "hairy" and ultimately as withering as a Sahara sirocco. For seventeen years he studied some thirty thousand of those pushy ones clambering up those man-trapped slopes, with results that should be scary for any woman who doesn't want to shave twice a day and have to wear a toupee for the rest of her life.

He demonstrates that the more aggressive breed of female is increasingly falling victim to the dread "stress disease." We already know what it does to the male—a living cinch for corpulence, coronary disease, and cerebral ailments leading to an untimely demise. But this is merciful compared to the fate of the stressed female. Those driving-type women who seek that penthouse office, access to the private dining room, and that perk of all perks, the four-button conference call telephone, are doomed to all the male consequences—and more.

For starters, the professor states, some of these women, as delicately female as Lena Horne, develop not only dizzy spells, acne, lapse of memory, and tremors but—zounds!!—"beards, chest hair, and baldness too." This is not only a shocking mirror image for the curlered morning eye opener, but ironically it must have a deterrent effect on the very goal she seeks. If every jock chairman of the board wants a clean-cut, clean-shaven, attractive vice-president, why should he settle for less in a female?

Perversely enough, to compound the frustration those achieving wonder*persons* develop, of all things, an insatiable sex drive (not at all unexpected, since stress masculinizes). This of course will rarely be satisfied by even the most aggressive of office harassers in her doubtful state of attractiveness. Any ordinary woman faced with hirsutism and eroticism in one conflicting package with nary a wink or proposition would chuck it all and crawl back in the pink-collar department.

So Dr. Mills pleads (as we chauvs have done for years) with some who try to break out of their natural female roles, to recognize their limitations. Maybe they can regress back to normalcy in the early stages, regaining some semblance of femininity and the ability to live out a normal female life—but not later.

Recently at least one part of the problem, baldness, was deemed solvable. Georgette Klinger on Madison Avenue says thirty percent of the working women in business lose their hair. She blames it on stress. She opened her scalp clinic just for these women at $25 a crack. She thinks she can help with massage, lotions, egg yolk, placenta oil, steam, and a pack composed of flax, oak, apple, and okra. But, as she puts it, "the woman also has to help herself." And as we see it, "female cure thyself"—if you can't stand the heat, get back to the kitchen.

## Katie Said It—We Didn't

Professor Phyllis Wallace of MIT agrees with Dr. Mills. She also blames these failures on the "greater stress in women" (as a natural complication to ambition) especially where the husband is also in management. But with or without the Mills syndrome, Dr. Wallace feels "it is tough to make it even to middle management, because most of those women still have the weight of family duties sapping their energies." And Katie Hepburn agrees. She's said she couldn't be a top-of-the-heap career women and still have children and "a marriage that would please me."

In trying to show that this is not just one chauvinist's opinion, Mrs. Fallows, assistant dean at Georgetown University, echoes, "Family and a prestigious career just does not work." And as we've always said, Dr. Fallows repeats, "The more glamorous portraits of the Successful Woman are not faithful to her whole life." Then to pile it on, their own *Working Woman* magazine takes it from there: "Even Superwoman Gets the Blues," either she'll fail in her career or fail as a wife and mother.

The worst is yet to come. As stress increases, so does the masculinizing male hormone. With that, those superdoers became almost monomaniacal and frequently ruthless and abusive to both children and spouse, usually winding up on the psychiatrist's couch.

### As Mean as J.R.

But as we know, regardless of what they have to face, a certain breed of the second sex take their chances—beard, bald, and all. And a certain few do make it. Most of those with an M.B.A. from Harvard (that seems to be the badge that admits them to the club) would rather "be in Philadelphia" than making a bed or wearing that starched pink uniform stamping out stars and crescents in a cookie factory. Some of those aspiring babes with dreams of glory, especially in the media, are as tough and mean as "Dallas" 's J.R. They get their kicks from nothing less than firing a male, merging a few conglomerates, junketing on company jets, and having a box at the World Series (even if they don't know a base on balls from a balk).

### Those Sisters "Superior"

Strangely enough, though the feminists pushed those doers all the way to the vice-presidency, there is no love lost between them. For predictably, once there, those VPs develop an acute case of amnesia. Now blondined, they're ashamed to show their dark feminist roots. They scorn the former hands that fed them, stow away their placards, let down their consciousnesses, and won't march down Fifth Avenue for anything less than their Mobil image. They imply that they would have made it without the "hysterical feminists" (of course we heartily agree with that), and do a cover-up that Haldeman would be proud of. Reversing the effect of this chronic stress syndrome is a complicated affair and not one as amenable to change as an Excedrin headache.

Of course those other fems left behind are not only *not* enthralled with those sisters "superior" but want to bring them down; witness the Cunningham-Bendix debacle. They would especially want to unseat those political traitors like Indira, Golda, Maggie, or even Senators Kassenbaum of Kansas and Hawkins of Florida. They are the ones who could have done the most good once they got up there, but didn't.

They are called "Queen Bees" and like the real queen bees they have their female drones work for them only as long as they are useful—then bask in the honeyed world of male lovers only as the drones die off.

So those true-blue militant fems couldn't give a hoot if those heretical turncoats get as furry as a gorilla or as bald as an eagle. And here in the U.S., try as they might, though the specter of their feminine deterioration may become a reality, becoming the boss rarely does.

Admittedly, the women really aching for Dr. Mill's troubles were inching ahead here in the U.S. until the last national election. But Nancy Reagan put the brakes on that. Nancy just isn't comfortable with the NOW, ERA lunch bunch, and has about as much rapport with the Steinzugs as a cobra with a mongoose. I don't know exactly, but I'll bet few of the thirty-four (out of 550) female presidential appointments made by Rosalynn are still around, if any.

## One Large Step for Mankind—Six Small Schleps for Man

But it seems that here in the U.S., hope lies eternal in that bushy breast. For knowing full well that they have only a slim chance of ever reaching just second best, there are some women (either very courageous or without all their marbles) who literally go for the stratosphere. After some fifteen years, six women (out of thirty-eight astro*persons*) were finally chosen for the space shuttle. Of course it was implied before they were chosen that they could only schlep along in the back seat. There is little question those women were hand-picked by the chauvs in charge with practical malice aforethought. As they well know, even in the modern pioneering of the atmosphere, there is always a plethora of everyday chores and duties that only a woman can do. Why should it be any different up there now than it was right here on earth during our pioneering days or right now in our split-level ranches?

First and foremost, as we know from Tom Wolfe's book, *The Right Stuff*, potential male cosmonauts are as permanently lecherous as a tomcat on his nightly prowl. So naturally the male planners didn't forget the sexual needs of our courageous volunteers. After all, they'll be spending six lonely months up there. Look what that ultimate chauvinistic Naval Academy did for their boys. Of course, they didn't expect the orgies to hit the front pages when the female midship*persons* were allowed in, but the girls certainly have served gloriously. The boys have never been so happy—even filming some of the goings-on—possibly for the class yearbook.

Sex becomes even more important in the stratosphere. They had to make some provision for relief of the male libido, if only to have them keep their minds on all that expensive equipment they are fooling with. (To digress a moment, just catching her and connecting, much less cohabiting in that weightless state, poses challenges not heretofore studied by Masters and Johnson or sketched in *The Joy of Sex*.)

However, not all of these astronaut*persons* were chosen merely as sex objects. Hard on the heels of this requirement to keep our astronauts sexually appeased came the need to think about the small comforts of life. The planners, knowing their males, chose one of the three women because she is a mother of three, with years of expertise in bedmaking and laundering; two are reasonably good cooks; and one is very handy with a needle and thread, and even makes her own clothes. So, on the longer trips when a woman will be a necessary asset, it seems to us that the predictions of the two Russian women leaning on their brooms will come close to realization. Of course we make no absolute assertion as to who will be fixing the zippers, flipping the weightless pancakes for breakfast, or cleaning out floating ashtrays, but we sincerely doubt it will be one of those former male test pilots or a Green Beret colonel.

## Executive Clemency

Now to get back down to earth and the world of big business. It appears that, even with more and more women in training on the golf course and at the country club bar, it has gotten tougher for females to reach the management level. It's mainly the green envy and blind jealousy of her corporate sisters that are boring from within. A case in point is the recent front-page saga of the unusually attractive Mary Cunningham (the exception—not bald at all). That Bendix female executive was denied advancement to the top regardless of how good she was in (or outside of) the office, with or without a very, very friendly sponsor, Chairman Agee. At least this is one female who didn't yell harassment when she didn't get what she wanted—especially in jobs. But who gave her the business? Not the chauvs in the office but her own sisters. Ann Fleming in the *New York Times* writes, "Her successful female colleagues in their gabardine suits and gold neck chains hinted around that Cunningham used her sexuality to get ahead. They were quicker than the men to ascribe her rise to her blond beauty and her romance with the board chairman." After this publicized cat fight, she had to seek employment *near* the top of another heap.

## The Sardines and the Piranha

But Cunningham is a realistic female and wasn't at all surprised at what happened. Though she does not now speak kindly of her fellow male or female colleagues in management circles, it's understandable. As she says, "busybodies [and we know which sex she's referring to] in business make it difficult for a woman executive to function as efficiently as her male counterpart." (This is probably true, but it's also true that as the harasser complaints increase, female corporate executives need not get there by brains alone.) As she puts it, "one can't even go on a business trip or a convention with a 'colleague' " without bitchy tongues wagging.

Mary Cunningham is no longer an employee of Chairman Agee (she wound up at Seagram's). And though it's reported she still sees the chairman, it could be the solid platonic male-female relationship she claims it was. It could rationally be surmised that some of those candlelight dinners now can still be working sessions, though Seagram's makes booze and Bendix space-age machinery. When last heard of, it seems nuptials were in the offing. So was it pet-otism or did she make it on her own?

### The Dollar, the Franc, and the . . . Yen for the Top

But by whatever means Mary got as far as she did, it's all legitimate gamesmanship up there in the world of the big dollar, the big franc—and of course the big yen for making it. However, whatever her excuse, she still didn't go all the way—in business, that is. So one must come to the glum conclusion (and we hate to mention this) that the big-wheel conglomerate aptitude may just be lacking in most women—no matter their degree of masculinization. Goodmeasure, Inc., a Cambridge consulting firm, reports in a recent survey, over forty business organizations expressed concern about the ability of the big-business achiever women they've hired. As Goodmeasure put it, "affirmative action and court decisions may put them into the pipeline, but the problem is moving them up."

Even in education, which should be the female's bag (the inevitable schoolmarm since frontier days), they can't seem to grasp and hold that top rung. Though they've all read the feminist books, like *The Management Woman*, on how to dress, act, and climb to power, they just can't balance on that top rung. The American Association of University Women states that ever since federal equal opportunity laws went into effect some ten years ago, only six percent of college presidents are women—this includes women's as well as the usual co-ed institutions.

Dr. Donna Shalala, president of Hunter College, put her finger on why there are so few female college presidents. "Women tend to stay in their (lower-level) jobs too long because they're happy in them." The obvious implication is that the top will make them unhappy, which little ole Dr. Mills warned them of. But then, imagine Jill Abrandt, advertising manager of NYU, saying at that meeting, "What we should do should be based on what we want to achieve instead of how happy we are." Well, as we've always said, every female to her own poison—even at the top.

## Bonnie, Sans Clyde

But however unhappy or shut out they may feel in some ventures, there are others wide open for the enterprising female. Now women may not be suited to bribe on an international scale, like the men at Bethlehem Steel, or to give illegal campaign funds to Nixon from the IT&T treasury, but they have shown some talent in other more specialized areas—not too removed. The U.S. Law Enforcement Association claims women are getting on famously. Their pictures are frequently on the front page and, by the same token, in rogues' galleries all over the world. They undoubtedly have been upwardly mobile in crime. Shoplifting and purse snatching are now small potatoes to women. Among the more gutsy *balls of fluff* the crime rate has risen a solid 246 percent, compared to the puny 22.8 percent rise for men.

Still, as in most other fields of high female endeavor, when they get near the top, they spook. This may account for more than twenty thousand female inmates languishing in federal, state, and local prisons, with only dreams of the excitement and the glory of "getting out of the house."

## In Their Hearts They Know We're Right

However, though the lowly unskilled woman behind the sewing machine or the few at the steering wheel of a tractor trailer still complain of their unequal pay for equal work, those stressful high-wire gals have an even more legitimate beef. For instance, at Columbia forty men and forty women were studied, all with

M.B.A.'s from the classes of 1969–1972. They were all similar in economic, social, and academic background. Starting off the same in 1972 at $12,130 per year, by 1979 the male moguls averaged $48,000; the women, $34,038. But, get this; not a gripe in sight. And for good reason: in their hearts they know we're right. As one of their own, Maryann Vandervelde, president of Pioneer Management, concludes, "Even professional and managerial women don't have quite the same commitment as do men."

## A Pap Smear—or a Light Beer

What about the female entrepreneur in this age of equality? Certainly those females can't complain that they've not had enough counsel and guidance. It's a bad week in Washington if there aren't at least half a dozen workshops that are supposed to show the ambitious ones how to get a grubstake and thus be on their way to independence and fortune. (It's not so small a business itself, with a six-hundred- to one-thousand dollar registration fee to advise on everything from starting up a female singles bar to a hang-gliding school (for menopausal women). Yet those women seem to miss the whole point on those get-togethers. Sure, they're there to learn a little something, but if they have ever studied men in such groups, they'd learn how to run these affairs. They'd never think of an agenda winding up with free vaginal examinations and pap smears. What a pitsy way to end a tough day of "how-to." Can you imagine a male conventioneer paying eight hundred dollars for a starter course, then standing in line for a prostatic examination rather than a topless bar after a day of panel discussions?

## The Paper Tigresses

Though we males have taken our knocks for obstructing the progress of feminism in business, there is one trade where the ladies have no gripes coming—not a leg to stand on. That is journalism. As the pusillanimous male editors rolled over for the liberators in the 70s, they literally grabbed at any female with a college education who could write a compound sentence and spell sexist with one *x*. But still, of the thousands of major daily papers in the U.S.A., there is no known female editor-in-chief. Here is the female with her lone aptitude in the verbal skills (even accepted by us chauvs), and she can't make it up the path which those ink-stained males smoothed for her. Not only that, but the male publishers and editors (under pressure to be sure) opened the opportunity gates with "Women's Pages," "Women's Features," "Junior Miss Sections," and lonely hearts and gossip columns from Liz Smith to Shepherd to Dear Abby; plus regular columnists like Ellen Goodman and Mary McGrory. Yet nary a one comes anywhere near the sleeves-rolled, tie-askew, "hold-the-presses" echelon. The furthest they ever got was at the *Washington Post* with their "house female editor," the mousy Meg Greenfield—securely employed under Big Boss Bradlee, or at the *Times*, with Charlotte Curtis, who probably went as far as her talents and affirmative action would allow as Op-Ed page editor.

Yes, we know that by affirmative action (or as some call it, preferred treatment) women have made it on the local TV news shows (if there isn't one black female as coanchor the FCC will have a sharp look at them). Where are the female Rathers, the Chancellors, or the Reynolds? Barbara Walters had a shot at it with Reasoner and lasted less than a year, going back to her Beautiful (if utterly boring) People specials with questions like, "Nancy, how did it feel when Ron first kissed you?"

Recently, when the president was shot and the top honcho at NBC, Bill Small, was in China, the store was left for a time in the hands of his executive assistant, Sylvia Westerman. It seems as if it was either one of those days for her or it was her best judgment that John Chancellor needn't have been seen on the screen for that teeny-weensy piece of news. So without even trying, CBS and ABC had it all to themselves all afternoon, and poor Sylvia, with her big chance scrubbed, is now caught in the "network."

## *Mzzzzz Lonely Hearts*

Though the gals do get close, it seems every time there is a little upward movement there's a downward flap that throws them from the editorials back to the obits. One such was in the

1972 presidential campaign. There was a bomb scare on a nominee's plane (which also carried the press). A scary buzzing sound was heard coming from the luggage compartment. The Secret Service got everyone off the plane, called in the local bomb squad, and narrowed it down to one female reporter's suitcase. It was touch-and-go as they gingerly opened it and pulled out a small elegant case with the buzzing culprit. Dousing it quickly in a bucket of water, it stopped the action. Then, with everyone breathing a sigh of relief, the case was pulled out and opened. There in full view was the lady's "personal" vibrator. The "sound waves" spread like wildfire, and the unprintable jokes were composed so fast and furiously that the female reporter disappeared from that campaign, never to return.

Then just a few years later, Abe Rosenthal of the *New York Times* had to yank Laura Foreman, a top-notch female reporter, from her political duties in Philadelphia. It was found that politics had made strange bedfellows. It appears that she was not only covering an elected official journalistically, but literally, in the most intimate breakfast-through-bedtime way. But that man had a heart—even supplementing her miserable female reporter's salary with a mink coat. She was fired. She then threatened all kinds of suits against the *Times*, but it was all dissipated when her boyfriend (a Mayor Rizzo crony) was indicted and went to jail.

## Cook-ed Their Goose

This little set-to didn't earn the cause of female journalism any kudos. And though they were making little progress after that, the situation now has retrogressed back to the sob sister days. After the great Janet Cook–*Washington Post* flap of 1981, the female journalists will be kept clear of the editor's desk and on the restaurant and fashion beat for years to come. And at least the fems couldn't cry discrimination when the prize for a feature story had to be returned because it was found to be pure fiction. Even Judith Crist, the eminent feminist critic, said "the whole *cooked up* story stank to the high heavens from the beginning."

There was not only the shame of it to every budding Ann Landers, but it put a big crack in the newspaper world's first-amendment Maginot Line. Who else but a female could get away with fabricating an eight-year-old junkie—and then brazen it out on her constitutional rights and refuse to give the source to the police and the mayor, much less her editor. They all smelled a rat, as some of the Pulitzer jury did. But then there were complicating factors. The paper had pushed the story for a Pulitzer for months. The Pulitzer jury was overruled by their board. Cook was not only female, but black, and allegedly had one of the higher-ups as a boyfriend. So why question it? But when she received the prize and much attention and scrutiny, they not only found that the story was fabricated but so was her whole background as well. So with great full-page apologies, the *Post* editors had to eat female crow, and that's one dish they don't thrive on.

However, contrition comes so routinely with the *Post*. A year or so back, the editor's then live-in, "poison pen" Sally Quinn, wrote about Chief Security Adviser Brzezinski pulling his zipper down with appropriate remarks and pictures—all of which proved trumped up.

## Busts at the Top

But why go on? The fact is the libbers have shown little but *busts* at the top. Of course they will have a dozen excuses, complaints, and rebuttals—but no record to speak of. They will admit no failures and will still plead, "Just give us another twenty years of equality and we'll show you." But why won't they accept their own history (past and recent), and give up the ghost? Don't they yet know that the delicate female brain, a beautiful instrument, can't be fast-franchised for a *buck* at the top? It's as much a product of evolution as the hairy body, big muscles, and the coziness of the male clubs. It took billions of Darwinian years to develop the mentality and push of the Rockefellers, Sulzbergers, Fords, Carnegies, and Nelson Bunker Hunts. A lifetime is a pittance, and there will be not many more female tycoons in another twenty years than in another twenty thousand unless a new ozone-breathing mutant of the female species evolves for the top.

## CHAPTER XIV

# Politics I—
# the Dominoes and Dominees

A woman politician is like a dog walking on its hind legs: it is not done well, but you are surprised that it's done at all.
*Samuel Johnson*

Politically, most women are still in the pterodactyl era. They claw, glower, and simper, and scheme and dissemble.
*Shana Alexander, columnist, feminist, television commentator*

IF TESTOSTERONE is the Hormone of Champions, it is even more the mother's milk of politicians. And if God in his hormonal wisdom had wanted women to be politicians, he would have infused them with that golden elixir. Then they could have appeared in the shape of a rain barrel like Tip O'Neill, been born with the integrity of Richard Milhous Nixon, or been caught disporting themselves like Wilbur Mills in the Tidal Basin. Not that androgynous types like Golda or Thatcher could not have run the Roman Empire. However, estrogenous women with neither the vices of the common garden variety of politicians nor the instincts of a puff adder could possibly succeed in the second oldest profession. They lack those inherent traits of leadership: the chutzpah of eight-time-loser Harold Stassen or William Jennings Bryan: the honorable pride of those poor entrapped Abscam victims; the messianic complex of a Charles de Gaulle or a Jimmy Carter; and all in all, that aura of "the world owes me a living."

As to the more practical aspects of politics, it would be difficult for her, on any given campaign day, to stand the gaff without the built-in capacity to knock off a fifth of that general-purpose back stiffener, "Old Grand*person*" (somehow Lydia Pinkham's compound just doesn't do the trick). Where else could she get the fortitude and dulled sensitivity to stand, frozen stiff at 5:00 A.M., in ten-below-zero temperatures, at a woodpulp plant in Wausau, Wisconsin, and last it out to wheel and deal in a smoke-filled room at 2:00 A.M. the following morning?

## What Makes Bella Run?

Loathe to cast aspersions on their faces, figures, or femininity, a few females like Bella, Indira, and Maggie do nearly fill the bill. But judging just from how they've gone about it, they probably have as much male hormone in their veins as Attila the Hun. Some of them even mimic the arrogance of their male counterparts, but the real stuff of politicians just isn't there.

If females have "come a long way," it would be mighty hard to tell from U.S. politics. Over the past few years there have been no more congress*persons* than before. So what kind of progress is that? As President Carter spoke his mind out in a church sermon, "Women have gone about as far as they ought to go." And maybe they have.

## 'Til Death Does She Start

Yet let no feminist try to pin the political failure tail on our chauvinist rumps. For in all fairness, with our inborn generosity, we did try (without much success) to dispense a modicum of political largesse. Not that we are that altruistic, but a few women sprinkled around the seats of power gives a healthier glow to our Jeffersonian democracy. Most politicians enjoy this imagery, but more, it gives the impression that we males do not control the political game lock, stock, and bottle. But as small a dent as the female has made on the national political scene, even with our tolerant attitude and noblesse oblige, we certainly weren't about to go all out to prevent their political hara-kiri in New York recently. What a beautiful exhibition of female solidarity it was, to see New York Democrats Liz Holtzman and Bess Myerson knock each other and that great Senator Javits out of the box and let a non-such Republican like D'Amato slide into the U.S. Senate.

But as little or as much as we did for them, the feminists never showed much appreciation for our efforts, even though nine out of eleven women who ever served as senators did so only because of the male—their loving husbands. When most of those honorable gentlemen departed this earth prematurely, who but their spouses finished their terms—and were even reelected on their husband's name and reputation alone. But what ingrates some of them were. Some did nothing but zing it to the very political males or central committee who, in memory of their esteemed colleague, put them where they were.

Most notable among recent past zingees was Jimmy Carter. Not only did a passel of congresswomen help do him in, but even his fem appointees in the White House jumped on him. Those imperious females (besides NOW et al.) claimed his tenure was a disappointment—regardless of his generosity in dunning Illinois legislators to pass the ERA, and even sending Rosalynn all the way to the lib convention in Houston.

Heretofore, in appointments too, when the tokenism of equality is called for, the one-hundred-percent chauvinist American politicians never flinched. Actually, from the time of the Declaration of Independence, there have been in those two hundred years an abundance of at least six or seven females appointed by male presidents to top posts. We vaguely remember somewhere back in the McKinley administration that a now long-forgotten female was appointed third assistant postmistress. Then FDR, in a sop to Eleanor, tossed them the secretary of labor bone (Ma Perkins); and Eisenhower gave in with Oveta Culp Hobby at HEW. Since then each president has had a "house female" stuck somewhere in the machinery of government where they wouldn't be too troublesome.

But now in the 80s, Ronnie is taking no chances. Though the fems are crowing over the new female Supreme Court appointment, it was the neatest trick he ever pulled. Getting all the glory, Ronnie submerged a woman at eight-to-one odds, staving off another female appointment to the court for another 192 years.

His other appointment, the hard-nosed Jeanne Kirkpatrick, safely buried at the U.N., seems to be following and bollixing in Andy Young's footsteps (and getting coronary attacks just like her male counterparts).

Our latest president, during his campaign, did make vague

noises about putting qualified females on the federal payroll. I'm sure he will have as many females—in the *right* places—in his administration as did General Grant or Warren Harding in theirs. For instance, even under Jimmy, the henpecked feminist, senior executive posts went up from 3.4 to 4.4 percent in Agriculture and 8.9 to 9.5 percent in State. Not earthshaking, so why should Ron do better?

But with the critical state of the economy, our weak foreign policy, and general low morale, Reagan knows it is no time to play female softball. Early on, he cleaned the White House of all female advisers on the problems of femaledom. After all, with forty years of experience with Hollywood women, what sort of advice could he possibly need from them?

## Spiro with Morning Sickness

So here they are, by virtue of fifty-three percent of the electorate plus our "helping hands," women in politics are still barely making it on the national scene. There are reasons for this, most of which are fairly obvious. At the risk of being repetitive, we must bring up certain inherent problems in the female not so amenable to solutions—problems not shared by most stars in the chauvinist political realm. Though the fems keep denying any kind of inner physiological functions that could make a difference, we'd like to see Spiro Agnew or the Ayatollah keep down a fund-raiser breakfast of hash browns and creamed chipped beef when retching with morning sickness. Or the roly-poly Speaker of the House matching drink for drink with the head of the bricklayers' union (usually a cinch for him) when wracked with menopausal flushes and flashes. Though we feel for their disability, can we help it if their hormonal vibes are not in sync with the ups and downs, the fevers and fervors of skimming the cream from the public milk bucket?

## Shorthand—a Congenital Malformation of the Upper Extremity

But there are even more cogent reasons for female failure in politics. With visions of political plums dancing in their heads while representing a majority of the population, females should be sweeping every election without registering a gravestone. They should not lose a single precinct, any more than the Kennedys could ever imagine losing a Boston Irish district, or Mayor Koch, a New York Jewish borough. From the arithmetic alone there should be a majority of females elected to the all-male political gravy trains and junkets to Paris, Rome, and Morocco on official business like the best of them. If only most women voted for their own. Don't they realize that if they did, there would be more of them inspecting the Berber postal system, getting that ne'er-do-well uncle a sinecure in the Small Business Administration, or hiring fourteen-thousand-dollar-a-year secretaries who think shorthand is a congenital malformation of the upper extremities.

It again brings back the research of Professor Lionel Tiger showing that women have too little bonding and too weak a leadership gene to ever make it big in politics.

As Congressman Barbara Mikulski said, the sixteen women in their political caucus group disagree about forty percent of the time. Which shows why, even if they get elected, their legislative power has been almost nil.

### A.B.F.—Anyone But a Female

What is the root of their problem? Why is it they do not vote for their own? Now we don't mean to pick on poor Bella's many campaign losses, but they are rich in clues. Studying them, one perceives the common feminine trait standing out in big bold letters: J-E-A-L-O-U-S-Y. Now Bella is, by all accounts, about as enviable to other females as a self-propelled rocket launcher. But our research shows that the marrow-deep instinct in every *feminine* woman worth her salt is suspicion of any other female—not only in getting her man, but getting her vote.

### Mighty Bella Had Struck Out

But jealousy is just another factor and certainly does not represent the whole ball of wax. As they say, failure breeds failure, and with one blow after another to female political aspirations on the national scene, it seems their failures have succeeded. With the torpedoing of the unsinkable Bella A. in her last three big ones, it was almost too much. Depression set in, from the National Women's Press Club all the way to the Watergate Beauty Parlor. It was discouraging to every potential female candidate bent on out-sucking the male at the public teat. It was as if voters had said, "She can't be trusted with a secret ballot any more than with over-the-back-fence gossip." Bella's campaign was supposed to be the feminists' political showpiece, ultimate proof that the female voter really would line up and back her to break into the Senate big league. They no longer wanted to depend on a husband in rigor mortis. In her first navel-to-navel engagement with Daniel Patrick Moynihan (an opponent about as ideological as the Reverend Moon, having worked for both JFK and RMN), the movement mobilized feminists from Maine to New Mexico. They raised funds, recruited volunteers, printed materials, stuffed envelopes, knocked on doors, and telephoned and chauffeured. In short, the feminist pols laid down their bodies in a great political *tour de force*, and the male machine (with the aid and abetment of the female voter) blithely rode over them.

## The Last Her-rah

Election Day 1976 was a sad one in Maudville—Mighty Bella had struck out. Not only that, but the ignominy of it all, she lost to a triple-A, one hundred percent, twenty-four karat chauvinist. Then, another female fault broke out: timing—not knowing when to cool it for a while. Even RMN laid low from 1960 to 1968, giving us those years to forget his Checkers speech. He came back to fool us again. But not Bella. She bounced right back for more blood—in this case her own. For after the formality of a less-than-genteel concession of defeat to Mr. Moynihan (in terms earthy enough to have gained the admiration of the unslung tongue of LBJ), she plunged into another battle where even she should have feared to tread—the mayoralty race in New York. This time it was quadruple jeopardy—taking on a four-square team of natural enemies of feminism. Here she was opposing not only *bachelor* and *chauvinist* Ed Koch, tainted with snide allegations of gay-ety, but also a *former Miss America* Sex Object (Bess Myerson, that type so abhorrent to any liberator). Here Bella's womanly instincts and her manly arrogance—a tough combination to beat—did her in. Starting about twenty points ahead, like a wrecker ball in the Hall of Mirrors, she alienated enough political leaders, newspaper editors, and more female voters to go down the drain—hat, pantyhose, girdle, and all. With fifty-three percent of the voters hers and hers alone, and the rest Jewish and liberal, if she were a male she "could have stood in bed" and enjoyed her landslide on television.

Then, like a missile on target, she couldn't stop herself. She came back for another unsolicited encore (a congressional seat) —her very last her-rah. She lost to an unknown Republican—and there she lies stone cold dead without the political benefits of Taps and an Arlington gravesite.

## Ms. Mean Jean

Another female characteristic which may help solve the mystery of the female political failures is also illustrated by our Bella. When things got down to the wire, not unlike top female business execs she got as mean as a mother asp. She even called a female reporter from the *Village Voice* "bitchy" (which is not only unladylike but a term abhorred by the fems). Then the brouhaha was prolonged as the reporter called her a sexist—which, of course, they both are and were. As author Irwin Shaw described Bella, she is the Lady Macbeth of her day.

So here we come up with another clue to the political riddle wrapped in the feminist enigma. Female politicians who go for the big enchiladas—not just county councils and PTA treasurers —are almost to a man, tough babies. Thatcher is no shrinking violet, nor Indira a crinoline-and-lace lady-in-waiting. Pants-suited, roly-poly Congresswoman Barbara Mikulski is another. Riding in on her ethnic district majority, she was a strict down-the-line feminist until she became entranced with some Australian woman's kooky philosophy about cottage industry in urban Baltimore. She hired the woman, and eight die-hard feminists in her office quit her cold. She just went on, hitched her heft a little tighter, and even refused press conferences—usually her favorite sport.

And with enough of the hair of the male hormone that bites her, Patsy Mink from Hawaii is as spiny as the skin of a ripe pineapple (she also lost for a Senate seat in Hawaii—to another chauvinist, yet).

Recently, in the lower house of the Italian parliament, fistfights, obscene language, and book-throwing (*The House Rules and Regulations*—weight, nine pounds) erupted when two radical women leaders had to be separated by security guards.

We may be wrong, but from their collective behavior, these women all seem to have been blessed with a little too much of our natural male meanness—of course, via the golden hormone. Coming from us, it's okay. But coming from a woman it not only alienates and confuses the feminine voter (is she is, or is she ain't), but the male voter as well.

## The Top of the Dung Heap—for Cocks Only

The big trouble with Bella, Patsy, and those others is that they forget their roots. Not their recent ones—their real deep roots. History and science show that, from the League of Female Earthworms to the African Violet Club of Neanderthalia, women just do not go for female leaders. As those Nobel Prize winners, Konrad Lorenz and Tinbergen, so candidly prove, the average female is a follower; and as we have shown a dozen times the average female rarely follows one of her own. Again, to put it in terms every fem can understand: Behind every good politician is a true-blue male hormone. And if they do not believe it, shoot testosterone into a female guppy follower and she'll lead the school; feed it to the barnyard hen and she'll take over the pecking order.

## The Tie That Bonds—for Men Only

There is a good reason for all of this. To endure, the male had to use every trick of his newly acquired primeval gray matter to conjure up and piece together a male mob. How else but as a team could he and his cronies compete with the leopard for a leg of antelope, or outwit another vandal tribe? Certainly the female, with child at knee, at breast, and in belly, was unfit for such activity. Back slapping and palm crossing was left only to the most wily and corrupt (virtues of the political fittest). Our neolithic brothers survived and passed those admirable traits along to males on Capitol Hill, the Bundestag, and to Number Ten Downing Street.

The male's ability to organize, inherited from the leaders of the flock, the pack, then the tribe, is the first prerequisite for any successful politician. That is why not only McSorley's bar, the New York Athletic Club, and the Kiwanis but every congress or parliament in the world today is bonded for men only—brother to brother—not brother to sister. And if you put two and two together, it is difficult to escape the conclusion that the last twenty years of female political freedom make Darwin's theory look good even to the creationists.

In the most civilized of parliaments and chambers of deputies or politburos anywhere in the world today, one can hardly count on a healthy if paltry aggregate of females. But most revealing is that great equal opportunity system the Soviets run. The motherland of female liberation begun by Marx and Engels shows not a sign of female anywhere near the seat of Kremlin power—much less on the Presidium. The Soviet male still measures out his political largesse to female politicians in little teaspoons, so there are now three females on the powerful Central Committee (among 130 males). Counting their blessings they boast, "It's at least three more than under the Czar."

## Lady, Beware

But ladies, beware. Politics is one merry-go-round with no free rides, and on occasion the urge to take over may be not only hazardous to a female—but deadly. So if by osmosis and the connubial bed a woman becomes afflicted with dreams of glory, she should be prepared to take the lumps. Marshal Tito's widow cast just one blue eyeshadowed glance at that seat of power and wound up in the dock, and then house arrest—allowed out only to put flowers on his grave. The last of the Madame Perons also tried, and she was a prisoner of political love for seven years, now exiled; and when Mao's widow, Chiang Ching and her "Gang of Four" naively tried takeover tactics—well, after her trial even the wall posters show her in stripes.

In the year A.D. 1982, no less than in 1982 B.C., overwhelming evidence suggests politics is hardly in the nature of the average female beast. It is just a plain fact of evolution, history, and genetics that leadership has little to do with conditioning. The Garth polls can tell it as it is, Scotty Reston and David Broder can analyze the situation down to a cinder, and IBM can compute it to the tenth power. But what it all comes down to is that politics is an instinct as male as football or war. Sure she'll make tiny inroads here and there, and there'll be some backing and filling, but when the dust settles she'll still be flying securely on our coattails.

Still, with no fear of flying, even in the face of evolution, genetics, and the added hurdle of our chauvinistic roadblocks, the female continues to bang at the forbidden doors of the all-male marble halls. And we men—gentlemen that we are, knowing in our politicized Precambrian marrow the name of the game—suffer in silence. With a lift of the eyebrow and a condescending smile, from precinct captains to prime ministers, we tolerate and even encourage the Patsy Minks and the Margaret Thatchers. For deep in our hearts we know that this too shall pass.

> Hers was not to reason why,
> Hers was not to plot and vie,
> Hers was then to follow camps,
> Hers is still to lick the stamps.

## CHAPTER XV

# Politics II—Skirting the Issue:
# Could She Be President?

Women in politics have masculine faces, figures, and manners; but when God transplanted a political brain to alien soil, only a little of the original "good earth" clings to the roots.

*Ambrose Bierce, 1881*

THEY MAY LOVE POWER MORE, but they love not their Cuisinart less. As the saying goes, you can take the skirt out of the kitchen, but you can't take the kitchen out of the skirted. To repeat, Prime Minister Thatcher, even at Number Ten Downing Street, isn't fulfilled unless she gets breakfast for the family. And Golda could only relax during the Six-Day War by doing the dirty dishes. Those few female political anomalies, though acting the part, deep down are as different from male politicians as horses from horse feathers. And the difference will out, whether on the hustings or during a missile crisis.

But make no mistake about it, that is not to say those ladies aren't tough—Daley tough, Tweed tough—and kitchen or no, they'd never have made it to the top otherwise. At first they'll start at anything, going out for sandwiches, or putting bumper stickers on telephone poles, to wangle themselves into the inner circle. Then they'll stop at nothing: sew on shirt buttons; chauffeur; or climb into bed with every elected Franklin, Ike, or Jimmy. They'll even go to the extreme of holy matrimony. Though this may sound as cold as a frozen salmon, Mrs. Anwar Sadat came right out with it: "I married my husband for politics."

## Handed to Them on a Catafalque

The waiting game wasn't always as deliberate as it sounds but nonetheless it was the usual, old-fashioned way to female political power. In the old days, the wives of political candidates were window dressing especially at election time. But in between, they were the Mothers Courage of the husting roustabouts. They stayed at home minding the kids, taking his highness's dirty clothes to the launderette every Monday, and patiently waiting up for him while he had his fun and games in the House, the Senate, or Lincoln's bedroom. And many finally got their reward. Such women as former Senators Margaret Chase Smith of Maine and Maureen Neuberger of Oregon, Congress*persons* Lindy Boggs (Democrat of Louisiana) or Lenore Sullivan (Democrat of Missouri), among many others (including Madame Bandaranaike, the former prime minister of Sri Lanka), were ladies-in-waiting till their positions were officially handed them on a catafalque.

Though many of the female pols no longer go the traditional underground route of burying their husbands to play the power game, some still do. Now we don't mean to imply that they actually wait around for his demise like some kind of vulture. And though it doesn't appear on the surface that personal ambition is the motive, some of those recent congressional wives do not seem exactly four-square behind their spouses. A patient woman like Mrs. Herman Talmadge shamelessly exposed her powerful spouse by telling of the shoe box where he kept those tens of thousands of dollars of "campaign funds."

Another congressional wife, Rita Jenrette, found a unique means of exposure to bring down her man, via the *Playboy* centerfold or on talk shows all across the nation. Now she's talking of running for public office on her own. The only real political experience we know of, as she revealed, was her successfully making love on the Capitol steps during a filibuster.

We repeat, we hate to imply that the female of the team is avidly waiting in the wings, but if I were a senator or congressman I'd play it close to the vest.

## Over Their Dead Bodies

Regardless of how it's usually done, the political shot is still there today for any of those wives. The longevity statistics are all on their side. If they wait long enough and have a lust for fundraising banquets and plant gates at the crack of dawn, they've got it made.

Then again, as we've seen, with their long years of experience mingling at the top, we're sure they would have no trouble snoozing through a filibuster or fulfilling their obligations on junkets to Rome, Dublin, and Israel. And if any of them were especially endowed with the Abscam mentality of their loved ones, plus a digestive tract that could take on a Greek communion breakfast, a B'nai B'rith seder, and a Harlem soul food banquet in any one day, they might be in for life.

It must be said, however, that of those ladies who came into congressional power over their husbands' corpses or by capitalizing on famous family political names, only the androgynous ones came up to the expected level of male mediocrity.

## Evita, Indira, and Nancy—the Name Is the Game

Of course some top female political leaders like Indira Gandhi, Madame Bandaranaike of Sri Lanka, and Madame Peron II of Argentina actually ran for office—but in these cases the name was the game. It is questionable whether Indira could have been elected as corresponding secretary of the Untouchable Chowder and Marching Society without the magic moniker of Gandhi. And the second Madame President Peron would not have placed in her high school beauty contest bearing just her maiden name. Even now, one of the two most recently elected female senators, Nancy Kassenbaum of Kansas, would have still been behind her Hoover vacuum cleaner had she not invoked the name of her grandfather Alf Landon a hundred times a day during her election campaign.

Until 1978, of the six female chief executives in the world (out of 178) only Golda Meir and Margaret Thatcher achieved prominence without the benefit of name or nepotism. But Golda was a female of another *choler*. As Ben Gurion put it when she came into his government, "Thank God I now have at least one 'man' in my cabinet." As for Maggie, she seems to be of the same hormonal ilk as Golda; the Soviet Union and the opposition Labor party and most jealous feminists aptly nicknamed her "The Iron Butterfly." And as the kettle calls the pot, Germaine Greer describes Thatcher as "an obtuse, humorless, merciless woman."

But the big question is, when and if they get there, can they lead? We know from all of our anthropological and genetic data that it has always been the male out front and on top. However, as usual, the feminists disregard all of that scientific claptrap— such as Leakey and Darwin spout—and say this time "it's it." The lady gurus have Ms'd the ramparts, whipped up the cadres, and cite John Stuart Mill's feminism as if it were the gospel.

As the lib litany goes, the intellect of the male and female is equal, so why shouldn't the females sit in the big house, have secret service escorts, and hear ruffles and flourishes ringing in their ears. But they don't understand. Even if the intellect part were true, which it isn't (as we've shown), what in the world do brains have to do with politics? As we know, the convolutions of the frontal lobe in politicians have had a disuse atrophy for centuries and are of limited use even to the male. Also, we have proved, as with the guppies, it's all up to the hormones. The hormone is king; so as testosterone goes, so goes the nation. Anyway, as the fems admit, they can't keep order in a white sale, a garden club election, or a female political caucus. How in the world do they expect to run a country?

## *The Feminist of the Species*

It does not matter by what public relations, pubic relations, or interments any of these ladies got on *first*: if we are serious (and believe me, we are) in the doubts we chauvs have about a female in the White House, we must be objective. Let us study a few of the female chiefs of state inside and out, as the Olympic Committee does with women athletes—blood test and all. Getting to the bottom of both the character and the record of those lionesses who have already made it, we should at least gain insight as to whether even a highly testosteronized woman can overcome her natural limitations and govern like a man.

## Political Subjects and Sex Objects

Starting with character, one thing can be said about female politicians—they rarely stoop to being sex objects just to be elected. The same cannot be said of some of our male leaders. Take Golda, for instance. She may have said women's lib is "a lot of damned foolishness," but when it came to being a sex object she stuck strictly to the feminist party line. Not once did she use her face or her figure to further her political ambitions. In fact, most female politicians, from that recently betrothed congress*person* Shirley Chisholm of New York, to former Governor Dixy Lee Ray of Washington State (no darling of the liberationists either), never go out of their way to exploit their physical charms. Luckily this has posed no insurmountable problems for most of them.

We never saw Golda in anything but her granny gowns, but judging from her stolidly endowed mass she easily could have been the model for tank traps on the Golan Heights. And nothing less than one of Omar the Tentmaker's creations could camouflage the expanse of Madame Bandaranaike. As for Indira, she has the advantage of the ultimate coverup—the sari. She may be as wraithlike as a Twiggy and have the legs of Shirley MacLaine, but swathed in those layers of Indian silks, who would ever know?

So it's obvious a female can't have all that male hormone and heaven too. Which explains why that gaggle of ladies would have more trouble getting past Elizabeth Arden's doorman than Arnold Schwarzenegger. They are unlike the modern male politician who now spends more time getting his teeth capped, hair plugs implanted, and eyes pinched than he does getting a pothole fixed. The ladies wisely don't even try. Admittedly, their options are limited. Even a plastic surgeon has never claimed powers of resurrection. Still, the delicate skills of that yet uncanonized surgeon who performed the miracle of Phyllis Diller always offers hope.

## Not a Kickback in a Carload

If the feminist politician does not have the greatest face or figure, one thing cannot be taken away from her: she rules with a minimum of corruption and no sex scandals at all. No under-the-table shenanigans and no nontyping congressional gigolos—which is a lot more than you can say for a host of male officeholders who by mid-career are in jail, out on bail, wading somewhere in a Tidal Basin, or being videotaped by a phony Arab sheik.

However, this admirable moral record of the female politician is not entirely of her own choosing. Deep down she has certain acquisitive tendencies, but it seems they are usually confined to furs, shoes, and jewelry. Also, there are built-in weaknesses in job preservation—to wit, former Congress*persons* Bella and Liz Holtzman. Despite the myth of womanly endurance, they didn't last long enough in national politics to get both hands deep enough into the till to raise an FBI eyebrow. Contributing to this political delinquency is the female's well-documented mathematical deficiencies. When it gets beyond the fingers and toes stage, she can never distinguish herself à la Tweed, Harding, or Agnew in the fine art of depleting the public coffers.

## Sinless and Sexless Madames of the House— and Senate

We know from the research of sociologist Lionel Tiger of Rutgers that women are more bonded to kin than to cronies. Though it ordinarily is considered a cardinal sin in politics to have less than half the staff reserved for family and friends, Madame Bandaranaike of Sri Lanka, who just lost her job, did overdo it. She had some 246 relatives on her "White House" payroll. When Indira let her politically inept first son get in on the boodle, he did so like a lay*person,* getting both mother and son into serious legal difficulties. Now with that first son's demise, she has his brother firmly ensconced on the government's payroll. Let us see if he learned anything from number one.

As to sex and the female politicians, you won't find even a

touch of the Wayne Hays-Profumo kind of sordidness (though many of them are husbandless and free; to wit Mayor Byrne of Chicago, Congressman Mikulski, Council President Bellamy, et al.). One reason for their sexual rectitude is, of course, as plain as their noses on their faces. It takes two to tango, which does not say that any of these single or widowed would not grab at any reasonable offer. As we have shown, there are not too many political temptresses with attractions that could inveigle any higher primate into a popcorn movie date, much less an assignation. So maybe Freud was right after all—at least about women politicians—"her anatomy is her destiny."

## The Blackest Widows

In delving into the female potential for the highest office, we cannot overlook the marital status of those who have made it. Luckily, though not Marlene Dietrichs in legs, loin, or looks, even in their youth, all of these aforementioned chiefs of state managed to hook a man. However, if any of those poor political husbands had known they were stepping in where a Hollywood stuntman would fear to leap, they would have had serious second thoughts. If they did know what they were getting into, one must conclude they either were desperate or suicidal. The record is clear: Four out of five of those "first gentlemen" are now stone-cold dead in their graves. The premature deaths of these political husbands may well have been merciful, yet there is little doubt that their life span could not have been shorter had they been espoused to one of the Manson girls. Not wanting to make a rash judgment that all "female excellencies" are husband eaters, our suspicion was enhanced when a fifth female chieftain recently took over Switzerland's highest office. Madame Blunschy's husband, coincidentally, has long since gone to his reward. Thus far, only Maggie's husband has survived, but from the precedent, Lloyd's would be scared to death to write his policy.

This brings to mind a rather macabre analogy from which the female has gotten the rotten reputation of being the deadlier of the species. It is a matter of scientific observation that the spouse-cidal black widow spider also wastes her mate not long after she has been properly serviced (the praying mantis—right during the act itself). This may be sheer coincidence, but it would appear that any male entranced by any woman in high politics should first see a psychiatrist specializing in Russian roulette.

## Love and Lincoln's Bedroom

The tarnished marital record of the widow leaders must have gotten around. After all, what looks like a pretty plush deal for some enterprising if indolent male seems to go begging. With all the luxuries of high office—ruffles and flourishes, state dinners, and foreign travel—none of those husbandless executives has been known to have had as much as a nibble, much less hook a live one.

*Au contraire*, any male president, at any stage of his chauvinist career—crippled, senile, or terminal—has almost never had a problem attracting the opposite sex. It is now known that Lincoln's bedroom was used by Harding, FDR, Ike, LBJ, and JFK for more than just meditation and prayer. Even Britain's venerable Gladstone in his heyday had standing (or lying) room only, upstairs or downstairs at Number Ten Downing Street, for some of his favorite females. Just as the sun never set on his empire, it seemed never to have set on his libido.

So the odds are that, if we have a female candidate (just like any female business executive) she will most likely be single, divorced, or widowed and stay so. And as strange as it may seem, though the feminists constantly fear and deprecate the exploitation of political wives by male leaders, it is the male who practically assures his spouse a long and esteemed widowhood. Bess (now ninety-six), Lady Bird, and Jackie (and the now-deceased Mamie and Lady Churchill, both over ninety) are or were around long after the demise of their political spouses.

## Guns and Bagels

Enough of sex and corruption. What about women and the grand sport of national leaders—war. When the great suffrage movement in its semicentennial surge surfaced again about fifty years ago, the feminist chant was, "Give us the vote and there'll be no more wars." Well, they got the vote, and the promise was not requited. There have been only sixty minor and three major wars since, and perhaps two dozen civil ones thrown in for good measure. The greatest game on earth even appeals to female politicians.

Just in the past ten years, three out of four of the female chiefs of state have not let us down. They carved out battle records as enviable as those of any male in the history of civilization. They were involved, instigated, and won better wars with a grander body count in a shorter period of time Tamerlane and Attila the Hun combined. Even Golda's record reflects no matzo-ball–chicken-soup type of leadership. She saw her finest hours in the middle of three hot wars. In her very own 1973 *blitzkreig*, she captured and devastated land twenty times the size of her little nation—how's that for the peaceful ways of womanhood?

Madame Bandaranaike, the drum-shaped former honchess of Sri Lanka, after taking over her dead husband's job, squashed three internal uprisings as if they were a cup of Ceylon tea.

## Indira—First in War, Last in Peace

When it comes to pursuing peace through war, Indira Gandhi was the pride and joy of every female lieutenant in the Israeli army, every female midship*person* in the U.S. Naval Academy, and that hardy lot of lady machine gunners in the glorious forces of the Soviet Socialist Republic. For here was one woman who was not only first in war, but last in peace, and still is. Though JFK, LBJ, and HHH were all labeled warmongers by Bella, Shirley, Gloria, et al., Indira was touted by the sisterhood as the true believer in peaceful leadership. She was their guru, their dove of peace. Then the fall. Now all is quiet on that feminist front.

When first elected to the highest office in populous India, on the name of the man synonymous with peace, she soon not only attacked little Portuguese Goa, but wasted Bangladesh as if she were a Cossack in a Moscow ghetto. She now is preparing for her big one—Pakistan. She acts with dedication and pride and, like any male leader, lets war take no back seat to any issue. Once she was a Pentagon pet, receiving two billion rupees for bombs before bread, and neutrons before butter for her hungry nation. Now in her second go-round, she is as nuclear as Three Mile Island.

## Gandhi, Gonads, and Raging Hormones

Though first a warrior*person*, Indira prided herself even more on her political talent. (In passing, it is interesting that in India, Sri Lanka, and Argentina where liberation has little to do with the female, they can find female presidential material to elect; while here in the U.S.A., which is inundated by the boring feminist political litany, there is not ever a female Harding or Coolidge in sight.)

No doubt Indira had the brass gonads of a Boss Tweed and showed none of the passive resistance nonsense that her Uncle Mahatma dished out when setting India free. She took hold of the second-most-populous nation in the world, held it by the throat like any good Honduran general, and never fainted at the sight of blood. And in the spirit of "her kind of democracy," when things got hairy, she threw the rascals out. She boarded up the libelous press; and imprisoned ten thousand males, friend and foe alike, lay*person* or priest, or anyone else with misguided ideas about how a democracy works (and sterilized any others she could catch).

But before her first fall, and maybe because of it, the Indian chauvinists (some of the best kind), began circulating the rumor that Indira's hormones were raging and that she was more to be pitied than censored. As they said, only the ravages of red-hot flashes and ice-cold flushes, with a few pounding headaches in between, could account for such awry malelike political judgment which ended her first term as chief herds*person* of the sacred cows.

## Direction from the Oval Womb

In the interest of fairness, let it be said: If by some quirk of political chance a woman can overcome her feminine nature, using evolution and a surfeit of male hormone—or can bury a husband, she could rule with the best of them. Treading in the footsteps of Indira and Golda with their natural compassion and abhorrence of violence, she could make as sensitive a president as Ulysses S. Grant. If, as Ambrose Bierce claims, she could bring all the female virtues of indecision, gossip, jealousy, and flightiness to the White House, would it not lend a certain charm to an otherwise colorless administration?

In this era of sexual quotas and equal opportunity, ready or not, even we chauvs are ready to give her a try. It may take four years out of our lives and foul up a few things, but it could at least clear up the whole affirmative action mess once and for all. Contrary to conventional wisdom and discounting physiological limitations, women may bring something special to the highest office in the land at least for a short time. They certainly could not do worse than Millard Fillmore. But the males around her must watch their P's and Q's. As Disraeli said about his queen, the tough Victoria, "She must be managed. I am a flatterer when necessary; I have found it useful with her."

Conditioned or not, a female president would still put the feminine *Good Housekeeping* seal of approval on everything coming from the White House. However, if the budget does not turn out just right—give or take a few billion—the U.S. Treasury cookie jar is right around the corner. If she can't write a few overdrafts, à la Bert Lance, who can? To lift her spirits on one of those crampy days of the month, she might just go out and buy us a dozen new B99 bombers or have the Pacific fleet painted robin's egg blue. No shopping for tanks, MIRV missiles, or subs in April when she can get twenty percent off in August.

## *Eavesdropping In, Tapings Out—and No Curlers at Cabinet Meetings*

Would not that chauvinist Congress bow to the fury of a female president scorned on her check-out-counter budget? Who says the female privilege of mind-changing should not apply to a newly packed Supreme Court or a Salt IV? We don't know if the *seance* adviser would recommend a Ouija board, but it could not produce fewer results than Billy Graham's prayer breakfasts. Needlepoint would certainly replace the Redskins on Sunday afternoon, and Wall Street would cry like a banshee with a phrenologist as chair*person* of the Council of Economic Advisers (they probably would predict economic trends more accurately than Nobel laureates Samuels or Friedman or any one of those know-it-all banker gnomes).

For obvious reasons, everything would be run strictly by the lunar calendar. This is not to say that those three or four days a month cannot be spent productively—measuring for new White House draperies or something—as long as she is kept away from that "button."

Secret Oval Office taping would be out, eavesdropping in. No hair curlers at formal cabinet meetings, and the presidential yacht not referred to as a "she." Also, if this chief executive is in that certain stage of life, all radiators are deemed inoperative at the first sign of a flash or a flush.

## But Now There Are None

So, though all's coming right with the world again as four out of six of the female chiefs of state in foreign lands are back where they belong, their leadership did serve a purpose. It gave hope to the Bellas, Lizzes, and Rosalynns that someday, somehow, it may happen right here in the good old U.S.A. Though we chauvinists may peck and quibble at the records of foreign leaderpersons, there is every reason to believe our own U.S. female chief could live up to the grand performance of those stalwarts of yesteryear —Calvin Coolidge or Herbert Hoover.

## CHAPTER XVI

# The True Confessions
# of a Razed Consciousness
# Help Stamp Out Men

Consciousness raising? I call it grievance mongering.

*Ariana Stassinopoulis, author of*
The Female Liberal *and* Callas

The rarified atmosphere of an elevated consciousness can be hazardous to a female's health—at times resulting in hardening of the femininity.

*E.B.*

ABOUT THREE NIGHTS A WEEK, most of us chauvs kill a few hours at singles bars just to keep abreast of the new fluff coming on the market. One of those evenings, as we stood shoulder to shoulder with fellow night crawlers, dawdling over a drink or two and watching the mating game, we were struck by a paradox. In the first place, why would even one of these newly liberated nonsex objects allow herself to be caught dead in the flesh-peddling marketplaces if she were not on the make? And if she and her sisters aren't there with their consciousnesses at pubic level, why has their decolletage descended below the umbilical frostline? Now you cannot tell me that these sweet young things or that mob of "gay" divorcees are flocking to those one-night stands with their skirts slit up to their rib cages just to have a drink with the boys and prove they are free and equal. Who do they think they're kidding? Just stepping into Maxwell's Plum demonstrates that their prurience overrides their pride. Let's face it: If their consciousnesses cannot be elevated much above the mons veneris, where does that leave their equality?

## Moon-June versus the Pelvic Engagement

Now we've heard a lot about raised consciousness, but with the females, consciousness raising is a bit more complex than it sounds.

Her mind work in instinctual ways. Liberated or not, there still lurks somewhere deep in her subconscious the Moon-June, "for better or for worse" syndrome. Now, the archfeminists consider this attitude just another sop to the male ego. But it goes deeper than that. I have seen fewer consciousnesses raised high enough to deny the mating urge. And it is no different in the romance of the orangutan female than in the Avon lady. Consciousness is still the slavish mistress of the hormones.

Now, mind you, we are not complaining. As long as sex is the bait, any chauvinist will take it; but what does that have to do with love, honor, obeying, and all that? And though in rare moments, when our guard is down, a few of us will allow romance to seep into our souls, most will not let it interfere with our primeval lust. And for those poor deluded lovelies with stars in their eyes who still equate lust with love, the cruel fact is that marriages may be made in heaven but only *pelvic* engagements are made in singles bars. So, through no fault of our own, after that blissful god-given animal act is consummated, it is only natural for us to turn over and peacefully snore the night away while our ever hopeful sleep-ins lie wide awake, tense and worrying if "he'll still love me" in the morning.

## A Hardening of the Femininity

Having observed this scene for some ten long years, we can vouch for the fact that few consciousnesses have really been raised for long, and most have long since fallen. And lucky for them that this is the case. There is ample evidence that if this kind of temporary insanity hangs on too long, the ultrathin atmosphere of a mile-high consciousness is hazardous to the female's health and happiness. It may, God forbid, lead to a Greer-born type of hardening of the femininity which insures that Saturday night will be the loneliest night of the week.

But never let it be said that we chauvs are stone cold when it comes to our women. We do have a feel for the plight of their consciousnesses—up or down. With a maximum of restraint we tolerate their temporary foibles, especially when they are ready to come down from the mountain. In fact, we usually treat them as if they had never been away. The compassionate shoe salesman or dentist who has cynically listened to her on her aggressive ascent to equality will just as silently empathize with her embarrassed comedown from that never-never land. We act the perfect foil—a psychological decompression chamber for the back-to-sea-level mind set.

## The Sexual Equivalent of War

As we now know all too well from the outpourings of thousands of those hoodwinked females, the brain which has weathered that grand hoax does not emerge entirely unscathed. So we pass along one of the very many true confessions—right from the tape recorder. Here goes, from Mrs. R.C. of Brooklyn, New York:

Back in the 60s, I was one of the original raised consciousnesses (R.C.), and I can only say, from what I see now, the few modern-day novitiates of that order are not what they used to be. There is just no more of that high-spirited "get those male *muthas* off our backs" sort of thing. Now, only ten years later, the present-day watered-down sessions are as acceptable as wife swapping (why not "husband swapping"?). These latter-day C.R.ers, now summering in East Hampton and wintering in the East 60s, would be pure Feminist Chic to some of my old, hard-liner friends from the movement. Now they go at it in a posh Madison Avenue boutique, serving white wine and Perrier and selling everything from T-shirts with clever feminist mementos from Bella's campaigns (left over from whatever office she may have run for). At these more fashionable Beautiful People sessions, the old uniform is out and designer jeans are in, with the East Hampton types holding forth with a memorized line or two on abortions (which they seem *too* well-versed in). It is of course all duly reported in *Women's Wear*, with a too-frequent op-ed piece solicited by one of their many female journalistic cheerleaders, Charlotte Curtis of the *Times*. Naturally the few female Queen Bee execs who have made it are always conspicuous by their absence.

As I see it, it's a cinch now. In my day, in the early 70s, it was risky business, sneaking into a crummy Soho pad with a dozen other jeaned, T-shirted feminist frowzies of the ilk that could turn a Joe Namath off sex for life. For one thing, it was tough just getting out of the house with some vague excuse (especially for the married ones), then ducking into *the session* like a tired businessman slinking into the neighborhood porno movie. But at that time it all seemed worthwhile.

There was nothing like coming out of one of those sessions with a hyped-up, wild-eyed consciousness, raring to spit in the eye of the first gent who pulled a chair out for us. In those early years it was nothing for me to venture forth in freezing weather, to march forty blocks down Fifth Avenue, carrying a placard heavier than two garbage cans and a vacuum cleaner, chanting "Liberation Now!" Yet I must admit even late in the game, it took a lot of gearing up, plus a few shots of Wild Turkey, to come home and tell my husband to wash out his own "ring around the collar."

## Warning: A Razed Consciousness May Be Hazardous to Your Credit Card

To show how scary the situation really was, it was not just coincidence that as the Friedan–Steinem gospel permeated the system and consciousness raising was put into practice, wife beating picked up considerably. After all, nagging a hungover husband to get behind a vacuum cleaner on Sunday morning when he looked like he should be in Intensive Care, brought about unhealthy consequences. Not only did contusions and abrasions (and an occasional ruptured spleen) abound, but worse yet, charge plates were canceled, credit cards blown away, and allowances cut to the bone. Still, we can't say we didn't go into it with our eyes wide open.

It was no secret that the Capitol police and New York riot squads don't use kid gloves in removing, respectively, a chanter for "abortion on demand" from a congressman's doorstep, or a lesbian rights sitter-in chained to an editor's desk at the *Ladies' Home Journal*. There was also many an abdominal brush burn from skimming out on a sawdust-covered floor when equalizing the all-male bars in the East Village.

## The Bathroom Squeeze Play

Of course, some of those arrogant jocks we plagued did not get off scot-free either. In the psychological warfare segment of every C.R. session, the efficacy of the Chinese water torture technique was not untaught. What a charge to peep through a crack in the bathroom door in the morning and see him in a fuming funk, just staring fixedly at the tube of toothpaste squeezed from the middle, with the top gone. It was a picture worth a thousand shiners.

But the risks were not all at home; some were at those very same C.R. sessions. Many of those highly conscious sisters, all in the uniform of the day (granny glasses, T-shirts, American flags sewed on the fly, and clogs), could scare a Mafia hit man in a dark alley. And to wear a dress or a skirt at those sessions would tag you as either an FBI agent or someone ready for unnatural sexual adventures. It goes without saying that to wear lipstick, rouge, or sheer pantyhose would guarantee a consciousness leveling proposition.

## Consciousness Up: Libido Down

But there was more to this C.R. business than met the mind. There were actual physiological changes reminiscent of the brain-washing of the Manchurian candidate. For instance, as my female consciousness was in the process of being raised I noticed my libido becoming depressed. My throbbing headaches at bedtime reached the stage where my husband would back off with just one glance, not knowing whether I'd reach for my diaphragm or an ice pick.

The next physiological phenomenon I noted was the Doberman hackle stage, and it reminded me of my Pavlov experiments in Biology I back at Bennington. The hair on the nape of my neck stood up whenever I heard certain buzz phrases such as: "Isn't dinner ready yet?" or "Don't turn that dial!"

At the next level I could actually hear the usually dulcet tones of my voice decibeling to the screech level until they could crack a ceramic ashtray at fifty paces. I then knew the power of C.R.

Along with the physiological alterations, there was a concomitant change in lifestyle. After about four weeks, not only were both Saks and sex out, but even window shopping at Bloomies was considered a sop to sexism. After the eighth session, without batting an eye, I could use the words sh-t and f--k with my minister and enjoy his every wince; and after twelve I spouted feminist clichés like an altar boy his catechisms.

## Crossing the Rubicon—Good-bye to Estée and Helena

From then on, things progressed by leaps and bounds, and I really knew my consciousness was in the clouds when I felt guilty accepting a pair of diamond earrings (given, admittedly, as a peace offering) for an anniversary present. In my own quiet way I was now one of them. I even practiced serving macaroni for dinner three nights in a row (one luke, two cold). By then, on the QT, I had already helped equalize three Irish bars down in the Village. I then attained the ultimate benchmark of liberation: I got out of the house. I landed a part-time job as a school bus driver, which my husband objected to, and which hardly paid for parking my Corvette at work. In my twentieth C.R. session I crossed the Rubicon—not the last one, but the next to the last. I canceled my regular Friday afternoon beauty parlor appointments, gave up *Good Housekeeping*, and began sending subscriptions to *Ms.* magazine as Christmas gifts. However, that's as far as it went.

Somehow, some way, something kept me from going the last mile—where you can't go home again. I never went to a marriage counselor and never got caught in a lesbian liberation march. Around fourteen months into the process, the Bergdorf-Bendel worm began to gnaw. Also, I began to burn for those cold blowy Sunday afternoons (post-season) under the sheets with my supersexist spouse. Next, the Jane Fonda movies became less appealing than the *Summer of '42* genre, and I had a yearning for those gossipy morning sessions on the phone or experimenting in the kitchen with the wok I received for Mother's Day.

## *Any Resemblance to an Earthmover— Hardly Coincidental*

But what really did the trick, pushing me off the perch and back to natural feminine reality, was the company I kept. Most of my acquaintances at the time combined the steel-trap mind of a Claire Booth Luce, the build of a ten-ton earthmover, and the genteel personality of Indira.

One of them smoked smelly, crooked Italian stogies and, when clearing her nasal passages, sounded like a disposal with a stuck peach pit. Another one (more typical and more repulsive) who was always shod in clogs, a symbol sewn on her zippered fly (you won't believe this), brought her own aborted fetus (in a small formaldehyde-filled bottle) to each session, along with her earthy rhetoric for abortion on demand. (The tiny preserved thing must have been about three months old and half-inch in size and as she proudly swirled it about to make a point, the little hands and feet bounced up and down. It looked like a tiny naked Santa Claus in a paperweight snowstorm.)

## *If It's Carrot Juice in a Peanut Butter Glass— You're in a C.R. Session*

The meeting places weren't exactly the Palm Court at the Plaza. Whether in New York, San Francisco, or Pittsburgh, they were all done up as if by one decorator—and it wasn't Billy Baldwin. The orange or electric blue paint on one wall was forever peeling, there was a fire escape sign on the rear window, and the only place for the hot plate was on the toilet seat. One could walk in blindfolded and know she was in the right place if she got a soybean canape on whole wheat bread garnished with unfertilized Swiss chard. There was no question at all if those "health" foods were served with carrot juice in a peanut butter glass. This kind of diet, by the way, is now known to stimulate intense aggression in female hamsters. It goes without saying that no matter how many chairs were spaced between the water beds, one always sat crosslegged on the floor.

## An Antitesticular Testament

Then there was the blue-plate polemic of the day, always one variety or another of an antitesticular testament: a psalm from Friedan's matriarchal gospel, *The Feminine Mystique*; a sonnet from Millet's short-lived *Sexual Politics*; or sometimes a feature from Steinem's little moneymaker, *Ms.* magazine. Then there were those scary "spontaneous" demonstrations that frequently popped up at the drop of the word "sexist." Or if they were really ripe, the more sallow ascetic types from the New School would team up with the ruddy melon-breasted fullback types (from the old school) and start marching around the crowded room, fists raised, shrieking "lesbian liberation." At first I ran scared and played their follow-the-leader game, even if I did feel like a damned fool. At that early stage my embarrassment almost overcame the felt need for a raised consciousness. I was beginning to waver.

As feminist Diana Trilling later described such sessions, "It was not so much up with women as down with men—all men: provider, lover or boss." And whatever gripes were aired—frigidity, varicose veins, menopause, obesity—we blamed it on those bloody chauvinists.

## AA and C.R.—Not a Gripe's Worth of Difference

In any event, at each session the case histories of male oppression were vividly exposed, allowing the group to share in each shocking sisterly experience. Innocent feminine eyes were opened to the whole male conspiracy. There was the sad story of the blowsy female stutterer who was turned down as an anchor*person* at the local television station. Masochism was rampant, some consciousnesses coming on like the confession of a Skid Row bum at an AA meeting. As we got to know each other better, one-upmanship became the name of the game, with fact indistinguishable from fiction. The venom flowed like wine, and from the looks on the faces it was self-intoxicating. If you hadn't been ravaged by your grandfather, put down by the delivery boy, or harassed by your oversexed boss, you felt left out.

## Training for the Green Berets

After a year or so a new note was introduced, we became politicized. The sessions became known as caucuses (as it turned out, another word for Bedlam). This was another step down toward disillusionment. With it came the talk of electing a female president (at the time it was tough getting a woman voted in as county clerk). Then we were recruited for the Washington Institute for Women in Politics. I went. It was my first and last meeting. There were seventeen others present, including a mother of eight, a Las Vegas blackjack dealer, a go-go dancer, and three who were of a suspicious profession that didn't lend itself to either an elected or appointed category, much less an FBI check. My sanity began to return and began to seriously erode the flimsy scaffolding of my elevated consciousness.

The politics increased in intensity, and discussions ranged from Bella to bombs. The Green Berets couldn't have been inculcated with more hate. Surviving a caucus, any one of us could have joined the Symbionese Liberation Army with good credentials. The sessions went from personal gripes to "tomorrow the world." Every ethnic ILGWU seamstress was told she could run for a congressional seat even before she knew how to register a recently dear-departed for the next election. Shirley Chisholm and Bella Abzug took advantage of this momentary lapse in the male mentality and actually got elected—for a while. Then, spurred on and inspired by another female—former Congresswoman Mink (soon duly rejected by even her female voters)—they picketed for a female vice-president (somehow they gave up on the presidency).

## A Wombskin on the Wall

To most of us, by the time we were fully accepted (our consciousnesses in the ozone level), the whole thing became a bloody bore. But even before the boredom, I was on my way. What finally made me strike down my tent and silently steal away was the *hints and how-to's* part of the sessions. This was a big drawing card for the working girls, especially to the feminists who didn't want to end up a wombskin on the Gyney's wall. As we were told, male gynecologists get some kind of a kinky sex kick doing hysterectomies—notching their curettes and getting paid handsomely for it, to boot.

But there was a dichotomy here. Due strictly to sexist conditioning, those rather untrusting females not only had no faith in female bus drivers, airline pilots, or bankers; they didn't trust a female gynecologist either. When it got down to actual cases, most females, especially feminists, couldn't see those red-lacquered fingernails tinkering with their innards, much less have confidence in their diagnoses. This pox on both their houses mothered the do-it-yourself Vaginal Examination Kit.

## Mirror, Mirror on the Floor

Usually, before we adjourned, there was a short lecture and a pitch to buy the handy little packet selling for $2.98 (swabs for Pap smears, spreading specula and, of course, a mirror). Along with the kit was a pamphlet on how to prop the mirror on the floor or at the head of the bed to get the best angle for an unobstructed view (a periscope arrangement would have been an improvement). There were also drawings of exactly what to look for, and a diagram with little red warning dots showing which orifices to stay away from—if you didn't want to wind up in an emergency room. Usually a gymnastic type of the high-wire Olga Korbut variety was hired to demonstrate. It's said that some of those chubby leading feminists failed their beginner's test twice, even with two well-placed mirrors and friends holding them in position. Bella took one look at the demonstration and sold her kit at half price.

I myself never reached the pink speculum plateau because, just when I was about to get the hang of it, I slipped a disk trying. Strangely enough, those three weeks I was in traction gave me ample time to think about my cloud-high, if cumulus-fogged, consciousness. I began to feel pleasant long-ago and far-away urges.

## From Ms. Jekyll to Mrs. Pride

About two weeks out of the hospital it started. I was beginning to break out of those *bonds of freedom*. My reenslavement became one of the happiest periods of my life. It began one day on the way to my last C.R. session and was precipitated by a series of Upper East Side coincidences. I noticed myself gritting my teeth as I hurriedly passed by the Plaza, then Bergdorfs, in jeans, sandals, and a bandana. Then, in the window of Doubleday's was a Craig Claiborne cookbook open to—of all things—a new recipe for Portuguese carrot cake. Further, as if meant to tempt me beyond reason, a new young Bennington libber came to the session all Guccied, Puccied, and Chaneled.

The morning after this, on a whim, I threw my special patched and faded consciousness-raising jeans (worn fashionably gossamer thin) and the tattered art deco T-shirt into a washing machine, which had only rarely seen those togs. Then, as if a sign from above, both totally disintegrated—and along with them, my raised consciousness.

Despite the sixty dollars paid to the Whirlpool repair*person* who unclogged it, I somehow became ecstatic. As if suddenly gone berserk, I rushed up to the bathroom, locked the door, and took a bubble bath. Before I knew what I was doing I had taken my husband's razor and in no time had my armpits and legs baby-bottom smooth. Pell-mell, one thing led to another, and with reckless abandon I tore into one closet after another, retrieving a long silk Givenchy creation—pre-1969. I put it on over my bare skin, and had the best orgasm (whether clitoral or vaginal I can't remember) since that last season as a drum majorette, behind the high school stadium.

Frantically scrambling through the bottom of the practically unused clothes closet, I got out a ten-year-old pair of Ferragamo spiked heels (which were then coming back in style), an old lipstick, and some eye shadow, and I became maniacal. It was like the panting, drooling transformation of Ms. Jerkyll to Mrs. Pride.

Getting up the nerve to stand in front of a mirror, I got a real shock. For the first time, I noticed my hair. I cringed. I saw what I had had no eyes for before—the ravages the movement had made on my once-burnished, brown tresses. No self-respecting crow would have nested in it. As if out of my mind, with not a minute to waste, I put on an old raincoat over the Givenchy (not to upset the neighbors too much after a year-and-a-half). Like a thief in the night, I ducked out of the house and took the first cab I could find right to my old beauty parlor.

## *"Hello Dolly"*

I cautiously opened the door of that *pamper room* expecting the worst, not knowing if they'd even accept me in my present state of coif. But to my joy and relief I was greeted as if I'd never left. It was like the whole menage bursting into "Hello Dolly." And who was the first one I saw as I took my old chair by the *Vogue* and *WWD* rack? One of my former comrades in consciousness. She was the one who had gone over the hill about 1972 after doing it all the way, and was never heard from again. It took me back to that heady day when she proudly announced her separation from her advertising executive husband of ten years, leaving two kids behind to fend for themselves, as the C.R. group gave her a round of applause. Later, how proud she was, landing a job in a filling station, coming to the sessions from work with more grime under her now-frosted nails than comes off a broiler after cooking a ten-pound roast. Then, as I later found out, came the winter of her disenchantment. It started with pumping gas and cleaning windshields in a February blizzard at ten degrees. It all came to an end as she complained just before she disappeared, "What's so different about scrubbing an Exxon bathroom or your own, especially at $2.35 an hour?"

There she was, looking radiant after a hairdo and facial, calmly exploiting one of her oppressed sisters who was giving the manicure (at five dollars a half hour). She was as cool as if she were picketing the White House for the ERA. She waved me to my old chair, and in a matter of minutes I was oblivious to everything except the fluffy suds and, later, the hot breeze from the hairdryer. To all of you out there who sought to break with the impossible, let me tell you: It was cold turkey for me, with the most delicious withdrawal symptoms. From there on it was all downhill: backgammon, East Hampton, 21, the works.

Once I was back where I belonged, it all returned so easily: the thrill of Robert Redford on the big screen; gossiping at bridge on Wednesdays; tennis on Thursday mornings; a husband with vaginal envy; getting loaded at the club on Saturday night; having my orgasms any way I damn please. This may all be treasonous, unaware, and insensitive to my sisters and the cause, but it happens to be *my* kind of consciousness, and I guess I'm stuck with it.

## CHAPTER XVII

# No Runs, No Hits, No ERAs

Snugly upon her equal heights
Enthroned at last where she belongs,
She takes no pleasure in her rights,
She so enjoyed her wrongs.
                    *Anon.: Known but now forgotten*

I don't care a doodley squat about the ERA.
                    *Gloria Carter Spann, President Carter's sister*

When Dolly Parton was asked how she felt about the ERA, she asked, "Is that some new kind of drug?"

AFTER WHAT WE GENTLEMEN WENT THROUGH with that palate-parching catastrophe called Prohibition, when it comes to constitutional amendments it is incumbent upon all of us to be chauvinists first and Americans second. Any man who ever took solace from a fifth of Jack Daniels should never forget the Women's Christian Temperance Union and its dedication to rendering illegal the thirst of an Irish cop. Since that ignominious affair, some eighty years ago, all adult males have every right to scuttle, bury, and do away with any addition to our Constitution proposed by the female of the species. How could we possibly forgive those dragon-ladies of the Anti-Saloon League for their ten-year-long nationwide nag (1910–1920), which wound up in the weaning of America from its national sustenance. That legalized abomination was not only in direct conflict with the First Amendment (by prohibiting the freedom of slurred speech), it also afflicted our great nation with a Death Valley kind of dehydration, relieved only by bathtub *gin.*

## The Weaning of America

Nevertheless, though the ERA now has about as much chance of passing as Shirley Chisholm at a Klan rally, and though we're naturally a bit gun-shy because of that bitter Eighteenth Amendment experience, we still shouldn't shoot from the hip with this one. Underneath the usual feminist flummery connected with ERA, there could be a fallout for us chauvinists that would make a Susan B. Anthony dollar look like a twenty-dollar gold piece. Even on the surface there seem richer possibilities for us than for the ladies.

Whichever way it goes, we can't lose. We'll find some way to turn it around to fit our fancy, no less than we did with the equal rights and equal pay legislation. Likewise, in our hearts we know that that amendment will have about as much effect on equalizing the sexes as the Eighteenth had on the lost weekend. Nevertheless, we're not taking it at face value; we've been weasled by those tender traps before.

## The Face on the Barroom Floor

What makes us especially queasy is that the selfsame feminist ilk that had its hormones up in arms in the 20s is with us again, some sixty years later, and they are no "Princess Daisies." So we don't doubt for a moment that they'll be trying to pull another one of their fast ones. They cannily vow that passage of the ERA is only symbolic; well, so is the Maypole (if only a phallic one), but that didn't take an act of Congress.

As with Prohibition, those ladies didn't just want to make for a better (if thirstier) nation. Nor, admittedly, was it (as some males contend) a vindictive move to deprive the male of that necessary "back stiffener" to face that five o'clock shadow he has to come home to. They had darker ulterior motives. The real purpose of Prohibition was not only equalizing the male down to the female's own (public) nondrinking level, but equalizing the female up—to the man's B.Q. (boozing quotient). And the ERA motive has a strong resemblance to that one. So no matter how good ERA looks to us now, we must be careful.

## We Was Snookered

In the 20s the ladies came on genteel and holylike: "Lips that touch liquor will never touch mine." But during those ten or twelve years of Prohibition, that same female not only proved that she could hold as much booze as a boatswain's mate on shore leave from a polar expedition—she could survive the worst of bathtub rotgut with the best of the male rummys. It was a shock then to realize how the fems had snookered us. Though we men finally buried that law some twelve years later, the ladies had already gotten exactly what they wanted. They can now get stoned right out in public. They can now show the most sexist of bartenders that (on one boilermaker) a lady with a bleary eye, weaving like a rudderless sloop in a nor'wester, can be as bragging and obnoxious as any boozed-up male. We've never forgotten it.

Yet what they're trying to prove with the ERA is still not "perfectly clear." Back in the Prohibition era we were more idealistic and naive about feminists, so we didn't know what hit us until it was too late. We still cannot quite predict the sneaky surprises they might have in store for us. Though as we perceive it there may be hidden golden nuggets for us in this ERA gambit, there could also be more booby traps than a minefield in Vietnam. What added to our anxiety was the American Psychiatric Association (eighty-nine percent male), which has voiced its doubts. And any time they have doubts about anything there is nothing doubtful about it.

## That Was No Lady—That Was Genghis Khan

On the surface, the proposed amendment doesn't seem to be as tough on us males as that Eighteenth before it. But as we've said, who knows how much the fems will twist that ERA knife once they get it deep between our ribs? This dread is real: as we know from their few successes in big business, women with authority can be both canny and ruthless. For a preview, what nonviolent male didn't get the shakes upon witnessing the International Women's Year Convention in Houston? Those ladies, under the guise of pink and powdered femininity, held that convention at smoking gunpoint like Billy the Kid. Set to the tune of "Hearts and Flowers," it packed, gagged, and railroaded those delegates through their ayes and nays as if Boss Tweed and LBJ were each twisting an arm.

Then there was that U.N. Decade for Women meeting in Copenhagen, where the Sabras from Israel and the female Bedouins of the PLO had a six-day war right on the convention floor. It looked like a replay of the Sinai battle.

So, all of you gentlemen out there, don't ever be deluded that the sweetness and light you're promised is necessarily what you'll get. It hasn't been called "possibly the worst pestilence since Prohibition" for nothing.

## Which Clone Has the Ax Handle?

Historically, this clamor for an ERA should give us gentlemen great pause. There is not only a similarity of motivation behind the two amendments but the subtle if diabolic continuity of it all. The present green berets of the ERA seem genetically cloned from Susan B. Anthony, who begat Elizabeth Cady Stanton, who in turn begat de Beauvoir, who begat Betty Friedan.

In the early 70s another breed gave us a jolt, perpetuating this scare. A passel of radical feminists had mastered the techniques learned in Haight-Ashbury and Berkeley of throwing a Molotov cocktail with the accuracy of a platoon leader and blowing up buildings and themselves in a literal blaze of glory for the cause. After this era of carnage receded, the common garden-variety–Village-intellectual dropouts materialized from their bunkers.

From there on, to perk up their cause, which was becoming as baggy at the knees as a worn pair of pantyhose, the new buzz term became ERA. The result was an inundation of our elected officials by as ungainly a mob of barefoot lobbyists as was ever seen on Capitol Hill. Both the sweat-shirted in shorts and the scrawnies in clogs were underfoot and overexposed. They seeped through every crevice of the Rayburn Building, plaguing every Senate reception room and, like a bunch of gypsy moths, were automatically drawn to the lights of the TV cameras. They even invaded the sacrosanct privacy of those little hideaway rooms in the bowels of the Capitol, so necessary for a male senator's mid-afternoon siesta or relaxing assignation.

## Bottled in Bondage

It must not be forgotten, if one is to be true to the history of this saga, that about twenty-six prior Congresses, over a half-century span, had had a similar amendment literally bottled in bond; for each considered it about as useful as the training bra on an eight-year-old. One old senator from Arkansas, who could hit a spittoon at twenty paces in a hurricane, used to convene the ERA subcommittee every St. Patrick's Day and call for a tabling when the few fifths of sour mash had all of their heads nodding "aye." The amendment would then be buried for another two years. Anyway, in those days they were too busy pushing through their own pay raises to fool around with something as repulsive to them as equal rights.

## Rip Van's Delirium

But this last time out the feminists hit it right—a presidential election year when everybody in Congress, including Fishbait Miller, thought he was presidential timber. Though Senator Sam Ervin, the great parliamentarian, cautioned that the ERA would initiate legal chaos, and although most constitutional lawyers and alcoholic legislators who had ever careened through the Prohibition debacle advised against it, Congress passed it. Strangely enough, after holding their sauce-wetted fingers up to the wind, the lawmakers found that it was *not* we chauvinists but mostly the female voters who were against it.

After the first seven years brought no confirmation by two-thirds of the states, the Congress, against all precedent and probably illegally, gave an extension of three years, until July, 1982. Now, ten years after this epidemic of democratic encephalitis began, not only have those lawyers in Washington awakened from their delirium, but so have the state legislators. Like sickly Rip Van Winkles, they had snored and tossed through a feverish thirty-five states, knowing not what they did. Now they want to rescind.

## R.I.P.—ERA

So here we are (as this is written), only a few months and three states shy before the amendment deadline. The feminist natives are growing restless. They're losing their cool and stooping to all manner of low male-ish tricks. Those lovely ladies even went to work blackmailing legislators and boycotting the convention business of every city on their hit list.

Then came the whirlwind. After forty years, the Republicans in Detroit huffed and puffed and blew their house in, ERA and all. With Ronnie's victory in November, R.I.P.—ERA.

Reagan administered the *coup de grace* with aplomb and finality. Knowingly or not, what he was saying was this: What's good for the chauvinists is good for the country. Since then, the nine old sexists on the Supreme Court (B.S.—before Sandy) added their requiem with the banning of the female draft. (From Ms. Sandra O'Connor's naturally ambivalent and indecisive record, one concludes that she would have gone along too.) So it appears it'll take the second coming and all the king's horses if that amendment ever hopes to see the light of day by July, 1982.

## We Have a Dream

The ERA thing appears to be trudging its last mile. But hold on to your hats; this may be hard to believe at first blush, but we chauvinists may even go to their aid. Now hear us out.

Though we know the whole feminist mishmash as a weird nightmare, and though we've never gone along with them on anything, we have a dream. Listen carefully. We must think positively—positive of number one—us. We're not concerned with the flimsy business of the ERA as a symbol. The important thing is, can we use it—or in simple male terms, what's in it for us? If that symbol means more leisure, money, comfort, sex and no military service for the male, who says we're against symbols?

After much deliberation and research by the top jock scientists and sociologists, we feel we can now turn this ERA business into the biggest male boondoggle since penis envy. Our investigators have found that beneath the ERA rhetoric and hoopla, there lies a sexist windfall bigger than singles bars, divorcees, the sexual revolution, and female coal miners all rolled into one. Our plan is simple, if subtle.

## *The Gentle Art of Avoiding, Evading, Twisting, and Turning*

First off, we don't have to make a radical 180-degree turnabout that would involve loss of too much pride and face. According to our scheme, we'll allow the ERA to pass, even though appearing as if we're really against it. Then, when it's on the books, we'll twist, turn, evade, and avoid as if we'd never heard of it. And there's a lot of precedent for doing it that way. Though the statute books are chock full of laws to limit our superiority and power, there is no written word on the thousand ways to get around them.

For example, the ERA couldn't possibly be as important as the Equal Pay Act of 1963, or affirmative action. Yet what did those laws really accomplish? Women were earning fifty-eight cents for every male's dollar in 1930; in 1980, fifty years later, women are only up to fifty-nine cents—advancing about two cents a century. Let's say we're generous and boost them another fast four cents by 2030—how much can it hurt? It's just a matter of how much we want to give up, not how many laws or amendments are passed. It's the old Russian tactic of retreating to victory. It beat Napoleon and Hitler—why not the feminists?

## *The Department of End Runs and Undercuts*

We know that, even if it gets them nowhere, deep in their dark liberated hearts the ladies will at least have pleasure in thinking that the ERA will be a sharp stick in the eye to us chauvinists. So we'll let them have their jollies; we're more interested in practical results. Whatever little gain the feminists may realize from the ERA, if it's a boon for the bedeviled male, then we're for it too.

What more enduring proof of this tactic than the example of that most equality ridden British Parliament, which adopted the

Sex Discrimination Act in 1970 and has done little but discriminate since. Women in the British Isles still lack the same citizenship rights as men.

Then there are the Swiss gentry—as down to earth as they come. That shrewd chauvinist society holds the world's money (charging, not giving interest), while profiting by every war since that of the Roses. They cleverly passed an ERA in 1981, knowing full well how they would render it useless. Why, even as they put it on the books, some of their cantons (provinces) still wouldn't let a woman vote.

However, the best example of a country making laws as fangless as a senile bobcat is Japan. We've learned a lot from them about end running, circumventing, undercutting, and generally disregarding those profeminist laws. It's one of the wiliest chauvinist nations in the world, where most females still dutifully walk six paces behind their husbands. Even though they've had an ERA for almost forty years, their schools rarely allow females the privilege of teaching their children. Aside from that little putdown, which is accepted by their women with the usual bowing and scraping, there is no such thing as equal pay for equal work. The best example of how they manage democracy is in the legal system itself: The few token female judges put on the bench for show are still expected to brew the tea for the male judges.

So if the British, the Swiss, and the Oriental chauvinists can sabotage their laws so well for thirty-five years, we'll have no trouble. With our knack for it and our track record (as shown by our handling of affirmative action, equal pay, et cetera), the ERA should be a snap.

## Loopholes Like Hula Hoops

If we play our cards right, we can use this ERA business to a fare-thee-well, and tomorrow belongs to us. We know our pigeons; we've pulled the wool on them before; and if our legal experts can't ream out every loophole to hula hoop proportions, who can? As we see it, it'll be a male renaissance unequaled even in Sicilian society. But it must be done carefully and under strict cover until it's passed; then, boom, we'll let them have it.

Brothers, as we see it, this amendment will roll off our backs like Chivas Regal down a wino's glottis. And we can't get hung up on all the caveats put out by Schlafly and Company. There will be no problem riding with any punch they throw, including homosexual marriages, unisex toilets, paying your wife for defrosting the freezer, and the rest of those right-wing scare tactics.

But we must also win over some of our own uneducated chauvinists—for instance, the fierce Mormon opposition to this good thing. They can't see that their male supremacy would be enhanced, not diminished. Even the bigamy in their hearts won't be touched.

Similarly, some of our Csonkas and Sugar Rays must have their confidence reinforced. They must know that no constitutional amendment going can make a male go into labor, wash diapers, iron dress shirts, drive carpools, or type seventy words a minute. Also, our high-rise-office jock brothers must be reassured that, when it comes to those working-late sexual vespers on Thursdays, those beery Saturday eves, and those football Sundays and Monday nights, that amendment can't lay a glove on them.

So no matter how the Supreme Court interprets it or John K. Galbraith supports it, or Arthur Schlesinger, Jr., stumps for it, or Donahue (with Marlo Thomas's prodding) goes teary-eyed over it, let's pass it first; we'll go around the mulberry bush later.

## Better Than Whiplash

With those red herrings checked out, we can see that, even if at first the ERA does little for our singles comforts and pleasures (which of course we shall rectify forthwith), it certainly will be an immediate blessing to our more beleaguered brothers: those Kramer versus Kramers plagued by alimony (even with the wife working and living with another man). Also, it will abolish the cruel judgments of the courts giving custody of the kids (paid for by the husband) to the wife.

On the other hand, to all those other males who've ever spawned a get with fear and loathing, pay attention to Mrs. Ann Ginger, an ERAer and dean of the New College of California Law, who said a divorced husband wouldn't have to pay for support of any snotty juvenile he didn't cotton to.

In fact, for the male (and it's about time), marriage could

guarantee an annual income better than whiplash. And for once, that dependent wife, who used to take us for all we were worth, will be on the short end of the stick in a court of law. Recently, the Supreme Court went a step further so that divorced wives of service men can't get their hooks into the thirty-year man's pension.

This amendment would straighten out all of these anomalous postmarital burdens of our brothers. For this alone we must rationally go all out in ERA support. After all, "there but for the grace of God go us."

## Different Strokes for Different Blokes

On a little different note, consider that, if dependency revolves around who is the breadwinner in the family, we could make that facet pay a king's ransom. For instance, if a gentleman of a more laid-back variety can swallow his chauvinistic pride, why should he not seduce and marry some unsuspecting well-paid, hard-typing spinster or a homely heiress of considerable income and give her the miserables for just a few months? Divorce is already almost doubled—it'll then be trebled. He's then home free, all downhill, living off the fat of her earnings (by law, mind you) with nothing to do but leisurely dope a scratch sheet in a Vegas massage parlor. Just recently, Maria Almendarez was the first woman ever jailed for refusing to make support payments to her husband.

## Money in the Bank

Other than those males who have been skewered by marital laws, there are other groups that might profit from the ERA, for instance the businessman employer. We think that ERA could make a case for getting rid of those *infirmative* guidelines that he spends precious time evading. If she can drive a tank, be a cop, and nurse her baby during the coffee break as a *fireperson*, she shouldn't need more than a weekend off to have a baby. As Ronnie Reagan would say, "How did her pioneer great-grandmother do delivering in a cornfield?" Why should management have to shell out for six months of maternity leave while she sits around the house in front of "General Hospital"? Under ERA, this can be turned around and be gone with the wind before you can say, "Oh, Mrs. Robinson." We also might press for a full-paid paternity leave to boot.

In addition, the male money-maker may be able to get rid of some of that female deadwood he had to hire under government edict, when he can show that their mistakes cost him more than her salary. As one delegate to the National Congress of Men said, "I'm for women working as hard as men; I'm sick and tired of being their wallet."

For you male lawyers out there—as Ms. Ginger explains—there'll be a flood of business not even the ten-second ambulance chasers could ever have imagined. There will be so many suits (by males) to interpret every comma and semicolon of the law—plus those ever-increasing divorce court cases—that any shyster six months out of law school will have his condo in Palm Beach paid for in a year.

The ERA would not only mean money in the bank for some of us, but also a load off the backs of most of our laboring chauvs. The hodcarrier and longshoreman's rank and file will be looking forward to the female carrying her full share of those hernia-producing loads that she's now declared too fragile to lift.

The National Congress of Men (unknowingly) seems to go along with much of our plan, if not the declared plan itself. They were instrumental in making Massachusetts the first state to declare higher insurance premiums for men (a form of sexual discrimination) illegal. Men's Rights, Inc., has brought suit in federal court charging what we charge: that the draft discriminates against men.

## It's an Ill Wind That's Not Drafty

Which brings up the *ne plus ultra* of our case in favor of the ERA—the military. Here we could have gotten it all, had it not been for that Supreme Court decision. Of all the things those nine dotty old men could have clobbered, they picked on the female draft. Imagine, wanting us to go back to fighting wars all alone!

206 THE COMPLEAT CHAUVINIST

As it stood before the ruling, feminists were *dying* for equal combat assignments in the armed services. Why shouldn't we have welcomed this with open arms? It could have been a godsend if handled right.

It may not be too late. It's possible—even with the court ruling —for the Congress (with our help) to put women back on draft status. Though we have seen no equality-minded women marching for the draft, they can hardly be exempted from it with a real honest-to-God ERA. After all, without a female draft it would be the worst sort of discrimination.

Even NOW is confused. Eleanor Smeal, their *very simple*, plain-spoken housewife leader who says "Our nation can't *deminuize* women" (*sic*), didn't know which way to go after the Supreme Court decision. In one breath she said, "Yesterday the Court held women in their traditional role" (wife, mother, non-draftee); then in the next, "Women in traditional roles have been penalized." Then in her third breath she calls Selective Service "sexist" and "racist," after which she reverses again, saying the decision "perpetuates the myth that we can't cut the mustard."

Well, with each female leader having her own kooky ideas on women in combat, who could possibly guess what the liberated rank and file feelings are? But we do know ours. And what a relief it was to hear Colonel Beckwith, who heads the Army Research Team, say, "Basic training for women is now being upgraded for combat situations." So the gals should be well prepared to die with the rest of us.

## Leave the Dying to Them

Our Pentagon reassures us that, even in combat, our ladies would be in no more danger than the men. "Women coming out of basic training will be versed in weapons handling, grenade throwing, everything." Though this should be reassuring to every mother in America, we have to think a little further along. It could kick back on us in civilian life, making "spouse beating" a much more dangerous game.

All in all we have little to be concerned about for women in the give and take of life in the field. It lets us breathe easier, for she'll

not only be relatively safe—but, as we'll see—she'll be supersatis-
fied as well. If things break right and the ERA passes, we may be
able to get the draft back and *revise* it so that females may get
the whole military thing, or at worst fifty-two percent of it. By
the year 2000, it could be a Utopian all-female army "and leave
the dying to them."

However, as it stands now, with female volunteers dropping
out of the service at about forty-six percent a year, our whole
relaxed nonmilitary future is dependent on that female draft.
Besides, with women at West Point and Annapolis learning to be
officers, the brass are going to have plenty of trouble making a
male dogface follow a skirt into combat. Only a woman soldier
might be foolish enough to follow a female shavetail, but even
that would set a precedent. But as Russell Baker puts it, "If a
civilized society can't draft women, how can it countenance a
female general planning mass carnage?" Personally, we see the
ideal fighting machine as a rear echelon general staff of males
calling the shots, with the women doing the shooting.

The more we get into it, the more we realize how important it
is for a female draft. The Supreme Court males will see the light
if they have one ounce of chauvinism left in their old bones. Even
the Israelis, who have had affirmative action and equal rights for
years, still have a female draft. Almost fifty percent of their
armed forces are drafted women. And as the legal department of
Israel's army has ruled, the sexy Sabra soldier's duties are not only
typing, filing, and cleaning up, but serving her commander coffee
as well.

## S.T.F.C.: Sexual Technician First Class

Which brings up the male libido factor—not unlike that inherent in the cohabiting atmospheric conditions of our astronauts.
The women will certainly not be doing cleanup and kitchen duty
eight hours a day. So why shouldn't they volunteer to serve in
other male/female ways, as on the U.S.S. *Norton Sound*. From
what's being publicized about that good ship, life in the military
is getting much more exciting for the female draftee. First, there
is enough sexual harassment to keep her blood from jelling (one

or two enlisted men have already been honored with accusations). Second, those old fuddy-duddy admirals must be loosening up: nineteen lady swabbies are up for lesbianism (which of course is a liberated right).

Speaking of excitement, what's duller than sitting in a foxhole hour after hour just staring at a male buddy waiting for a command to charge? Though Phyllis Schlafly says, "We do not want our daughters treated like sex playmates in the armed forces," what's wrong with playmates? With a female draftee companion in close quarters, and with the utmost in privacy, all sorts of noncombat options are open to keep our fighting men and women content and relaxed until the time to fight. If, as they say, one can get religion in a foxhole, why not satisfaction?

## Corporal Paychec Reporting for Duty

With the military thus being made more congenial for those of us who couldn't get out of it (so far), imagine the heaven back home for those males who could beat the rap. If we can only get this draft thing turned around, just imagine the setup in our next Vietnam. There we lounge, not a bullet within dodging distance, no fifty-pound pack gracing our rounded shoulders, no jungle rot, and no KP with dishpan hands. Sitting securely back there on the home front, we'll be having our fresh orange juice with our bacon and three-minute eggs, while the little woman gloriously slogs it out on C-rations. Her family allotment (with combat pay) would be coming in regularly to the one she left behind. All we'd have to do is drop her a card once in a while telling her how tough rationing is back home. We might send a few Uneeda cookies and scrape up an old passport picture to send her around Christmas time. When the spirit moves, we'll whip up an occasional three-pager bursting with undying affection, especially when there is trouble with the surrogate *live-in* resisting the Monday wash chores—or when she, too, gets her greetings from Uncle. Of course, no matter what, every card and letter should have that last caution—inch-high—"give plenty of notice before you're rotated home."

## *The Flag-Draped, Tear-Stained Lump Sum Solace*

There is much more to this female GI thing, if we just don't get too sentimental about it. We must explore her patriotism to the bitter end. For instance, regardless of her fine training and even her moral support from the home front, the little lady overseas takes her chances like every other GI. So it's possible that she could be one of the unlucky ones, catch the big *B*, and be borne home flag-draped. Even here it's an ill wind that doesn't blow some husbands some good. In his grief there is some solace in the lump sum of GI insurance, and a bit more consolation in her pension checks which will help relieve his loss and suffering. Even with the chore of looking for temporaries (somewhat younger) to fill her shoes and assuage his hurt, in his heart he will know that she served her country well.

If, however, she comes through unscathed and by chance he's found something more to his liking in the interim, there is a bill before Congress to extend the sharing of retirement benefits with the divorced spouse.

All in all, if the ERA goes through, we should fight the Supreme Court decision for the draft down to the wire. But if the amendment doesn't pass, we'll just have to forget it and work on getting back to those halcyon days of the nonaffirmed 50s. Disregarding the lesbian problem, the family problem, and the abortion problem, ERA not only may *not* be the holocaust it has been cracked up to be, but it may be a blessing in disguise. Knowing which side our bread is buttered on, we just can't let our chauvinist pride or anything else stand in the way of their losing this amendment for us.

All told, we are led to this judgment: Any chauvinist who doesn't at least respect (if not love and honor) the ERA should be safely ensconced in an institution. No matter the complaint of Anita Miller, President of the National Association of Commissions for Women, who said that ERA will bring a hell of a mess and "we'll be debating this in court for the rest of our natural lives"; let's pass the amendment. With each debate, we males will be sitting deeper and deeper in chauvinist clover.

## CHAPTER XVIII

# A Ram in She's Clothing—
# Twenty-three Ways to Spot One

What are little feminists made of?
Hardly sugar and spice and everything nice;
More venom and acid
Thus, not so placid.

*E.B.*

The way to fight a woman is with your hat—grab it and run.

*John Barrymore*

WHICHEVER VERSION of genesis one believes, whether biblical or Darwinian, it's a sure thing that neither God nor evolution could have fashioned both Bella Abzug and Sophia Loren from the same clay. As we have maintained all along, "feminist" is as different from "feminine" as arsenic from old lace. So to be an expert fem-spotter we must know not only how and from whence she came but what it did to her on the way, from day one.

As we see it, neither theory supports the various feminist contentions that a woman is equal to the male. The California rebirth of the creationist movement has forced us to reexamine woman's biblical beginning, especially if we are to be convinced that the rib story is anything more than an "old chauvinist allegory." Through our eyes, there is ample evidence that Eve sprang fully formed from Adam's skeletal frame. The only dubious part about it is (knowing the male's inordinate pride in his beachboy physique), we're sure he wouldn't want to spoil his symmetry. Yet, though knowing it was God's will, Adam was so malelike! If he absolutely had to give up any bone he would hardly give up one of his better ones. He certainly would never consider parting with his lusty loin bones—the fount of all his erotic pleasures—even for a full "10" sex object like Bo, much less for a pudgy equal rights object like Betty. So it was not unexpected that, when the chips were down and he had to give some part of his osseous structure, he would only relinquish that undistinguished soul food bone—the rib. That plebian bone from whence she supposedly came may be highly touted in Harlem's fast food franchises and Texas barbecues, but it's rated the lowest of low in every other kitchen in the world, including that of the Namibian cannibals. It is not only greasy, gristly, and highly vulnerable in contact sports, but is almost meatless. It is thus easily expendable, there are twenty-four of them, and is no more prized by us males than that ignoble bone we sit on, the coccyx.

## From the Jawbone of an Ass?

We chauvinists, of course, feel her extremely fortunate if she sprung as an offshoot from even the least of our male anatomy. Some of our more wry sexists insist that, with her penchant for prattle, her origins must have been the jawbone of an ass.

On the other hand, though giving the creationists their due, we cannot completely eschew the more prevalent scientific theory of the origin of the female species. Paying homage to her roots, the tiny shrew (as in "the taming of") was not only the first mammal to suckle the human in the raw, but to portray woman as she would be. She was the epitome of all females—part feminine, part feminist. On the one hand small, soft, and cuddly, she is the essence of Goldie Hawn, but as the immortal bard implied, she was also as nippy and bitchy as the worst of the Steinzugs. Today, though somewhat hidden, the worst of her is obvious to the professional chauvinist. It just comes down to which twin acts like Yogi.

So from way back then to now, though the masculine and the truly feminine were easily identifiable, not so the masculine and the feminist. Even if by their looks some feminists seem almost female, they are still as schizoid as Barnum's Bearded Lady. It has been suggested by scientists that this hard-knocking female with proportionate masculine and feminine hormones circulating in her bloodstream is closer to Mean Joe Green than Liberace, and is thus more frequently leaning toward making war than beds. Our best examples are, of course, Prime Minister Margaret Thatcher, the "iron lady" of British politics; Rosalynn Carter, the so-aptly-monikered Steel Magnolia; Madame President Indira Gandhi, that great male sterilizer; and of course, most of the feminist leadership.

## Ms. Inbetween—More Foul Than Fish

To really get a handle on the modern feminist and identify her in a flash of the eye, let's look at her sisters of recent past. For those Ms. Inbetweens only come completely out in the open every fifty years or so. So we tend to forget what that *barber-ous* Delilah or those police-battering suffragettes really were like. If we remembered the latter, not only for their acts but also for their formidable figures and lethal hatpins, the memory would strike terror into every masculine heart. It would bring back visions of those buxom, pillbox-hatted ladies whacking the constabulary, and wrecking those legitimate sweatshops where women were making a small but honest living. Even the modern goon squads learned a trick or two from those whaleboned old ILGWU feminists. Management never forgot it. Professor Henry Higgins in *My Fair Lady* wondered, "Why can't a woman be more like a man?" Well, Professor Higgins, there are some who are.

We are not referring to the sweet young feminist of the stirred-up Vassar variety going nowhere as an assistant editor in a publishing house, nor even the crochety old maid who missed her one good shot at connubial bliss and is still pounding an IBM. They are essentially average women who go bonkers on an equality binge—but only temporarily. They're not the ones we're concerned with. Those who are a worry, not only to the ordinary chauvinist but also to the real woman and to society at large, are those who seem unhappy that they're females, and who would need a chromosome test to get into Helena Rubinstein's.

## A Ram in She's Clothing

But even among those, there exists a grab bag of feminist breeds as varied as their hormonal mixtures. For instance, there are feminists such as the former governor of the state of Washington, Dixy Lee Ray, who may look the part but are not out to castrate us one and all. Then there are some real *rams in she's clothing*, as comely as Gloria Steinem was during her bunny days (now a bit long in the tooth)—but rare to be sure. Another example of that infrequent ilk—a pretty face and a pick-ax-mind —is that petite once-congress*person* from Hawaii, Patsy Mink. In her there lies a personality as cutting and abrasive as an Oahu coral reef in which lurks the deadly barracuda. Then there are other types much less camouflaged, such as the long, lanky Germaine Greer, or the manliness of the tough-talking congress*person*, Maryland's Barbara Mikulski in her double-knit pants suit stretched to capacity.

## *Like an Albino Rodent—Surly, Tough, and Sterile*

In any case, contrary to feminist propaganda, neither conditioning nor male oppression makes those latter trencher*persons* what they are. They were the tough part of the schizoid shrew from the beginning of time. And they received their nasty little genes dictating the personalities of the Minks and the Abzugs. But lucky for us, they are small in number. Obviously they were no feast to Peking man's raunchy libido and lascivious eye, and thus they were of low productivity. In those days, when competition was keen among Neanderthal sexpots, that Precambrian brute was not about to hook up with a breed of cat who could slingshot a five-pound boulder dropping a moose at one hundred yards. After all, his turn could be next. But even if those tough female aboriginals had a shot at a hard-up male with a chance to reproduce their kind, they had few maternal urges. With a testosterone level at male altitudes, nature doesn't look kindly on their making babies.

Naturally this macho jungle female, hacking it alone, unloved, with no protector and no provider, had every right to be surly and tough. It's understandable how she matured into aggressive, crabby human status.

And hardly being bonded to her more feminine sisters, the apple of the all-male eye, she had to compete with them to survive. She rarely could. This further reduced her numbers. Though she may have been tougher than a spiny iguana, when there was a bad day on the hunt or food was in short supply, she was the first to be fired—frequently on a slowly turning spit. To have gotten through all of those lethal trials up to now proves a lot. We must take her seriously. Though she is small in numbers, she is living proof that she is a worthy opponent. We should take note that it will be she who probably will outlast the cockroach if a nuclear holocaust comes upon us.

## Jacks of Both Genders—Masters of None

These female jacks of both genders (and mistresses of none) are themselves no less confused than is their sexual status. On the one hand they try to masculinize the feminine, and on the other, feminize the masculine. There's nothing new about misery loving company, but so far they've had little success in taking the female out of the kitchen and almost none in putting the male back in. Nor have they ever influenced (for any length of time) either the young or old female to forsake being a rock groupie, mourning Elvis Presley, or turning away from the Avon lady. (More females visit Elvis Presley's gravesite in a month than attend NOW meetings in a year.) Nor have they penetrated at all that extra thickness of the jock skull to get them to forsake their tastes for hard porn or massage parlors.

## The Trojan Filly—and How to Tell One

So we don't take these present-day birds of a feather lightly. Though knowing that we are onto them and the jig is up, the arch-feminists are still trying to make some inroads. But now they use much more sophisticated techniques than their predecessors. Lately they have come on with new ploys, some picked straight out of the male bag of tricks. Obviously, the fruits of Gloria Steinem's CIA training (which she can't cover up any more than her Playboy bunny days) are being passed along; and so is Jane Fonda's long experience in acting and makeup, both in Hollywood and Hanoi. But we red-blooded chauvs weren't born yesterday, and we can generally spot those militant Trojan fillies. What we're worried about are those naive housewives, "Cliffy" seniors, and, especially, our regular lovable one-night-standers. They too must be on the alert to penetrate the disguises behind which the fems lurk. And that's why NATCH—the National Association of True Chauvinist Hounddogs—has come up with the *New Unabridged Instant Fem-Spotter Guide.*

This little pocket reference, mainly for the bedeviled males (but, to repeat, also for the misguided female), could be his or her survival kit. It has surefire clues on how to tell a barracuda from a mermaid and what to do if caught by a female "jaws." It may not always deal with cases of life and death, but at the least it is an invaluable aid to avoid boredom or emasculation. Only a rabid antifeminist like the New York critic John Simon, who has studied this species inside and out, should dare walk among them without The Manual.

## Fem-Spotting

Here, briefly outlined, are some of the more helpful hints which may be memorized (or kept close at hand) for speedy reference:

I. Body and Other Languages
  A. If something redundantly fleshed and muscled comes on like a Land Rover but resembles a female, is raucous as a crow, and spews forth some choice four-letter words—be wary.
  B. At the other end of the spectrum, if you should bump into the Greerish fidgety variety, chain-smoking Gaulloises or small Italian stogies—with both mammary and buttockal secondary sex characteristics almost nonexistent—watch out.
  C. Any female bulging out of Levis, hiding behind mirrored sunglasses, knocking Robert Redford, Bloomingdale's, hair curlers, Clairol, or Dr. Spock is a dead giveaway. Also batten down the hatches if she "just loves" Jane Fonda, and Robin Morgan, or has ever voted for Bella Abzug.

Now there are borderline cases. At a cocktail party, for instance, if you are suspicious but not sure, bide your time and head for your third martini. It might make that nervous wait tolerable. Sooner or later they give themselves away.

D. As Mary McCarthy once said, the trouble with archfeminists is, "they never smile." If one wants to flush this type out, begin the conversation by referring to a Doonesbury cartoon, or repeat an old Groucho joke. The response of the feminist is predictable—grim. To clinch it, tell an off-color chauvinist joke, like the one about the traveling sales*person* and the farmer's transvestite workhand.

E. Unless her husband left her with money to burn, be on your guard when she makes out a check on the First National Woman's Bank.

F. If she still subscribes to *Ms.* magazine, has a female surgeon, or insists on paying her own way to the movies, give her the fishy eye.

G. Those frequently found in occupations with minimal human contact, such as legal assistants, zoo attendants, or veterinary assistants, should be avoided.

H. Never trust a strange female at a dinner party whose only historical reference is Joan of Arc, Queen Elizabeth I, Kate Millet, George Sand, and Billie Jean King, or whose only scientific reference is Marie Curie. You are definitely in the hands of the Philistines when they still hold Indira Gandhi up as a political heroine.

I. When it comes to using certain buzz names—don't. It sets them off like a smoke alarm. Get in the habit of monitoring out of your conversation such names as Freud (even to those women whose only salvation has been ten years on the couch). In our experience it has frequently initiated a salvo of invectives that would embarrass the madam of a Portuguese whorehouse. Mention Ted Kennedy, and if a sneer develops, you've got one on the hook. Drop Pope Paul's name (and his nil of the pill), and if their eyeballs become bloodshot and twirl like a swizzle stick, head for the hills. Quoting Norman Mailer, that wife batterer (a stabber, yet), also sets up their hackles.

J. In ordinary conversations there are certain phrases to be used at your peril. Complimenting her that she "thinks like a man" or even thinks "like a woman" can set off an explosive chain reaction. With no other female can you get into trouble by flattering some part of her anatomy, especially breasts, legs, or buttocks; the face is usually out of the question.

K. If she is at all mechanically inclined, can fix a running toilet, a lawnmower, or can adjust a carburetor—see her only when absolutely at wit's end.

L. If she's divorced, a college graduate, white, and under the age of twenty-five, statistics show she will most likely be a militant one.

## II. Chemise or No Chemise—There Is No Question

One of the surefire giveaways is the dress and ornamentation of the feminist. Even the cultural anthropology of Margaret Mead (a clotheshorse she wasn't) has yet to delve into the bedizenment of this tribe. So far, neither Paris nor Seventh Avenue seems excited by their fashions.

A. First of all, cosmetics, scents, and lotions of any kind are avoided as if those fancy bottles and jars contained pure cultures of bubonic plague. Lipstick and eyeshadow are out unless, through some rank error, she is propositioned by a male —any male. It goes without saying that lacy lingerie is unknown, and that pantyhose is of the Army surplus variety.

B. The dress and accoutrements vary with the age of the emancipated—the younger, the weirder. But occasionally an old one flies off the handle in costumes seen only at the Mardis Gras. Being Ms. Inbetween, their styles (styles???) fluctuate somewhere between "*haute* Schwarzenegger" and "*bas* Mae West," frequently both at the same time. For instance, the more maleish of them can range from a transvestite in reverse to one so normal you couldn't tell her from Mark Spitz in drag.

C. On the more feminine side, the uniform of the day was most commonly the gypsy look-alike; this is uncommon today except with New York Village fems and recent high school converts. It consists of voluminous, brightly colored skirts trailing the ground, and an embroidered bodice, off the shoulder, in harmony with the most romantic campfires in Romany. To make sure that not a trace of design is showing, a leather-fringed vest may complement this uniform. Their feet are usually bare, the color of asphalt, and, occasionally, sandalized. The topper is a tight bandana of the Aunt Jemima variety that does double duty. First, it is a badge to show the spirit of the road and, second, hides a head which is as unkempt and unshampooed as a Russian wolfhound just back from a briarpatch.

Robin Morgan, the movement's self-proclaimed martyr*person*, has come a long way. She now says she is "so liberated she can wear a skirt without a twinge of conscience." Gloria, true to her constituency on the college lecture circuit, is still in her declining years suited in her tailored denim and T-shirts except after six, when she slips into a Givenchy for her real people, the beautiful ones. Bella, of course, is a cockatoo of another feather—usually garbed in a combination of off-the-rack Gimbel's basement, in tentmaker yardage. Behatted she is; Rebecca of Sunnybrook Farm she isn't.

D. One must be on the *qui vive* for some of the older Janie-come-latelies who have no shame at all, before certain festive occasions they even dare to enter a beauty shop to get scrubbed down and temporarily camouflaged. Another is the rather rare family-type libber who only ventures into her costume after the family has gone for the day. However, to avoid a husband's less-than-flattering glares and also, like Cinderella, to avert turning into a black-and-blue pumpkin if he catches her, she reverts back to girdle, bra, and skirt before the stroke of five—the witching hour.

E. Feminist jewelry is, of course, another true sign of the unenslaved. The left ring finger is always unadorned with that mark of Cain. But all other fingers (especially both thumbs) are encrusted with one, and sometimes two, modern-design pieces of jagged steel or silver with semiprecious stones—the weight of which could cut a secretary's speed below thirty words a minute. Toes occasionally come in for a ring-ing, and if it weren't painful and also symbolic of virile bulldom, the nose also would probably be ring-ed. The freeform necklaces of bent wire with or without a Peace, Jewish, or clenched fist charm are too familiar even to discuss.

III. The Test of Tests
A. Of course, one of the surest tests, absolutely unequivocal and as reliable as a blood test or an electrocardiograph, is the TMT (the three-martini test). It's very simple, but if it misses and the female is really feminine, it could be very embarrassing. So it should be done in a bar where you're not well known and in a slack time of day—say 3:00 P.M. Take the suspect there under any kind of guise—business, relaxation, or just "getting to know you." Order a martini—straight up—for each of you before she has a chance to order a Pink Lady or

a glass of Perrier. The first toast would be "bottoms up." If she goes for this, get two more down, within an hour and a half, with any other type of subterfuge. Then sit back and watch. If part way through the third her eyes become glassy and her eyelids begin to droop, she lists to either port or starboard, and she knocks over the water pitcher and her chair on the way to the john, she is probably not a feminist. If she makes it back to the table at all and her pantyhose are twisted at least 180 degrees—forget it: She is a real woman for sure. However, if she is as clear-eyed as a tiger after the final one and says she just thinks she'll get back to the office and take forty winks—steer clear; you've got a live piranha on the hook.

So these are the feminist types in origin, habit, and habitat, and how to spot them—even at a distance. We hope we have hinted at how she thinks and what she wears, and how to deal with her or at least to survive her. Always remember: Every crowded room, cocktail party, sit-down dinner, or casual street-corner meeting could be a potential minefield. Use the recommended handy guide. It should provide at least time for evasive tactics if not surefire protection. Even with these helpful hints, pick your way carefully, or you could have two of your most prized possessions blown to smithereens.

Frequently the feminist is born to it and more to be pitied than censured. If her plight is the result of conditioning by her peers, only she can be held responsible. In any case, forgive her—she is only a female. But from here on in let no man complain that he wasn't warned and briefed in her history, psychology, habits, differences, powers, and frailties and given the ammunition to refute each and every one of her numerous and devious ploys.

"A proud admission of male chauvinism should in no way be construed as a personal pique against the archfeminists for remembrances of things past," writes Edgar Berman in his foreword, "A Chauvinist's Paean to the Feminine Female." "Some of the more shrill Steingreers will naturally bring up my international chauvinist ranking and indict this book as a subtle ploy to bolster it. Nothing could be further from the truth. First, my respect and admiration is unbounded for that marvel of reasonable and skeptical womanhood who neither needs nor heeds the hot and heavy urgings of the Abzugians to the left of her and the Schlaflyites to the right of her. This book is only a defense manual against the ravings and ravages of that more androgynous species—the militant feminist."

Berman is only half kidding. In *The Compleat Chauvinist* he exposes and skewers his feminist "enemy" in bare-knuckle fashion and with the broadest of humor. "Equality? Who said there's anything wrong with equality? But between sexes?—balderdash!"